PHOTOGRAPHY: CRITICAL VIEWS

A Dream of England

PHOTOGRAPHY: CRITICAL VIEWS

SERIES EDITOR
John Taylor

Department of History of Art and Design
Manchester Metropolitan University

This series explores the historical and contemporary uses of photography in sustaining particular social, class-located, institutionalised and gendered positions. Whereas modernist photographic history confined its study to the celebration of unique works of art produced by creative artists, this series shows how photographic meanings are produced in the social formation of knowledge. The series looks beyond the smooth narrative of selected 'masters', styles and movements. It rejects the idea that technology is the driving force spreading photography outwards. It refuses to allow the idea, found in illustrated history books, that photography is a straightforward 'window on the world'. The series aims to develop the subject area of photographic history, theory and criticism as an individual discipline. At the same time it crosses disciplinary boundaries and draws on the methods of art history, literature, film, cultural studies, anthropology and cultural geography to situate photography in its intellectual context.

A Dream of England

Landscape, photography and the tourist's imagination

John Taylor

Manchester University Press

Manchester and New York

Distributed exclusively in the USA and Canada by St. Martin's Press

Published by Manchester University Press
Oxford Road, Manchester M13 9PL, UK
and Room 400, 175 Fifth Avenue,
New York, NY 10010, USA

Distributed exclusively in the USA and Canada
by St. Martin's Press, Inc., 175 Fifth Avenue,
New York, NY 10010, USA

British Library Cataloguing-in-Publication Data
         A catalogue record for this book is available from the
         British Library

Library of Congress Cataloging-in-Publication Data

         Taylor, John, 1945-
         A Dream of England : landscape, photography and the
         tourist's imagination / John Taylor.
                  p.   cm.
         ISBN 0-7190-3723-9, -- ISBN 0-7190-3724-7 (pbk,)
         1. England--Geography, Historical, 2. Landscape photography-
         --England--History, 3. Tourist trade--England--History,
         4. Travelers--England--History, 5. Landscape--England--History.
         I. Title.
         DA600. T39 1994
         914.2--dc20   94-3826

         ISBN 0 7190 3723 9 *hardback*
         ISBN 0 7190 3724 7 *paperback*

Typeset in Sabon
Design by Simon Meddings, Lionart, Birmingham.
Printed in Great Britain by Redwood Books, Trowbridge.

Contents

Acknowledgements

I want to thank especially my friend and long-distance correspondent Laura U. Marks of Rochester, New York, for her criticisms and her ability to turn my sentences into what I mean to say. Similarly, I am indebted to David Peters Corbett, my friend and colleague at Manchester Metropolitan University, for his encouragement and specific suggestions. I am also grateful to my editor, Katharine Reeve for her continuous support, and to Peter James, Steve Edwards and Deborah Wynne for reading and commenting on early drafts. Peter James also helped me with his knowledge of the Warwickshire Photographic Survey archive in Birmingham Central Library. A number of people contributed to this book in ways they may not recall. Among those I wish to thank are Michael Brandon-Jones, Marianne Fulton, David Greysmith, Grant Kester, Valerie Lloyd, Terry Morden, Lavinia and Geoffrey Orton, Pamela Roberts and Roger Taylor.

Much of this book was written during a sabbatical funded by the School of Humanities and Social Science at the University of Wolverhampton, and I want to thank the Faculty Research Committee for awarding me this grant.

The large number of illustrations was made possible by a grant from the Arts Council of Great Britain, and the generosity of photographers, archives and agencies in supporting academic publishing. Every attempt was made to obtain permission to reproduce copyright material. If any proper acknowledgement has not been made, we would invite copyright-holders to inform us of the oversight.

Preliminary versions of chapters of this book first appeared in the following journals: part of chapter 3 was published as 'Behind every landscape is a woman: P. H. Emerson's and the anxieties of class and gender' in *Afterimage*, 21, 8 (March 1994); part of chapter 4 was published as 'Kodak and the "English" market between the wars' in *Journal of Design History* , 7, 1 (1994).

List of illustrations

Introduction

Chapter 1 Landscape record and reverie

13. The Kodak factory, Harrow, *c*.1890. (Courtesy of The National Museum of Photography, Film and Television).

14. Workers 'spotting' negatives, Kodak factory, Harrow, *c*.1890. (Courtesy of The National Museum of Photography, Film and Television).

15. 'Outing to Kinver, Staffordshire', Warwickshire Photographic Survey, *c*. 1890. (Courtesy of Birmingham Library Services).

16. Harold Baker, 'Moor St, corner of Dale End, Birmingham', 1880. (Courtesy of Birmingham Library Services).

17. 'Outing to Tysoe', Warwickshire Photographic Survey, 1891. (Courtesy of Birmingham Library Services).

18. 'Compton Wynyates', Warwickshire Photographic Survey, 1891. (Courtesy of Birmingham Library Services).

Chapter 2 Shakespeare land

19. W. Jerome Harrison, 'Cottages, Broom', Warwickshire Photographic Survey, *c*.1890. (Courtesy of Birmingham Library Services).

20. J. L. Williams, 'First glimpse of Kenilworth', from *The Home and Haunts of Shakespeare*, 1892. (Courtesy of Birmingham Library Services).

21. J. Walter, 'Anne Hathaway's cottage, Shottery – back view', from *Shakespeare's Home and Rural Life,* 1874.

22. A. Leeson, 'Picnic party on the Avon, 14 June 1890', Warwickshire Photographic Survey. (Courtesy of Birmingham Library Services).

23. H. Snowden Ward and Catharine Weed Ward, 'The tumble-down stile', from *Shakespeare's Town and Times*, 1896.

24. J. L. Williams, 'At Shottery Brook', from *The Home and Haunts of Shakespeare*, 1892. (Courtesy of Birmingham Library Services).

25. J. L. Williams, 'Waiting for the ferry', from *The Home and Haunts of Shakespeare*, 1892. (Courtesy of Birmingham Library Services).

26. J. L. Williams, 'The old chair mender', from *The Home and Haunts of Shakespeare*, 1892. (Courtesy of Birmingham Library Services).

27. J. L. Williams, 'When we were boys', from *The Home and Haunts of Shakespeare*, 1892. (Courtesy of Birmingham Library Services).

Chapter 3 Travellers, tourists and trippers on the Norfolk Broads

Chapter 4 'England' as a reliable make

Chapter 5 Documentary raids and rebuffs

Chapter 6 History under fire

Chapter 7 At home with Fox Talbot

Chapter 8 Pleasures of the imagination

Chapter 9 Wastes and boundaries

Colour plates

Introduction

TOURING AND TIME-TRAVEL

THE RHYTHMS of the working day are set by the clock, and measures of time relate to measures of production. Tourists, along with the infirm and the unemployed, stand outside workaday time. But unlike other groups, tourists wilfully enter into the pleasures and dangers of time-travel. They seek to alter their relation to it just as they alter their relation to production.

When tourists travel across space, or even sit in their cars and gaze at the view, they take part in the type of time-travel which is commonplace in reading and writing. Then time slows or quickens as stories are compressed or expanded, apparently moving at speeds unrelated to 'real' time. In the acts of writing and reading, as in touring, time becomes elastic; or at least it is changed from its fixed measure in the working world (Stewart 1993: 3–14; Thompson 1967).

Changing the scales of time-keeping is one of the pleasures of touring, though tourists are never totally free of the 'real' time of work, and depend on its schedules for their trains or flight connections. Much anxiety attaches to tourism, and some of it comes from this antagonistic dependence upon (and simultaneous loosening from) work-time.

In its ideal form, touring is like dreaming. This suggests a period which is magical and free of volition. Tourists expect the working schedules to protect them and allow a degree of relaxation, opening on the chance to dream. In the

A river in Buckinghamshire, as seen from an InterCity train.

With some peace and qui t, you'll ave less rouble concentrating on your ork. If you've a report to write, the extra comfort, privacy and tranquillity you get in First Class is not a luxury. It's a necessity.

FIRST CLASS   *INTERCITY*

1. 'A river in Buckinghamshire, as seen from an InterCity train', British Rail advertisement, 1991.

advertisement for British Rail reproduced here, the landscape outside contrasts with the imagined warm interior. The photograph of willows on a foggy day shows that Britain may be cold and clammy outside, but inside the train it is so warm and pleasant that the traveller begins to nod off, suggested by gaps and other imperfections in the accompanying text – which in this case are a typographic equivalent to dozing or day-dreaming.

Outside appears to be 'dreary', but it is not alien or threatening. Willows beside a brook and autumnal fog are stock signs of the English countryside, reminiscent of the pre-industrial countryside, the poems of Keats, and the turn-of-the-century vogue among artists and art-photographers for low-lying wetlands (see page 266). The advertisement reinforces the rhythms of the train with a familiar scene which is inherently indistinct. This may be an effect of fog, or a sign of the speeding train, but it produces a visual equivalent to the sleepy text. Together, text and picture suggest calm precisely because the train is 'taking the strain'. In this pleasant day-dream, text and picture are reassuring signatures of speed and leisure, of trains and England.

Photography and language is conventionally used to keep a dream of England before waking eyes.

In miniature, these are the themes of this book: the use of texts and pictures in representing England in ways tourists might wish to see it; tourists' experience of 'reading' signs, and how they enter the game of travelling in time; how landscape and photography are implicated in this game, and how the game contributes to a sense of national belonging. When talking about landscape, photography and tourism, I include the armchair tourism enjoyed through books, albums, brochures and holiday guides and, as I explain below, I confine my argument to landscape in England. All these themes are interrelated, which makes a forbidding complexity. To make sense of it, I have found it useful to concentrate upon the act of looking, how this relates to comfort and anxiety, and I shall now explain how these concerns fit into the overall framework.

OUTLINING THE FIELD

I have chosen to write about photography and landscape in three different periods, each separated coincidentally by about fifty years. The first period is *c.*1885–95, when mass tourism and mass photography had a new and discernible impact on the idea that traditional ways of life in England were rapidly disappearing, and needed to be preserved or recorded for posterity. The second period is *c.*1925–42, when England appeared to be feminised, reliable and coherent, despite plenty of evidence to the contrary. This coherence made it strong enough to withstand the topsy-turvy experience of wartime on the home front. The third period is *c.*1982–93, when ideas about celebrating England's heritage served the need for unity, and at the same time contrasted with ideas about disunity.

Themes which are common to each section include the mass production of entertainments for tourists, such as trips into the countryside in search of treasured landscape, taking its photograph, or simply looking at it in pictures. Looking at landscape successfully is one way for tourists to join in a national pastime. When tourists look and see what should be seen, they confirm that England is essentially content. Moreover, this peaceful scenery is ancient, and looking at the real thing or at photographs invites imaginative travel into more or less distant pasts. I use the convergence of photography and tourism to gauge the use of the past in England. In both these practices, the past is the source of nostalgia rather than danger, though danger of a psychological and social sort is inherent in tourism. Becoming a tourist is to risk the failure of not feeling or perceiving whatever is expected. To forestall failure, tourists prefer to see landscape in the prescribed manner, and so overcome anxiety and set aside the potential dangers of meeting the 'other', whether in the form of unsympathetic locals or fellow tourists.

Though these themes of contentment and anxiety are common to all sections, they have different weight in different chapters. For instance, my interest in tourist anxiety in various forms is clear in the first three chapters; it is less evident in the following section – specifically in chapter 4 on ' "England" as a reliable make' (about Kodak and amateur photography) and chapter 6 called 'History under fire' (which is about responses to English landscape in the early years of the Second World War). I have less to say about tourist anxiety in these chapters because I wish to emphasise the effects of commodities and the urgency of national identity in producing an apparently coherent, stable view of England. In the final section, I take up the theme of anxiety again, but show how it was displaced or muffled by an effusion of 'Englishness' in the celebration of 150 years of photography held at Lacock Abbey, the home of Fox Talbot. Contentment and anxiety exist side by side in chapter 8 on 'Pleasures of the imagination', and in the final chapter, 'Wastes and boundaries', the theme of anxiety is paramount.

There is continuity in the way English landscape has been seen by tourists over the last hundred years. This centres on the idea of a stable England, despite all the evidence pointing towards the idea that the nation is fractured and potentially unstable. At the same time, even the imagined stability of the country cannot be taken for granted, and has to be remade constantly. The idea of England, or what Benedict Anderson calls the 'imagined community' of the nation, is always in the process of breaking down and being renewed (Anderson 1989) (see page 20). The causes of breakdown and the sources of renewal shift over time. For example, in the late nineteenth century some of the greatest fears attached to social mobility. The greater differentiation among the middle- and lower-middle classes, exemplified and measured in the use of commodities, brought about new and often unwelcome class collisions. In this period, the source of renewal was the belief that the 'record' (or documentary) value of photography could preserve the idea of 'old England' from the growth of suburbs, commuters and tourists. At the same time, there was a flourishing trade in pictures which showed England to be wooded, magical and deeply rural, exactly the way tourists wished it to be.

In contrast, the anxieties which attach to the idea of England in the late twentieth century (as I argue in chapters 8 and 9) come less from disturbances associated with class than from beliefs about race and gender, or the fear of ecological disaster. The sources of renewal continue to draw on ancient signs or sites of 'Englishness' (such as Stratford-upon-Avon or the Lake District) which were already talismanic in the 1890s, though in contemporary times the struggles and uncertainties of a hundred years ago have been forgotten and replaced by our own sense of loss and nostalgia for the past. The late Victorian period is widely used in advertising and tourist guides to produce a sense of England at peace with itself. The urgency of renewing the idea of the 'imagined community' is so great, and the costs of failure perceived to be so threatening that, in the public realm of tourism, images of calm and contentment obliterate those of disarray and discord. Pictures of discord are found largely in the editorial sections of newspapers, or in exhibitions and catalogues of photographers who are critical of the idea of cosy 'little' England in which everything is in place. Consider for example John Kippin's photograph 'Hidden, National Park, Northumberland', in which the view of the peaceful or unspoilt countryside sold to tourists is shown to be inadequate, since the Park contains the ruins of military aircraft (see colour plate 1).

In writing about three diverse periods, I have not attempted to account for change between or within them. Instead of writing a chronicle, or accounting for a model of causality, I have chosen to present a collection, a non-developmental argument in which each moment reveals a distinctive aspect of the English obsession with landscape. I choose to present this collection rather than to offer a comprehensive overview, either in periodisation, geographic space, or photographic practice. I present the three periods and nine cases as examples of moments that impel people to use landscape in the (not always successful) attempt to define themselves and establish their security and sense of belonging to the nation.

Obviously, travel and photography are used to represent experiences of nationhood in numerous countries, including other nations within Britain. My decision to cut the book in three, and to stay in England, is in itself an expression of that wilful, almost capricious pleasure of armchair travel – the kind of travel across time and space in which I decide where I want to stop and how long I want to stay.

This type of touring, which I can do from home, or through libraries, second-hand book shops and photographic archives, seems at first sight to be a kind of 'unpackaged' touring. It is essentially private, and is widely enjoyed from cars. According to David Lowenthal, speaking at the opening of the Robert Gordon University Heritage Convention in Aberdeen, 'most people admire the landscape... from cars' (Wojtas 1993). This 'seated' enjoyment of landscape seems free of constraints and most dangers, though this freedom is an illusion, and the constraints and dangers are real. They might not be life-threatening – like driving and also peering at treasured landscapes from cars – none the less there are social and psychological constraints and dangers associated with touring, identifying landscape and then using photography to record it.

The logic of tourism divides the terrain into two unequal parts: the space occupied by the host culture, and what it becomes when it is invaded by tourists. The arrival of tourists is an invasion because aspects of the local culture are turned into commodities for tourists who take advantage without necessarily having to pay for the 'service'. For instance, they provide authentic or picturesque subjects for photographs, but tourists often 'take' them without obtaining permission or expecting to pay for the privilege. Locals find themselves overtaken for the advantage of other people's profit, and their culture expropriated without any necessary benefit for them. Following the final line of argument advanced by John Frow, tourism involves the progressive extension of commodities, along with the consequent imposition of social relations. Characteristically, these sustain 'inequalities of power between center and periphery, First and Third Worlds, developed and underdeveloped regions, metropolis and countryside' (Frow 1991: 151). Tourism encourages structural underdevelopment because this is what tourists often seek (see page 68).

Furthermore, the 'place' of tourism is subject to further division since tourists are highly differentiated among themselves, each group seeking to fend off the others. There are three main groups – travellers, tourists and trippers. The three terms denote a hierarchy in touring. Travellers are the most serious and dedicated explorers. They expend more time, money and attention to their practice than tourists, who set out to confirm what they already know through tour guides and brochures. The lowest position of all is occupied by trippers, who characteristically have the least time, the least money and the most superficial interest in the place they are visiting (Boorstin 1962; MacCannell 1976; Fussell 1980; Culler 1988). Of course, the hierarchies of touring are not fixed, but applied by those groups and individuals who wish to mark themselves off from those whom they wish to avoid or condemn. Further, the hierarchies of touring are neither objective nor distinct. They overlap and, since they are self-definitions set against others, they are decided by numerous, often minute differences.

In addition, the terms have to be qualified in three other ways. Firstly, each of them is subject to refinement, so that travellers may be explorers or adventurers, conquerors and colonialists; tourists may be packaged or 'unpackaged', in the manner of 'adventure overland' expeditions to far-flung places; trippers are different from each other if they travel by train or coach, or stay away for a day or an afternoon, or go to the seaside or a stately home (Ryan 1991). Secondly, the 'profile' and activity of any one of the groups alters according to gender, age, race and social class, which makes for a heterogeneous experience which sociologists, geographers, historians and literary critics have tried to describe (Ousby 1990; Urry 1990; Barnes and Duncan 1992; Prentice 1993). Thirdly, these conditions alter according to specific historical circumstances, localities, and ways, means and intentions of travel, tours and trips. I intend to mitigate, however temporarily, the extreme instability of these terms. Firstly, I use case-studies bounded in time and place. Secondly, I confine my analyses to the types of travellers, tourists and trippers who in various ways use photographs to direct them in what to see, or to prove that they have undertaken specific journeys. Finally, I turn my attention away from the scene in itself towards the ways that individuals or groups are *looking*. My concern is with sight, and with observation.

TOURING AND LOOKING

There is no position of innocence from which to see or speak. Words used to define space – such as position, location, situation and mapping – immediately suggest relationships, hierarchies, and the possibility of oppression or repression. The spatial metaphors of exploration, for instance, have their roots in imperialism, while other terms, such as centre–margin, open–closed, or inside–outside, describe the 'geometrics of domination' (Keith and Pile 1993: 1). These metaphors, often applied to colonisers and their objects, are part of the rhetorics of looking and writing which for centuries have been used in the production of the unmarked, universal man.

An example of this ancient, colonising and universal way of looking at landscape is the testimony of a contemporary traveller in the USA, the geographer Jonathan Smith. He looks at the landscape in these orthodox ways, but he attempts to present them in an ironic light. His account is also a useful and clear introduction to some of my other concerns, including the relation between landscape, time and memory. Smith describes his experience, or what he calls a 'common reverie':

> I was driving east from the village of Canandaigua towards Geneva, which stands at the foot of Seneca Lake in the state of New York. The road undulated over swells of glacial drift, while the setting sun turned the corn stubble to gold and threw crisp shadows over the fields. Infatuated by the scene, I wished it could be somehow transfixed. I did not want the sun to drop, or spring to come, or the road to end. I wanted to continue through a silent landscape where everything stayed the same, where there was no substance or consequence, where there was only stylized motion through a stylized scene.
>
> (J. Smith 1993: 79)

His journey is less significant than the ways in which he chooses to recreate the view for his readers – placing himself at the centre of the scene, laying it out piece by piece while interpreting its significance. This strategy – the common ground, as it were, of so much landscape writing and observation – forces viewers to accept the vantage points and preoccupations of authors.

Jonathan Smith is specific about his location, but makes nothing of the names of places. For him they may be simply a matter of locating the scene, but at the same time they recall European culture and expansion, as well as mixing together villages, cities and states with mountains and lakes. The author's reverie happens in a complicated, evocative space which he pretends is much simpler by using a misleadingly innocent but revelatory device. He writes that 'the eye that has been properly educated' sees 'landscape present itself as a spectacle'. This spectacle 'situates its spectator in an Olympian position', rewarding the onlooker with 'the pleasures of distance and detachment and the personal inconsequence of all they survey' (J. Smith 1993: 78–9). Smith describes how he was turned into 'a species of voyeur' whose first pleasure is aesthetic: 'the setting sun turned the corn stubble to gold and threw crisp shadows over the fields' (J. Smith 1993: 79).

Smith aligns himself unproblematically with the Romantic imagination. This approach to the world insists on aesthetic pleasure and control, from the detached position of the masculine 'educated eye'. The Romantic imagination remains what Patricia Yaeger calls 'a masculine mode of writing and relationship...concerned with self-centred imperialism, with a "pursuit of the infinitude of the private self" that we, in the twentieth century, regard with some embarrassment and keep trying, epistemologically if not politically, to amend' (Yaeger 1989: 192). A critique of Smith's approach, and its consequences, is a leitmotif of my book.

The disengaged look of the universal man was (and remains) the look of mastery; gazing was (and is) a masculine attribute. Anyone in the historic periods under review standing actually or metaphorically on promontories and taking in the view looks with a masculine eye of survey, ownership and control. As I discuss in the first chapter on 'Landscape record and reverie', this gaze was always that of explorers and adventurers, conquerors and colonialists (Pratt 1992). It was extensively used by writers in the nineteenth century, such as Thomas Hardy who used the roving and controlling eye of the tourist to describe his women characters (Nunokawa 1992), and it was widely used by photographers to colonise their subjects (Alloula 1986; Bate 1992; Ballerini 1993). Women could borrow this way of looking, though they found it uncomfortable: it never belonged to them. Women in the nineteenth century found it difficult to establish a look of their own (Solomon-Godeau 1986), and it is only recently that photographers have begun to question the assumption that the gaze is a masculine attribute to which women must submit.

For instance, in 'Untitled Landscapes', one of a series of photographs by Susan Trangmar, we see that (in the words of Susan Butler) 'this observing woman remains obstinate in her refusal to be revealed, to be the object of our look' (see colour plate 2). According to Butler, Susan Trangmar refuses to accept 'the traditional pattern of looking in which an (assumed) male glance has access to a mute feminine appearance', and insists upon 'her own right to look' (Butler 1989: 11) (see page 269). This interrogation of the dominant, masculine look is of recent origin in landscape photography, and as I intend to show (especially in chapter 9 on 'Wastes and boundaries'), it is one of several ways in which independent photographers have questioned mainstream ways of looking.

None the less, the structure of the dominant look is intact, and I intend to investigate it further. Smith's second pleasure also results from his detachment, but inflects it differently. It is linked to his desire to stop the passage of time. He writes, 'Infatuated by the scene, I wished that it could be somehow transfixed. I did not want the sun to drop, or spring to come, or the road to end. I wanted to continue through a silent landscape where everything stayed the same, where there was no substance or consequence, where there was only stylized motion through a stylized scene' (J. Smith 1993: 79). Had Smith photographed the scene, he would have had a contemporaneous but imperfect measure of what he remembered and later chose to record in words. A second leitmotif in my book is the desire for the possibility of stopping time, or appearing to do so, in photography. The medium caters for armchair time-travel, in which the viewer has the illusion of entering some other place and period through a magical window. At the same time, the viewer stays safely in place, and the act of time- and space-travel is purely speculative, encouraging day-dreams and reverie. Travelling in this manner is an imaginative act, an act of memory and reflection. The only danger arises from the capacity of photography to stir up or encourage dark thoughts about the passage of time. This desire to stop time is given in the nature of photographs, which Roland Barthes calls 'clocks for seeing' into the dead past. Looking at photographs (in which time appears to have been frozen) invokes in viewers the recognition that time does *not* stop, and leads consequently to thoughts of mortality. Susan Sontag writes that photographs are 'reminder[s] of death'. Once again, this thread runs throughout my book, coming to the surface for examination chiefly in chapter 2 on 'Shakespeare land', and in chapters 7–9, which comprise the final section on various aspects of photography and the past.

Mortality, though, is not uppermost in Jonathan Smith's mind. On the contrary, Smith uses his 'reverie' to move it into yet another register of meaning. He opposes his desire to stop time with the wish to think of the past as a time of safety and repose. He likens the frozen scene to the 'pleasures of retrospection' in which the correspondence of scenery and memory invokes 'the sense of detachment and the luxury of indifference' (79). He decides that the landscape was 'like a setting for life remembered'. What happened to him on that journey was a moment in which he rose above 'the temporal flux', and imagined the landscape and his past to be complete, stable and permanent (attributes which David Lowenthal identifies as valuable counters to the perceived uncertainty of present times) (Lowenthal 1985: 62).

Jonathan Smith is amused by being the author of the scene. He acknowledges that his description of this episode is an act of 'spectacular egoism', but he does not reflect that this viewpoint is an important part of the process of identifying landscape and ascribing meaning to it. For him, the pleasure in the landscape is aesthetic only in the first instance, and only because it is the prelude to a dream of immortality. The idea of the fixed scene permits his indifference to time, giving the illusion that he has the capacity to rise above, even while remaining within, 'the temporal flux', striking a deal with death to pass him by. What his egoism allows him is a flight of fancy, escaping time, denying his mortality, standing on the promontory and viewing the parade with god-like indifference. This attempt to 'transcend' time and place through verbal and photographic records – a position which is very hard to sustain – is a third leitmotif of my book. Indeed, Jonathan Smith recognises the transitory nature of this moment of transcendence, and tells how the peace and power of the voyeur did not last for long. It was spoiled when 'a truck loaded with crates of cabbages lurched into [his] path' (J. Smith 1993: 79). This ended the reverie as suddenly as it had begun, with his educated eye forced to focus for the sake of life itself on this unlovely, commercial and wayward trespasser.

LOOKING AT LANDSCAPE

I intend to argue that the category of 'landscape' is primarily not a phenomenon of the natural lie of the land, or human geography, but an attribute of sight. In her article on the origins of sightseeing, Judith Adler warns against linking a single sensory perception to a specific historical period, because the same period easily accommodates different travel styles, each of which may deploy the senses in different ways. Tourists in 'minor travel traditions' may set out on journeys not to see sights but for the sake of hot springs, mineral waters, music, or a breath of fresh air (Adler 1989: 24). Similarly, travellers of all periods have placed at the centre of their discourse the word and not the image, the ear and tongue and not the eye. However, as Adler makes clear, by the seventeenth century vision was placed at the top of the sensory hierarchy: 'hearsay' was no longer legally admissible as evidence, and the ground for valid judgement was now occupied by the 'eyewitness'. The ear and tongue were no longer the primary senses of travellers, and were superseded by another tradition which 'gave preeminence to the "eye" and to silent "observation"' (11). At its inception sightseeing was not immediately attached to aesthetic interests, but thought to be a branch of history, 'history being understood, in opposition to fable, as a true account of the facts, based upon first-hand observation' (16). The 'eye' was disciplined to emotionally detached, objectively accurate vision. Its authority in the public realm of historical knowledge was not put at risk by travellers' 'personal' responses. Yet by the end of the eighteenth century, the traveller's 'eye', hitherto bound by the normative discourse of science, became increasingly subject to a new discipline of connoisseurship, gauging the merits of works of art. At this point travel itself became the occasion for the display of 'taste' (22).

In the eighteenth century the aristocracy and gentry of England thought that landscapes were places which directed ways of looking. English parks and gardens were full of signs referring to classical myths and current intellectual concerns. These signatures of civilisation demanded a kind of observation which Norman Bryson has defined as the activity of the gaze, a 'prolonged, contemplative [look] regarding the field of vision with a certain aloofness and disengagement, across a tranquil interval' (Bryson 1983: 94). Walking in the landscape, or taking in the view, required learning and time. The landscape was not to be seen at a glance but had to be brought into focus and 'read' in order to be seen (Paulson 1975; Pugh 1988).

Using the gaze, the eighteenth-century viewer was encouraged to travel in time and across continents – making connections with the deep past of the Greeks, the Italy of the Grand Tour, and the library of literature in the great house. Taking in a landscape required the tourist to be an eyewitness, though this did not necessarily involve direct experience, with all its difficulties and dangers. Taking in a landscape was always (and often solely) a cerebral activity. Landscapes could be taken in by surrogate viewers, and later presented to their audiences, who viewed them at a safe remove from the originals. Landscapes could come already fashioned for readers or viewers into accounts, poems, or pictures – and from the mid-nineteenth century they appeared in the forms of photographs.

By chance, the words site and sight in English sound the same, and their meanings can overlap: landscape is both a site (as in a 'place') and a sight (as in 'view'). This accident of the English language is matched by another, in which the noun 'eye' and personal pronoun 'I' signify the privilege of the observer, who always stands at the vantage point and commands the view, conjuring it up to be read, written or pictured. To be able to gaze across an interval is a sign of leisure, education and seriousness. Gazing seeks to confine what is elusive, and counter the fleeting moment with a prolonged look which in itself is a sign of permanence. It stands in strict opposition to the glance, which is a subversive and furtive look.

A hierarchy of different ways of looking is attached to the three levels of touring that I discussed earlier. Travellers practice the gaze, which is contemplative and penetrative; tourists glance, which is accumulative but shallow; and trippers see everything (if they see at all) in disconnected blinks, blurs or 'snaps'.

The three broad categories of touring and looking have appropriate technologies for recording sights, which in the periods under review and in the most general terms range from plate cameras to snapshooting and disposable 'fun' cameras.

The gaze, glance and blink are clearly not characteristics of machines, but are ways of looking which might be ascribed to different machines or formats. For instance, any camera which is used according to the rules of perspective and linear–planar space produces the equivalent of the tranquil gaze. Similarly, any camera which is used to create tilted or blurred images, or distorts natural lighting through flash, is equivalent to the quick glance or the momentary blink, as if seeing from the corner of the eye.

To complicate matters, any photograph, whatever its composition, may be looked at for a long time or only for a moment. The length of time spent looking at the scene or the photograph is crucial: it suggests more than the fascination of the viewer, and endows the scene or picture itself with special, perhaps mystic significance.

None of these photographs or ways of looking at them is tied forever to any particular meaning: in other words, the permanence of the image which usually signifies 'the tranquil look across an interval' might discomfort, subvert or exaggerate the traditional gaze, as in the work of Susan Trangmar, Keith Arnatt or John Davies. In a similar vein, Martin Parr and Paul Reas seem to imitate the quick glance by tilting the camera, but they produce exhibitions and books where the images come under the prolonged gaze of viewers. In various ways, including the use of flash, these two men draw attention to their own relation to the scene, perhaps distancing themselves from their subjects or incorporating themselves into the pictures as tourists by adopting the quick, 'flashed' glance. Either way, they demonstrate their presence and point of view in the ways they choose to look.

Because my interest is in ways of looking, and how looking is related to a sense of place and history, I am only interested in rural and urban landscape as an effect of looking (rather than resulting from town and country planning). My pursuit of sight, which in touring is intricately tied to spaces known as 'sites' or 'beauty spots' and also to a sense of historical time, means that I shall sometimes turn away from considering landscape to be an attribute of the countryside towards the urban scene (as in chapter

5 on the work of George Orwell, Humphrey Spender and Bill Brandt in the 1930s), or the interiors of factories (as in the discussion of Kodak in the 1890s in chapter 1). The term 'landscape' in relation to the urban scene is useful because it continues to differentiate whatever may be seen from that which should be overlooked. I use it to underscore the characteristic act of touring, which is to insist on difference and mark it by various techniques of observation.

The phrase 'techniques of the observer' is Jonathan Crary's, who in his book on the historical construction of vision and the status of the observing subject draws a distinction between the spectator and the observer, which in common usage are effectively synonymous. The Latin root for the term 'spectator' means to look at, but has specific connotations of passivity which Crary wants to avoid. Instead, he chooses the term observer mainly for its etymological resonance: to 'observe' does not literally mean 'to look at' but ' "to conform one's action, to comply with", as in observing rules, codes, regulations, and practices' (Crary 1990: 6). The nineteenth-century observer was one who saw within prescribed sets of possibilities or conventions within a 'shifting field' of discursive, social, technological and institutional relations. Indeed, the observer was an *effect* of this 'shifting field'. The key element is the 'ceaseless and self-perpetuating creation of new needs, new consumption and new production [and far] from being exterior to this process, the observer as human subject is completely immanent to it' (10). In this system 'vision itself became a kind of discipline or mode of work' (19). It was used to assess 'normality' in the fields of medicine, agriculture, industry and economics long before the development of photographic procedures and mass-production techniques. By the late nineteenth century the idea that vision was a mode of work, organised according to convention, was matched by ideas about the mass production of goods for mass markets, including tourism.

My narrative begins in the middle of things, when most of the apparatus required to produce photography was made in factories. Advertisers often used images of factories to demonstrate the excellence of their products, as we see in this drawing of a dry-plate factory printed in the *Amateur Photographer* magazine in 1887 (see illustration on page 16). The picture of a factory organised along rational (or reassuring) lines, with light and airy buildings settled in the countryside, was a visual equivalent to the verbal testimonials about giving 'satisfaction'.

Orderly factories were regularly visited by journalists, who then praised them in the photographic press. In revealing the beauty of the industrial process, journalists

2. 'Britannia's Factory', *Amateur Photographer*, 20 March 1887.

combined older rules about seeing nature's beauty in its symmetry with their observations on a corresponding precision and multiplication of simple forms in methods of manufacture. They demonstrated how aesthetic pleasures were enjoyed in factories as in nature, since both places were governed by similar systems of observation. Wherever they stood in the chain of factory production, or whether they came to report for the press, those watching the industrial process utilised vision as a mode of work. This was the source of their authority and productivity, different only in degree from the overseeing authority of factory owners observing the rules of expenditure and profit. The modern observer lives within a discursive field already organised by capital, and exists in its investigative, disciplinary and organisational modes.

Since this idea of observation is so central to my book, I often avoid 'landscape' in the sense of countryside, and concentrate on the relation of rules and looking. In order to underline the centrality of convention within the realms of looking and producing, I begin chapter 1 not with a description of a successful landscape photograph but with accounts of two photographs that failed. These failures reveal as much about the relation of looking and work as any successful picture. Following this,

I discuss the integration of looking and producing in accounts of factory production in the late nineteenth century before going on to discuss survey work in Warwickshire. My purpose in spending so much time in factories rather than in the treasured landscape of countryside is to place the category 'landscape' in the realms of work and governance.

ENGLAND AND THE PICTURESQUE

Taking aesthetic pleasure from landscape is not widely recognised to involve work at all, though actually it depends on 'good taste' gained through education in the ways of certain social classes. The most important aesthetic distinction for photography is the idea of the picturesque (Andrews 1989). In the eighteenth century, the cult of the 'picturesque' among the leisured classes was already a mongrel term, mixing delight in the gentle ('beautiful') effects of nature with the extravagant ('sublime') feeling aroused by wild nature. In his book on the early history of tourism in England, Ian Ousby describes how writers used the terms picturesque, beautiful and sublime 'almost interchangeably' for any landscape of mountain, rock and water which could not be appreciated by referring to the symmetries of neo-classicism. But the term 'picturesque' never lost touch entirely with the fact that it meant, 'at its simplest, "that kind of beauty which would look well in a picture"' (Ousby 1990: 154). Landscape was not just anything seen from the top of a hill, or from a low vantage point: it should be composed, improved and imagined. The capacity to see landscape was not open to everyone: it was a privilege enjoyed by the gentry, who understood both art and touring.

In the latter years of the century, the Reverend William Gilpin published a series of 'picturesque tours' through England and Scotland which listed alongside art works the natural scenes which satisfied pictorial canons of beauty. Tourists carried Claude glasses (focusing devices named after the painter Claude Lorrain) that they could look through to colour and frame a view. By the early nineteenth century numerous 'picturesque tours' had been published, and the ways of looking at entire geographic regions had become conventional, and were enjoyed by increasing numbers of professional, middle-class groups.

More than half a century later, these widened social groups used photography to 'take' a landscape in an instant rather than using Claude glasses to help them sketch it. Even so, photographers still had to compose and choose their subjects. As H. P. Robinson wrote in 1869 in *Pictorial Effect in Photography*, the power of this 'art' was limited: 'the sublime cannot be reached by it', and 'its power is greatest when it attempts the simplest things' (Robinson 1869 [1971]: 53). What Robinson meant by 'simplest' was pictorial, which was the translation of the picturesque into the unusually realistic medium of photography. In order to carry out a successful pictorial photograph, the artist-photographer must obey many of the tenets of traditional art forms, including the absolute rights to construct the scene, select whatever was to be included, and be ruthless in excluding whatever would spoil the artistic 'effect'. He claimed that 'picturesqueness has never had so perfect an interpreter' as photography (15).

In the same way that the gaze is meaningful in relation to what it is not – the glance – so landscape is a relational term: calling something 'landscape' places it in a superior position to whatever is *not* designated in this way. 'Pleasing prospects' rewarded the educated eye, whereas everything outside the park or garden could not be read, and had no meaning as landscape. What lay outside was either heath or worked land, which was never perceived to be landscape by those privileged to see and read it. As Raymond Williams observed, 'A working country is hardly ever a landscape. The very idea of landscape implies separation and observation', both of which imply differences of place and hierarchies in social class (Williams 1975: 149).

The emphasis on the gaze and ways of looking turns inside out the common-sense idea that landscape is something existing 'out there', in some absolute form. The term 'landscape' is an honorific title granted by viewers with specific, if unintentional or unconscious, ends that correspond to and reinforce the hierarchies of social class, gender and identity. As Grace Seiberling writes in her history of amateur photography in the mid-Victorian period, pioneer photographers knew what was worth looking at and recording. Their knowledge stemmed from their social and economic status within the dominant class (Seiberling 1986: 46). They did not choose all possible subjects, but stayed within a narrow range influenced by 'cultural convention' governing pictorial tradition. Seiberling recounts that when, in 1852, the first exhibition by members of the Photographic Exchange Club was held at the Society of Arts, a reviewer described how different their pictures were from recent French work. Whereas French photographs were largely architectural:

The English are, for the most part, representations of the peaceful village; the unassuming church, among its tombstones and trees; the gnarled oak, standing alone in the forest; intricate masses of tangled wood, reflected in some dark pool; shocks of corn, drooping with their weight of grain; the quiet stream with its water-lilies and rustic bridge; the wild upland pass with its foreground of crumbling rock and purple; or the still lake, so still that you must drop a stone into its surface before you can tell which is the real village on the margin and which the reflection.

(cited in Seiberling 1986: 46–7)

Photographs confused the difference between reality and reflections, and this was the source of their authority. They transcribed and held the English scene in view forever, as if by magic. In the above report, readers were given a catalogue of objects already resonant with English values, already archetypes of the home landscape, and they remain so today. The stability of the set is equalled by its easy transference across class boundaries, becoming a source for national identification among people who would never own such landscapes or even visit them.

Later in the nineteenth century the picturesque was still being used to reassure people that England was as beautiful as ever. There was a consensus among writers on artistic photography that landscapes were improved or enlivened by figures, and photographers were exhorted to include them in their pictures (Robinson 1897 [1973]: 80). Figures and landscape must be in harmony. Photographers engaged in subterfuge in order to achieve this end, substituting the children of the gentry for poor children in bucolic scenes because the poor never looked the part, nor did they understand what was expected of country types (Pringle 1890: 13). The search for landscape most often involved the search for an equivalent to social harmony, regardless of real conditions: it reflected the desire of the dominant groups to maintain social authority without interruption or challenge. This created a stability in the definition of what constituted landscape, enjoyed by the tourists who bought mass-produced prints by Francis Frith or the work of George Washington Wilson (R. Taylor 1981). For these audiences, modern reprographic techniques resolved the difficulties of travelling and remembering. The modern methods of photography and printing allowed them to see an ideal England that was permanent, if only in memory. A conventional, ideal England is readily available today in thatched cottages printed in calendars or on place-mats, jigsaw puzzles, and chocolate boxes (see colour plate 21).

ENGLISH LANDSCAPE WITH COLLIDING FIGURES

The need to sustain the rural idyll derives from the need of the English to define themselves and remain united as a nation. I have chosen to discuss landscape only in England because it is a distinct arena within which groups regard certain landscapes to be defining parts of the 'imagined community' (Anderson 1989). Anderson argues that the nation is imagined because it is not directly experienced as a community, but rather is joined together by images held in the minds of its fellow-members. The crucial point, however, is that communities are distinguished not by the 'falsity/genuineness' of their shared images, but by the style in which they are imagined (15). Hence, I do not look at landscapes in order to guess whether or not they are false or genuine representations of what England is 'really' like, but to examine the preoccupations and methods of those observers who contributed images to the shared, national pool.

England offers a discrete area, and a discrete and highly developed sense of community – what Anderson calls 'a deep, horizontal comradeship' (16). This sense of belonging was crucial to marketing photographic products. After all, the purpose of reliable film and cameras was to reach amateurs who were more interested in collecting souvenirs than in pursuing photography as a serious hobby. In 1888, one year after the drawing of the dry-plate factory was published (see illustration on page 16), George Eastman marketed his first Kodak camera, with celluloid roll-film created for it, and made his promise of trouble-free photography (Coe 1976: 52). By the 1920s, when the mass markets for photography and tourism were extensive, Kodak declared that taking pictures was child's play, as easy as 'gathering buttercups in a meadow' (*Punch* 23 March 1927). Moreover, Kodak enabled tourists to join with the deep past of the country by recording 'the beauties of Britain', as we see in this illustration of 'the lovely and ancient town of Guildford' in Surrey (*Punch* 29 June 1927). Kodak promised easy access not only to memories but also to British history: 'The old towns of Britain have stood for centuries looking on at history in the making. There is romance in the very stones [and your "Kodak" pictures] will always speak to you of a time that is gone and of a spirit that is deathless'. Thus Kodak showed how its customers could enjoy 'a deep, horizontal comradeship' with other Britons, and link themselves to historical time (see chapters 4 and 7).

3. Kodak advertisement, *Punch*, 29 June 1927.

Furthermore, as Anderson argues, the feeling of comradeship is achieved 'regardless of the actual inequality and exploitation that may prevail' (16). England, then, is not at all a single category but a set of relationships. The nation exists in tension. Its fellow-members remain deeply divided among themselves, but at the same time they constantly prove themselves ready to unite around certain issues, talismans and images. The greatest divide exists between the north and south, though there are numerous other divisions and distinctions within regions. In order to be able to discuss ways of looking, I have decided to concentrate on certain localities at specific times,

21

and attempt to chart how these local distinctions, allegiances and rivalries are made manifest, and how the resulting imagery fits into the preferred pool of representations which have national significance.

Englishness, which is a set of relationships, exists not only in tension but is always in flux. Its definition is inseparable from the non-English, and this separation begins within the island: England defines itself against the distinct nations of Scotland and Wales which are bound together with England only in the formation of 'Britain', a concept or an entity which is not identified by a 'deep horizontal comradeship'. On the contrary, the definition in Fowler's dictionary reads 'no Englishman, or perhaps no Scotsman either, calls himself a Briton without a sneaking sense of the ludicrous', or (according to Gowers's revised edition) 'hears himself referred to as a BRITISHER without squirming' (Fowler 1926 and Gowers 1965 cited in Lowenthal 1991: 209).

If England is defined sharply against Wales and Scotland, and there is little identification with Britain, the position of the United Kingdom is even less secure. It includes the 'province' of Northern Ireland, which is part of the sovereign territory of the 'Kingdom', but which geographically, culturally and conceptually is even more distinct from England than Wales or Scotland. Neither the United Kingdom nor Britain exists at levels of deep, horizontal comradeship. In my endeavour to see how imagery is used to sustain a feeling of community, the decision to stay within England comes from the clarity with which the English define their relationships with what they consider to be peripheral regions and cultures.

The hierarchy of distinctions does not begin at the borders of the 'other' nations of Britain, but is measured within England in terms of distance from London, and what are called the 'Home Counties' immediately surrounding the capital. When the British Association for the Advancement of Science established a series of committees (known collectively as the 'Racial Committee') between 1875 and 1883, the aim was to investigate by means of photographs the 'national or local types of race prevailing in different parts of the United Kingdom'. By 1880 over 400 photographs had been collected, mainly from Wales, Scotland, and the remoter Celtic regions of England such as Cornwall. These areas were defined against the dominant and normative Anglo-Saxon or 'Teuton' race living in the south of the country, and not at too great a distance from London (Poignant 1992; 58–60). I examine the observation of some sectors of the peripheral English by other, more culturally powerful groups coming from London in chapter 5 on documentary observation in the 1930s.

4. John Davies, 'Victoria Promenade, Widnes, Cheshire, 1986.

This constant tension and flux within England is the other, under-represented side of the wealth of conventional, ritually peaceful landscape photography. The relative absence of tension in traditional or central photography, in which landscape is a view across a tranquil interval enlivened perhaps by a single figure or harmonious group (Street 1989), requires that throughout this book I turn to pictures where the photographer draws attention to disharmony. For example, John Davies's book ironically titled *A Green & Pleasant Land* is full of pictures of the historic impact of industry and engineering on the inhabited land, for instance in the picture reproduced here called 'Victoria Promenade, Widnes, Cheshire, 1986' (Davies 1987). My attention is fixed on scenes where I see the landscape full of colliding figures, by which I mean individuals and groups competing with each other for the use and meaning of the place – competing ostensibly for leisure, but also for identity and a sense of history. Once again, my interest in them is not so much in the social and historical implications of these conflicts but in the ways of looking which these groups or individuals have used to lay claim to fixing the meaning of the ground (for historical and social accounts see Mingay 1976; Newby 1979; Mingay 1981; Marsh 1982; Shoard 1987; Mingay 1989; Howkins 1991).

Looking back to the nineteenth century, at first sight it appears there were no arguments over who made landscapes. The conventions for observation were in place. For instance, in 1886, photographers were encouraged to take a trip to Dorking in Surrey, which was a cheap train journey from London and easy to reach on a half-day holiday. There they would find exactly what they were looking for – 'picturesque nooks, woodland glades, old-fashioned cottages, extensive prospects, and some charming scenery' (Brown 1886: 19). Tourists with cameras, by discovering the types of picturesque subject matter every day, proved that it really existed. They could forget their workaday lives, forget the discomfort of travel, and take pleasure in the experience of rediscovering a more delightful England, which they could photograph and take home to prove their experiences.

In behaving like this, tourists could escape from urban life. By the 1880s, this was already a standard response among people with leisure and taste. Over the next twenty years, more and more people from different stations in life were determined to show that they too knew that the picturesque was an imaginative form of escape from the city. Though different class fractions clashed, as I explain in chapter 3, and a large amount of capital and energy was spent in maintaining the differences between the subdivisions of class, the common pursuit of the picturesque had important ideological impact. Instead of splitting groups apart, it helped draw together competing class fractions into the 'imagined community' of the nation – a common shared history made evident in photographs, and a contradiction to social differences.

Nevertheless, the search for the picturesque in the late nineteenth century was driven by different groups and for different motives than in earlier periods. The mode of representation changed from engravings to photographs printed in books. At the same time, by the end of the century the category of the 'picturesque' flourished among new types of tourists who went around England with a special agenda – the determination to save the countryside in what they called 'survey' photographs, which I discuss in chapter 1 on 'Landscape record and reverie', and in chapter 2 on 'Shakespeare land'. These supposedly objective surveys did not simply break with the notion of the picturesque, but often used 'record' to capture the 'picturesque' content of a scene (see the photographs of the village of Pembridge and Moor Street in Birmingham by Harold Baker, pages 36, 53). The need to survey and record old

England was an indication of the struggle for the playing grounds, the pressure on the countryside as a site of leisure. Active class fractions living in the suburbs of London and of fast growing industrial cities such as Birmingham were increasingly in competition for the treasured landscapes which they considered to be sites of significance and leisure. By the 1880 and 1890s, the category of the picturesque implied a whole new set of relationships – most of them deriving from class consciousness, competition for space and the right to define the appearance of the country. Most critically, the picturesque is enlisted in the definition of what the country means: it becomes a patriotic term, a touchstone of national characteristics. Again, this sort of redefinition is not entirely new, but it became endemic because of the systems of mass production and touring then in place.

Comparing two views of Kenilworth Castle in Warwickshire (reproduced on pages 26–7), we see how the picturesque was transformed into one of the late-nineteenth-century forms of the photographic art of 'pictorialism'. The engraving of the landscape painted by Sir Henry Warren (1794–1879), and reproduced in a book published in 1870, depicts a leisurely moment in the countryside, with a cowgirl leaning on the fence and cattle following on (James Taylor 1870). In this pastoral scene, the manifestations of England's history and present order appear in a single picture, indissolubly linked in a narrow range of tones. The unity of subjects and the soft light evoke an England which is rural, deeply tranquil, and untroubled even by time.

The contrasting photograph of 'Kenilworth from the west' was taken by James Leon Williams and published in 1892. It is closer to P. H. Emerson's naturalism of the late 1880s (in which all composing took place in the field and darkroom work consisted of accurate printing) than to H. P. Robinson's combination prints of the 1860s and thereafter (in which he used several negatives to build up artistic scenes in the darkroom in order to overcome the limitations of photography to capture land and sky on a single plate) (L. Smith 1992). Williams's picture is unmistakably a photograph – but in comparison with the engraving of Warren's painting it has less composure and is less assured about the unity of the scene. What we see is no longer a pastoral delight, in which country folk and their animals wander along a lane beside a ruined castle. The pastoral signs have been displaced by the appearance of an artist, busily working on his canvas in the open air. The place is *seen* to be less than an idyll and more of a beauty spot for the artist/tourist.

5. Engraving of *Kenilworth Castle* from a painting by Sir Henry Warren, in James Taylor, *The Family History of England*, 1870.

Moreover, Williams demonstrates that two kinds of artist/tourist frequent that spot – the painter and the photographer, who, although their work is quite different, are associates. The difference in their work, however, is significant. The photographer accepts that his picture will be made in the conditions then prevailing: the scene is harshly lit, the time of day specific, the picture taken in a single plate exposed for the landscape and therefore leaving the sky overexposed and blank. Because of the action of light on the photosensitive plate, Williams's work remains a record which is apparently independent of him and therefore a closer link to the material world than the painter's work on canvas. What Williams shows is that moment in the history of looking at landscape when it moves from painterly interpretation to record work in photography. This was a double movement, breaking with some of the conventions of painting landscape in order to establish some of the characteristics of landscape photography, while remaining within the broad conventions of appropriate subjects for tourists to visit and turn into pictures.

Williams photographed a tourist spot of considerable significance in England,

6. J. L. Williams, 'Kenilworth from the west', from *The Home and Haunts of Shakespeare*, 1892.

redolent of Elizabethan glory and the historical romances of Sir Walter Scott, as I discuss in 'Shakespeare land'. Kenilworth had what Walter Benjamin called 'aura', a mystical significance which separated it from social usage, and left it subject to ritual or mystic uses. This quality remained part of favoured historic sites or treasured landscapes. Yet, at the same time, the desire of tourists was to close the gap between themselves and unique objects of the past. This desire was encouraged and met by rational recreation, which became possible by means of the local and national provision of utilities such as libraries, galleries and museums and the development of the tourist industry through maps, brochures, guides, tours and so forth. The integrated and overlapping systems of self-improvement and self-management produced a progressive and calculated detachment of objects from their aura, or their quality of singular or unique presence. Reproductions of these objects offered this sort of immediacy, in the form of commodities without aura (Benjamin 1973: 225). By the early 1890s when Williams visited Kenilworth it was well established as a busy tourist attraction – a fact not evident in his photograph, which suggests the place is exclusive to artists.

From the testimony of Henry James, writing about the castle in 1877, it seems that aesthetic experiences at Kenilworth were hard won against a backdrop of tourists and the trades catering for them. The difficulty for educated tourists such as James, which worsened progressively because holiday crowds increased, was to find places of interest which kept some degree of social exclusivity. James wrote that from a distance Kenilworth looked like a 'perfect picture', in the manner of paintings by Claude. As he walked closer, however, the vision disappeared, since under the walls he found hawkers selling keepsakes for tourists (including photographs), paupers, and young men sprawled on the grass in front of the beer shops. The entry price kept these people outside the castle, but inside he encountered different social embarrassments. Children were running around, their parents were eating from newspapers, and someone was reading aloud from the guidebook. His only escape was imaginative: he found there was 'still a good deal of old England in the scene', with a 'quaintish village' and 'dark, fat meadows' nearby. He was willing to pretend the modern vagrants were Shakespearian clowns, and was on the point of 'going into one of the ale houses to ask Mrs Quickly for a cup of sack'. He had resolved the 'richly complex English world' by deciding the present was always seen '*in profile*', and it was only the past that showed itself '*full face*' (H. James 1905 [1981]).

Henry James exhibits several of the characteristics of tourists, particularly his self-styled distinction from others at the same site. Unlike the author himself, these trippers were unable fully to appreciate the aura of the place because of their youth, class or (what James considered to be) their stupidity. England was complex – the social structure was highly visible yet allowed for new degrees of movement, notably among sections of the lower-middle class. James found this disconcerting, but he found a way around the problem, which became a conventional solution to the problem of touring. Those who organised the commercial life of historical sites tried to keep the present in profile (by hiding its signs) and to show the past full face (by foregrounding what they presented as its authentic signs). Tourists accepted that the price of entry tickets, or the costs of travelling to special sites, enabled them to see rather less of the present and rather more of the past. They expected the guardians of such sites to provide them with a marked degree of isolation and exclusivity from the outside world. In order to ensure that they saw the past full face, in the manner of serious travellers rather than casual trippers, they sometimes banded together in specialist groups. They claimed they were qualified to examine the sites by virtue of their investment in expensive photographic equipment, or by virtue of an unusual degree of shared intellectual commitment to ideas about history and heritage. These groups set the standards, and put pressure on landowners and Government alike to cater for their needs. In the end, though agreement has never been final, the disparate groups saw landscape as a means of unifying significant forces around the idea of the proper aims and characteristics of the nation. They agreed, after all, that England was an 'old country', and signs of its age were worth preserving (Wright 1986).

The signs of age are always signs of something else, and some old places seem to be more 'English' than others in tourists' imaginations. For instance, sites which have 'deep' and authentic histories in their own right, such as Kenilworth, Stonehenge, or the Lakes, are quintessentially English. Places which are old but recently and fortuitously 'left' as bequests to the nation, which include most of the houses held by the National Trust since its foundation in 1894, are only essentially English. Contemporary theme parks or concocted 'heritage centres' represent Englishness least well, appearing to be more of a response to recent reversals in the economy than emerging from and belonging to the past. They remain popular among tourists who are looking for entertainment rather than edification. Thus the hierarchies of looking, touring, and places are interwoven.

THE COLLECTION

Each of the three sections looks at three aspects of travellers' experiences or preservation methods in relation to photographic practice within a narrow time-frame. The first section is confined to c.1885–95. In the opening chapter, entitled 'Landscape record and reverie', I discuss how the standpoint of distance was used to describe factories so that they looked rational and reassuring. I then examine how the record and survey movement (in particular the Warwickshire Photographic Survey) tried to show that photography could be used for what photographers supposed to be the objective, 'scientific' work of gathering factual 'historical' information. The photographers who developed these practices tried to pretend there were no colliding figures in the landscapes they surveyed. Photographers and writers showed how modern systems of visiting, telling, and *repeating* allowed England to be known in its imaginary and idealised aspect.

In chapter 2, called 'Shakespeare land', I look at how the Shakespeare industry developed in the period under review. The chapter continues to use the case-study of Warwickshire Photographic Survey, but looks at guidebooks illustrated with photographs, and expensive books such as J. L. Williams's *The Home and Haunts of Shakespeare*. Williams was an American, and the significance of 'foreign' touring is examined. The search for Shakespeare has implications for using photographs as the instruments of time-travel, or 'clocks for seeing'. I discuss this along with the ideas of tourism, photography and *memento mori*.

Chapter 3 concerns 'Travellers, tourists and trippers on the Norfolk Broads'. One result of the increased opportunities for holidays was a new mix of classes messing about in boats on inland waterways. The classes consisted of many fractions who, though they wanted to avoid each other, were increasingly coming face to face on the Norfolk Broads. There was much friction, embarrassment and social comedy. The chapter explores the complexity of class relations through different experiences of photography, each with its basis in different leisure activities and different class fractions. This sets the scene for an extended class and gender analysis of the work of P. H. Emerson, a traveller and social anthropologist who was interested in marginal spaces, areas of underdevelopment which allowed him to create an acceptable bohemian life for himself while remaining firmly of the bourgeoisie. He was constantly in search of the 'low' (especially women), but was determined to avoid 'degeneracy'. He tried to adopt a documentary or record mode in relation to his objects, but this constantly broke down for reasons of class, sexuality and fascination.

The second section covers the years *c.*1925–42. In chapter 4, I discuss the idea of ' "England" as a reliable make'. The photographic industry disguised itself in order to fit with inter-war conservatism, moving closer to the centre of domestic life by continuing to expand the market for amateurs. Photography already had a base in the family, but now that common-sense beliefs about what mattered in life were more firmly anchored than ever to the private and individual, the trade was well placed to take advantage of the new circumstances. This chapter looks in detail at four ideas and conditions which shaped the market: the idea that Englishness was 'feminine'; how touring in England was promoted in guidebooks; Kodak's appeal to the lower-middle class through popular snapshooting; and the use which was made of the idea that photography was a universal language.

Chapter 5 is called 'Documentary raids and rebuffs'. Here I look at how photographs were used to provide evidence of working-class life in three key texts: the two-part project of Mass-Observation, which listened to mostly lower-middle-class people in its National Panel of diarists, and invited Humphrey Spender to photograph the inhabitants of Bolton in the late 1930s; George Orwell's *The Road to Wigan Pier*, whose original edition was published by the Left Book Club in 1937 with what the editors considered to be self-evident photographs of deprivation; and Bill Brandt's book of plates called *The English at Home*, which looks across the whole panoply of class relations (Brandt 1936).

The landscape of the working class documented in such works was more than an emblem of economic slump. It signalled that the story of an antique 'Beautiful Britain' was an insufficient measure of modern times, when harsh realities would no longer stay in profile but demanded to be seen full face. In order to signal their difference from the tourist market, Orwell, Brandt and Mass-Observation needed to tell the story of the economic wastelands in a different language from celebrations of English life. The storytellers needed to use different techniques of discovery than simply travelling the roads to the holiday resorts and into the countryside to photograph or describe quaint customs and places. They established their difference by placing great value on witnessing the here and now – on being there to see what they understood to be the actual, real conditions of life (though Brandt, as we shall see, was more interested in fiction than actuality). Mass-Observation and the Left Book Club used what they believed to be factual, 'documentary' photography, and aimed to bring to light the spaces of the working class.

Of course, all three projects existed within tourism, since their authors observed the 'other' from positions of authority and power. Nevertheless, their intentions were closer to those of serious travellers than tourists seeking entertainment. In their different ways, these middle-class photographers were trying to discover something about the 'other', though at the same time as observers they were bound to define themselves sharply against their subjects.

In chapter 6, 'History under fire', I discuss how England at the beginning of the Second World War was both strange and familiar. The country was made strange by war and made familiar by a massive advertising campaign emphasising the history of English freedoms in an English landscape. The countryside blanked out, forbidden or unvisited during the war was the countryside prepared against invasion. Locking it up in this way protected it. At the same time, these practices placed the countryside in an unexpected light. Whereas the landscape had been taken for granted as a holiday haunt, or fought over as a social amenity, now the Ministry of Information and the press demanded that British people see that it was their own, and see that Britain was a nation (so the story went) successfully defended against military invasion since the Norman Conquest of 1066.

In the third and final section I look at some aspects of tourism and photography between c.1982 and 1993. In chapter 7, called 'At home with Fox Talbot', I discuss the celebration of 150 years of photography at Lacock Abbey in 1989. I examine the converging but disparate interests of the National Trust and Kodak, both of which promote traditional photographic techniques in quintessential English scenes. The main concern of the chapter is the way the celebration confined the long time-scale of Lacock Abbey (which the Trust normally promotes) to a shorter and less glorious period. This era was begun by the mid-nineteenth-century 'invention' of photography, something which later became a mass-produced product not normally foregrounded as part of England's heritage and not considered to be central to its values. In order to overcome this lack of conscious interest in photography's ability to represent English history, the 'place' of Lacock was endowed with an unusually specific view of the English past. During the celebration, a theatre group re-enacted Fox Talbot's photographs of his family and servants in an odd recapitulation of Victorian values at the end of a decade of 'Thatcherism', when such values were at a premium. Amateur photographers recorded the re-enacted scenes, placing these revived Victorian values within a general celebration of English ways of life.

Chapter 8 is called 'Pleasures of the imagination', and in it I discuss ways in which photographs of the English landscape have been used to promote both comfortable and disturbed feelings about the English past and its contemporary uses. I examine the 'heritage industry' to see how photographers use orthodox imagery and everyday tourist practices to attack what they take to be the misrepresentation of 'England'. I also discuss other problems of identification with core values of white, middle-class Englishness, and how photographers signal their sense of exclusion and dispossession. The debate over the 'heritage' counters any simplified or relaxed history of the country.

In the final chapter, entitled 'Wastes and boundaries', I look more closely at the sense of disintegration which surrounds so much of the current work on landscape. I look at landscapes which tourists generally avoid – empty, spoiled or destroyed landscapes commonly called wastelands, which contemporary photographers have found ways of seeing. I examine the historical nature of wasteland as a sub-genre of the picturesque, though I turn away from spoiled landscapes in their objective forms, and examine how they remain subject to the masculine look of the gaze. From this position of authority, landscape is treated as the body of a woman. To foreground this usage, contemporary photographers often turn to wastes and boundaries as the sites of symbolic rape or assault. The view of landscape at the end of the book contrasts deliberately with that of nineteenth-century travellers who had at their disposal what they took for granted as the certain process of discovering fecund nature. In contrast, the unease of contemporary landscape photographers about themselves is expressed in the attention granted to marginal and peripheral space.

1

Landscape record and reverie

WRITING LANDSCAPE

IN THIS CHAPTER, I shall look at some of the methods which photographers and journalists used to imagine the landscape and write about it in the last years of the nineteenth century. I shall examine the language of landscape writing, and the attempt to survey landscape. The main features of writing and surveying were to conceal the author, to place the viewer at the author's vantage point, and to represent the view as the result and sign of order. Discovering a high level of order was the precondition of looking and also its main effect. Order was supposedly self-evident in scenery which was empty of people, or in which workers were shown applying themselves to steady production in the workplace (suggested by these photographs of women engaged in daylight printing and girls labelling boxes at Kodak's factory in Harrow sometime after 1890). Reporters of all kinds adopted what they took to be 'objective' ways of looking and seeing. I shall argue that the representation of order was widespread in journalists' accounts of manufactures of photographic 'goods'. In parallel with this, amateur photographers set out to record Warwickshire in apparently objective photographs. We see an example of this practice in the photograph of Pembridge taken by Harold Baker working for the Archaeological Section of the Birmingham and Midland Institute and also for the Warwickshire Photographic Survey (see illustration on page 36). I shall discuss the attempt, and examine the failure to achieve a pure version of historical 'fact'.

7. Workers daylight printing, Kodak factory, Harrow, *c.*1890.

8. Girls labelling boxes, Kodak factory, Harrow, *c.*1890.

9. H. Baker, 'Pembridge', Warwickshire Photographic Survey, 1893.

This expectation of orderliness was repeated and discovered so often because it was intended to dispel an unacceptable degree of anxiety. The mass production of products created leisure among the middle classes, but this pleasure had its drawbacks. In 1876 a lead article in *The Times* remarked on the 'mingled mass of perfectly legitimate pleasures' then available, but considered that 'all together' they made 'continually increasing demands upon our time, upon our money, and not least, upon our strength and powers of endurance' (cited in Bailey 1977: 7). To counteract the feeling that 'modern amusements' must be destructive, by the mid-1880s owners and advertisers viewed the factories and machines which produced them, and which now proliferated in England, in a positive light. They encouraged users to enjoy their products and not worry about the implications. Modern commodities and leisure were legitimate, and this was proved by the ways they supported one another. Trains, bicycles and cameras were united through timetables and standardised parts, with increasing ease and reliability of use.

Modern England was no longer sublime, and it was becoming less than picturesque, reformed into suburbs by the railways and the demands of the modernising life of the country. The garden of England was now part of the machine world, exemplified by these two illustrations of the country site at Harrow before Kodak was established there, and the idealisation of the factory. The countryside was now interspersed with railways and commuters, while the neat suburbs matched the

10. Drawing of Pinner Drive, Harrow, the site of Kodak's factory built in 1890.

11. Drawing of the Kodak factory, Harrow, c.1890.

timetables, the filing cabinets, the interlocking and replaceable parts of the urban and commercial centres. The modern experience was speed, mobility and an apparently rational order producing a cornucopia of 'goods'.

Of course, the success of such links did not end anxiety. Pleasure trips had to be planned in some detail to match the timetables, giving rise to the modern terrors of missed connections. Worse yet, as Henry James discovered at Kenilworth, newly mobile sectors of the working class and lower-middle class invaded the reserved space of the once-secure middle class. Leisure became vulgar or 'common'. Moreover, leisure among people of similar interests led to crowded resorts or beauty spots, and their ruination. This was illustrated in the *Amateur Photographer* (*AP*) of 1887 by a cartoon showing 'the photographic craze', in which tourism is seen to destroy the object of its desire (see illustration on page 38).

Though the tension between the classes associated with leisure and goods has never ceased, in the late nineteenth century many published accounts of production and holidaymaking aimed to dispel customers' fears. Just as the countryside was being rationalised, so were ways of observing and reporting on landscape. Travellers joined together various machines (of moving, viewing, writing and publishing) to ensure that landscape was easy to see and not threatening. Whether the scene was countryside or industrial, it was visited by outsiders and then described in the photographic press in language which had been honed in the writing about discoveries overseas.

THE PHOTOGRAPHIC CRAZE : A VILLAGE BESIEGED.*

12. 'The photographic craze', *Amateur Photographer*, 10 June 1887.

Mary Louise Pratt discusses this writing in her book on travelling and imperialism. Analysing 'Victorian discovery rhetoric', she identifies three conventional means which created value for explorers' achievements. Firstly, explorers turned what they saw into landscape by recreating it in the form of a painting, and so making it *aesthetically* pleasing. Secondly, they provided *density of meaning* in the passage, ensuring that the landscape was extremely rich in material and semantic substance. Thirdly, they sought *mastery* over the view. What the author (or photographer) 'sees is all there is, and . . . the landscape was intended to be viewed from where he has emerged upon it. Thus the scene is deictically ordered with reference to his vantage point, and is static' (Pratt 1992: 204–5).

Writers on photography also aimed to take aesthetic pleasure in the sight; to reproduce the sight, more or less purely, in one or other of two modes of discovery rhetoric – either technical or artistic. They characteristically slipped from the scientific to the sensational, from the neutral and matter-of-fact to the experiential and sentimental. They thus kept the view or landscape under their control or governance in the manner of observers. This is not to say that they always achieved the ideal of perfect control, any more than the combination of systems of travel, journalism and photography were realised in perfected forms. There were class and social tensions among the groups who professed an interest in landscape, and the culturally active groups competed with each other to control its representation. At the same time, much energy was spent in looking at the landscape and writing about it in ways that pretended that there were in fact no such tensions.

Even more important, because this was a shared assumption, was their belief in the authority of what they 'took' in photographs to be hard evidence or truth. They assumed this authority to be derived from the way photographs had a closer one-to-one relationship to reality than any other system of representation. Photographs were relatively difficult to take, develop and print to this standard, demanding a high degree of control on the part of practitioners. They combined the belief in truth and control with other systems of knowledge, such as the taxonomies of natural science, which were also the languages of domination and distance. They anchored their beliefs about seeing the landscape in how they wrote about it, and in the plans they made for photographing it. Indeed, the work of writing and photographing the landscape went hand in hand as new opportunities for both practices became available. A proliferation of journals accompanied the huge growth in the production of materials for producing photographs and reproducing them in publications (Harrison 1886a, 1887; Clark 1891; Boni 1972; Harris 1979; Johnson 1990). What is so striking is the way this writing and seeing was directed outwards, projected on to classes other than those of the photographers themselves. Even as they recorded the landscape, they remained largely hidden in the accounts and in the pictures. Stationed behind cameras, and directing secretaries at typewriters, they were in the best positions to control and repeat whatever seemed important to them (Briggs 1990: 413). Just as discovery rhetoric enabled explorers to leave out everything which disturbed their view of the landscape, so these same devices allowed authors and photographers to leave out all disturbing social conflicts, or enabled them to comment on them in a way which tried to persuade readers of their point of view.

This apparent unity of authors and readers was characteristic of travel writing, and was crucial to its success, along with its appeal to sentiment, its dense materiality, and its claims to responsible control. Most of its effects are at work in the following brief descriptions of landscape which were published on a single page in a photographic journal in 1885, where two adventurers told of their photographic failures. A submarine photographer named John Ingham and a landscape photographer called Major Verney wrote their landscapes within the conventions of discovery rhetoric. They used the imaginary neutrality of scientific or technical accounts; the claims of art upon the sensibility of the viewer; the text made dense with language and rhetoric, making it materially 'thick' with meaning; the view (and ideological viewpoint) kept under the author's control. With their skill in practising these tropes, they turned their failures in photography into small triumphs in discovery writing by making readers share their own point of view.

John Ingham, in an attempt to photograph shipwrecks without the use of divers, placed his camera in an iron stove and lowered it more than thirty fathoms to the bottom of the sea. Describing his technical methods, he ended with the admission that his pictures showed nothing. He expected to try the following summer using artificial light (Ingham 1885: 102).

Ingham's thoughts and methods were amateurish in the honorific sense of the word in use at the time: he was a hobbyist with an experiment in mind. His idea for submarine photography was purposive but speculative, trying to push one technology to the point where it could replace another and its human operative. Had his project succeeded, Ingham as inventor would have been centre-stage only during the period of heroic experimentation. Once successful, he could leave the rest to those who accounted for losses: 'photographs of wrecks would be a great help in Board of Trade inquiries' (Ingham 1885: 102). His was the small-scale version of a proven and increasingly rewarding gamble, namely, the exploration of inhospitable regions (such as the polar regions or Africa), their systematic mapping with resilient instruments, and laying claim to resources seen only from a distance. What made submarine photography inviting was that the surrogate eye of the camera extracted knowledge without the current dangers of diving. Its use in searching for wrecks would mean 'the services of a diver would not then be required' or would be maximised (Ingham 1885: 102). Everything in the unknown territory could be won back through instrumentation, and the application of what would become a rational, mechanised trade. Ingham's idea set out the benefit to business of the urge to see and own.

Ingham's hunch was correct. All that was lacking from his excellent colonising prospect (and it was almost everything) was the capital to pay for the adventure, the money and backers to finance its development. His capacity for technical innovation did not match his foresight in this direction, and it was left to others at a later date to reap the rewards. To this extent he failed as a capitalist adventurer, but he was successful in a much smaller way. He followed the method of writing and pitching a tale, using the persona of the self-effacing producer of information, the scientific prospector of land (Urry 1984).

Printed immediately after Ingham's pitch was a second and different kind of failure, that of Major George Verney. In traditional adventurist style, the Major carried a large-format camera into North Wales in an attempt to capture what he knew to be 'a difficult landscape' view – a slate quarry. He failed because the place was too dark, and was only one colour, 'a dull slate colour, without a bit of green'. There were no ordinary features of a landscape to relieve the gloom and monotony, not even a single tree. He was defeated by the slate: there was 'nothing but slate – slate rocks, slate huts, slate wagons, slate ballast on the lines of rails, and even slate-coloured faces and clothes'. What the Major failed in was the production of a 'good' exhibition print, being forced to settle for nothing more than a 'slatey smudge' (Verney 1885: 102–3).

However, before the Major spoke of himself as artist-photographer, he made the slate quarry the object of rational order. He minimised the presence of humans and made them blend with the natural material. He placed himself in the position of the disembodied eye, which saw that the quarry was visually pleasing, and worked all by itself: it was 'one of the finest sights to see a slate quarry in full work, with the hill side cut into galleries tier upon tier, extending from deep excavations in the valley to the top of a high mountain'. Even when workmen were mentioned, they were something that 'may be observed', so just as the quarry seemed to have produced itself, the position of the observer was similarly hidden in a passive construction. The account seemed to have been produced not by the traveller but by the face of the country presenting itself to a neutral, panoramic gaze. The Major hid himself in language, choosing to write of the quarry not as a place under active construction but as a ready-made motionless spectacle. Even when he began a sentence describing men at work, by the end they had disappeared into an intransitive construction of his making, workmen being replaced by waggons: 'Hundreds of workmen may be observed extracting the slates, filling the diminutive waggons with them, and dispatching them to a central station, where they are sorted previous to being sent to their destinations' (Verney 1885: 102).

The Major then changed from an objective point of view to an emotive one, placing his readers beside him: 'standing on the brink of a sheer precipice the view is truly imposing. At your feet is a vast abyss [and] in front of you stands a tall, needle-like shaft of rock'. Dispensing with the landscanning eye, he shifted to look at his readers, addressing them directly, and so placing them at the edge of the quarry, with the abyss at their feet and the rock rising higher at their front. The Major thus created for himself and his readers a great distance from the workmen. He forced his readers to adopt his perspective, so that they too would share the experience, or at least the sensation, of seeing workmen 'scarcely looking larger than flies'.

When he revealed that the site was dark, which meant he was bound to fail to make a 'good photograph', the Major began to use the pronoun 'I'. This completed his account's journey from supposed objectivity to the sentimental inclusion of the readership in a common experience and point of view; he drew his readers from 'prospecting' (as in mining) to 'prospect' (as in a view of a landscape). From this point of view, the real 'absence of light', as he put it, was matched by an equivalent absence in the humanity of the quarrymen – who were distant and small as flies, or indistinguishable from slate.

These types of writing, and their ways of imagining and controlling the landscape, are benchmarks for what follows. As I shall argue, photographers sought the mastery of John Ingham and Major Verney, but the larger their project, and the more comprehensive their attempts to scan the land, then the more likely were they to fail to keep the rhetoric within bounds. As I shall show later, this failure was especially true of survey or record photographers, because they were trying to apply a method of annotation taken from the natural sciences to gather what they took to be the straightforward 'facts' of history. Their search for objectivity was an attempt to separate the links between art, science and nature which had engaged writers and artists in pre- or early photographic periods (Cosgrove 1979; Pointon 1979; Stafford 1984). They deliberately set themselves against photographers who considered landscape to be picturesque or emotive (Robinson 1869; Hissey 1887; Robinson 1888; Robinson 1897; Seiberling 1986; John Taylor 1979; Vertrees 1982; Kemp 1990). On the contrary, survey photographers took what they intended to be impersonal records, which would benefit future generations of historians by showing objective facts.

Even so, complete control of the scene eluded the survey photographers, who concerned themselves with country villages, and is most evident in descriptions of the layout of factories. Describing and picturing factories was left to those with vested interests in showing them to be reassuring places. These photographers combined Ingham's and Verney's ways of seeing, which ensured that the landscape of the manufactory was subject to the order of discovery rhetoric.

13. The Kodak factory, Harrow, *c.*1890.

THE FACTORY IN THE GARDEN

I intend to discuss the use of discovery rhetoric in looking at the layout and production methods in factories making photographic goods. It might be perverse to open with a discussion of factory floors rather than with the proper landscapes of countryside scenery, but my aim is to show the integration of tools for looking and ways of looking. Factories making cameras or photographic film were aesthetically pleasing, and the subject of enthusiastic reportage as the essence of modernity (Marx 1964). Despite this, journalists did not write about everything in factories – they certainly made no attempt to include factory landscapes which threatened the air of smooth-running mechanisms and the domesticated nature of labour. Accounts of efficiency in factories were a fillip to businessmen who were interested in publicity and present success. In contrast with the amateur survey groups such as the Warwickshire Photographic Survey, which I discuss in the next section, journalists' accounts of factories did not appeal to 'history': they were intended to give meaning to the 'here and now', bearing eyewitness to the wishes of the audience for order.

Writing in 1894 about the Kodak works, built in the countryside at Harrow on the north-west fringe of London in 1890, an anonymous journalist remarked on its size, even when seen from a speeding train (see illustration). Having been shown around the site, he was impressed by the 'amount of work performed, and the extent of the machinery and labour employed'. The journalist wrote, 'It is a big industry, and one entitled to rank amongst the mills of Yorkshire, or the factories of Birmingham' (Anon. 1894: 4). Celebrations were in order because industrialists had transformed photography from what the socialist author John A. Randall called 'a simple unorganized cottage industry towards that complex and highly organized condition which is manifested in the factory system' (Randall 1896b: 360). Looking back from 1908 at the development of the industry over forty years, a different, unknown journalist said that in 1870 there were only 700 people employed in it, whereas now 'the world has half a dozen concerns, each employing that number of persons in one business'. Whereas 'a camera factory, even in later days than 1870, was said to consist of "a master, a man, three boys and a lot of glue-pots", today it is organised like the factory of a great staple industry' (Anon. 1908b: 118). In addition to making cameras, there were large factories making chemicals, plates, and paper, as well as printing and developing; there were innumerable smaller works engaged in the production of mounts, frames, related accessories and fancy goods.

The celebration of the 'development of photography into one of the ordinary industries of the country' (Randall 1896b: 360) required an appropriate form of expression. Unlike the tensions between science and art which (as I shall show) remained unresolved in the methodology of survey work, the pictorial and journalistic methods of representing the photographic industry were not problematic. Just as 'sylvan' scenes gave way to suburbs in which factories were part of the everyday scene, the celebration of the edenic and pastoral was often replaced in capitalists' writings by what Mary Louise Pratt has called a 'modernizing extractive vision best exemplified by a trope one might call "industrial revery"' (Pratt 1992: 150).

There was nothing new about this by the late nineteenth century. Whistler had defined the industrial city for the artistic audience in his famous 'Ten o'Clock' lecture of 1885. He said that wayfarers and pleasure-seekers, as well as wise, cultured and working-men 'ceased to understand, as they ceased to see' the 'exquisite tune' of 'Nature' at nightfall. Artists alone recognised that at nightfall chimneys became Italianate bell-towers, warehouses were transformed into palaces, and the whole city was alight and hanging 'in the heavens' like 'fairy-land' (Whistler 1967 [1888]: 144).

Disregarding this artistic response, industrialists took great pleasure in factories as they were, imagining them to be altogether more practical than palaces or bell towers, and more magical in their productive capacity than the mystification of 'fairy-land'. To express their satisfaction, they relied upon the expertise of writers to represent the dream, according to the modes of discovery rhetoric. The language of discovery, with its formulae of aesthetics, density of description and domination or control was borrowed from landscape and applied to factories. The journalists wrote with great clarity about the factories, always maintaining an objective stance though mixing it with wonderment at the efficiency of the establishments. In the accounts of manufactories, we see the landscape rhetoric deployed by John Ingham and Major Verney used in the service of complacent self-interest.

Firstly, the writers made the work-force disappear, seen in this description of camera manufacturing in 1896:

> Passing from the woodworking department to the metal-working tools, there was much to be seen of absorbing interest. The capstan lathes making the pinions, the nipples, and other small turned parts by the gross, the milling machine with a cleverly designed attachment for cutting the eccentric ends on the speed-setting spindle, the machine for cutting the teeth of the small brass wheels, and the punching presses for stamping out the sheet-metal parts – all these tools were busily engaged in performing the special duties allotted to them. The various parts so made are produced in large quantities at a time and then passed into the stores, from whence they are taken out as required for fitting up.
>
> (Thornton-Pickard 1896)

We can recognise here most of the techniques used in the landscape description of Major Verney, especially the scene that creates itself, and the trope of the hidden, scanning eyes of experts and masters.

Secondly, the site of manufacture was always materially dense. The above passage is thick with nouns and active verbs which set out to convince the reader of the actuality of numerous machines and their whirring, productive actions.

Next, the factory at work was aesthetically pleasing in terms of 'cleanliness, order, and method' applied to chemical processes and air flows. We see this in the description of a dry-plate factory in 1886:

> The drying arrangement is very perfect. The walls are hollow, and no air is admitted to the drying rooms that has not been deprived of its moisture by transmission over chloride of calcium. This air, after percolating the plates racked in the drying room, and becoming saturated with moisture, is drawn off by means of a large fan, which is rotated with great velocity, creating a constant circulation.
>
> (Anon. 1886b: 780)

14. Workers 'spotting' negatives, Kodak factory, Harrow, *c.*1890.

In the factories the controlling gaze of managers was perpetual. Sometimes they escorted journalists around, who always adopted the management's point of view, reproducing its order in the trade journals. The managers' gaze was constantly reproduced by employees charged with the control of workers. Supervisors decided whether or not an item was correct; overseers 'examined' fitters' work, and they in turn were answerable to the 'head of the department' (Thornton-Pickard 1896). In an earlier account of glass-cleaning in another dry-plate factory, we learn that the 'girls' were 'seated at a long bench systematically arranged for expediting the work'. They were 'supervised by a forewoman, who watches over them with a jealous eye, as upon her is thrown the responsibility of seeing that the work is properly executed' (Anon. 1886a: 414). In addition, the workers themselves were incorporated into the inspectorate, because they had constantly to look at and check their work.

Workers, situated in specific places and performing set tasks, were like the parts of a machine. If they failed to work they were disposable, exactly like the malfunctioning parts of a machine. In its ideal form, the factory maximised its cost-effectiveness, seen in this description about replacing machines: 'Every machine bears its respective number, and is treated for cost purposes, just like a workman.' Using the intransitive voice, the author of this passage wrote, 'If it is found that a certain machine does not pay', then it would be 'scrapped'. The only difference between the treatment of machines and men was in the choice of verbs: machines were 'scrapped', while workers were 'paid off' – it amounted to the same thing (Anon. 1908a: 94).

When photographers were employed to illustrate the articles, the factories were sometimes shown empty, or more usually the workers were at their stations, apparently absorbed in the job, seen in the image of women 'spotting' or concealing the imperfections in negatives at Kodak (see illustration on page 46). In these cases, the visibility of the workers did not destabilise the idea of the managed scene because everyone was in her proper place. The camera was an extra eye confirming the organisation of the space and power of mass production – the docility of labour, or harmony of people and machines on the factory floor. The photographs also functioned rather like Major Verney's shift from the intransitive into the address of personal pronouns: the photographs were versions of 'I' and 'you', a means of drawing the readers into the scene.

Unlike the photographs which were taken to illustrate the articles (and which were deliberately posed to suit the purpose), the photographs from the Kodak factory occupy an ambivalent space (see illustrations on pages 35 and 46). They were taken over several years as part of a sporadic but methodical record of the various departments and types of work carried out in the Harrow works. They generally showed employees at their station, though some include people who stare at the camera, and are not occupied. A few were used in publicity booklets, but they seem not to have been taken deliberately for that purpose (Kodak 1897; c.1906). The publicity use appears to have been an afterthought, though since the workers were orderly they eventually served the purpose of industrial reverie.

The fullest realisation of this dream could occur because of the way the factory was organised, requiring the division of labour into specialisations. The dream of order required that everything be known and predictable. Since the division of labour was the basis of rational order and maximum profits, it was also the source of reverie. As John A. Randall said, in 'the rudimentary stage of manufacture' the individual worker was responsible for the whole piece from start to finish, but 'as any industry progresses, this primitive method of production becomes unsuited to the demands of the case, and the business is subdivided into various sections. A special class arises, who deal first with the raw material, and we have the plate-maker and producer of sensitive papers; after these, many skilled men as operators, retouchers, enlargers, and printers, each making a speciality of operations previously done by the single worker.' So the workers become experts and their 'daily output is largely increased. Practically, there is no limit to this process; and, the greater extent to which it can be carried, the more productive does labour become' (Randall 1900a: 618). As an example of further subdivision, Randall also cited a job which formerly was done by one unaided printer, and now in one of the larger firms was carried out by eleven separate assistants: 'paper-cutter, printer plain, printer vignettes, boy to fill up printing frames, boy to carry them in and out of printing-room, washer before toning, toner, fixer and washer after toning, mounter, spotter, burnisher'.

While some of these repetitive jobs were small-scale, required no initiative, and were carried out by 'lads' or 'girls', some positions within the factory demanded a wide range of expertise from the worker. For instance, the operator would have to know how to use many different types of camera, plates and developers. The retoucher had to be expert with the pencil and brush, and conversant with innumerable colours and processes. The printer had to be able to use various papers and know many different methods of making prints by development (Randall 1900a: 619).

Specialisation was not dangerous from the employer's point of view. On the contrary, subdivision also meant the workers were divided among themselves. Since none had all the specialisms, any one of them could leave and quickly be replaced. Only a minority of workers believed that their reduction to specialisms would be an advantage to them if they could combine into a trade union or co-operative movement. Although the workers never succeeded in this, John Randall said that photography in its factory phase was already a co-operative movement, just 'like the wheels in a watch': 'to produce a photograph our methods must be so adjusted that they work like a well-arranged machine' (Randall 1896b: 361).

Randall was interested in the well-run or beneficent factory, but he was not interested in reassuring the readers of the photographic press that factories were orderly. On the contrary, he knew that factories were dangerous and exploitative, and his main interest was in improving conditions. He was especially concerned by photographic workers misused as 'servants' or 'chattels'. Managers expected workers to perform all sorts of duties, and so they were denied the opportunity to specialise. They could never become experts in anything, reducing their chances of improving themselves by gaining work in better factories. Adopting the language of management, Randall fought for assistants to be recognised 'as a wheel in a machine', and therefore crucial to the smooth running of the factory and the maximising of production (Randall 1900a: 618).

Randall spoke optimistically about matching the needs of workers and employers within factories, but the latter knew that workers were like wheels in machines. Some managers exploited workforce and machinery till they failed and then replaced them. In trying to promote the interests of workers, Randall applauded well organised factories, and set himself only against the worst employers. Through his writing we see how often the idealisation of large, successful factories was not matched in the smaller establishments which were never featured in the press. Instead of possessing a rational shape, a long building of one or two storeys, the poorly managed factory might be in a house with many floors, or with outhouses in different streets, all compelling the workers to waste time in travelling back and forth, reducing their efficiency and the profits of the company. In such places, the assistants were likely to be badly treated (Randall 1900b: 809).

'Assistants' grievances' were published in the *British Journal of Photography* (*BJP)* ('Victim' 1896: 126), and sometimes there would be a short article on them, or commentary on the assistants' unsuccessful attempts at organising themselves into a union (Anon. 1896: 306–7). Similarly, trade unionists would write proposals for action which were also printed in the photographic press (A. Field 1890; 1894; 1897; 1898; E. Field 1894; 1895). So the journals were full of different types of imagining and experience, each with their preferred manner of eliciting the support of readers. Randall's use of 'hard cases' among the assistants, and their own, sometimes anonymous letters complaining of how they had been swindled or sweated in 'miserable dens of workrooms' brought to light what industrial reverie left out (Randall 1896a: 271; G. Brown 1895; 'Operator' 1895).

None of this 'grievance' or combination material spoiled the reverie, which was a regular feature in the editorial body of journals – the space of owners and managers. Their way of narrating the space of the factory floor was in terms of a reassuring landscape. They invested their perspective in the scene and reinvented the factory in the process. They changed the landscape of the industry from decentralised, handicraft modes of production still common in the 1870s to centralised and mechanised systems which were common twenty years later. The size of the establishment resulted in economies of scale, which came to count for less than the speed of production. Profits depended on the speedy movement of raw materials into the factory, their speedy transformation into goods, and their speedy transfer from factory to warehouse to shop. The velocity of industrial production, so prized in the factory system of mutating and moving goods, also produced individual workers who were isolated from each other and from the products. Everything about the factory, including its workers, was disguised in the final product. Transferred to shops, the goods appeared as if from nowhere, and the links with factories were broken.

For owners and managers, velocity was at the heart of production and so had direct bearing upon the reverie as smooth-running and dependable as clockwork. In the reverie, the speed of work was worthy of comment, like all things related to it 'up to the point where it would be necessary to begin commenting on human movements, skills and contact with machines' (MacCannell 1976: 67). Writing about smooth-running machines took its place in the apparent correspondence between numerous machine parts and multiple divisions in the labour force. The complexity of operations was a source of anxiety for managers, journalists and their readers because machines and workers might fail to work. The escape route was industrial reverie, in which everything continued to work without agency.

THE DUTY TO SURVEY

The manufacture of photographic goods was not an end in itself, and the use of goods was a matter of concern. Leisure must have a moral dimension, and since photography was able to stop time, its specific task was to record those objects, persons, ways of life which the centralised, complex factory systems were destroying. Since factories had their own logic of making, controlling and looking, then the goods produced there must also have a place in that system. Outside the factories, the duty to investigate for the sake of efficiency and profit was matched by the duty to survey for the benefit of posterity. This was felt most keenly among the county record or survey photographers who were interested in country landscapes and buildings, and whose interest in the lower classes was different from that of factory managers, social reformers or local officials such as medical police or sanitary inspectors (McGrath 1984; Tagg 1988). The survey photographers were concerned about ways of life which were vanishing: from their positions in the middle class, they regretted the disappearance of what they considered to be the quaint, unspoilt lifestyles of different and lower-class people.

At the same time, and for similar reasons, these surveyors were equally interested in the manor houses and other residences of the gentry and aristocracy. Yet, unlike the labouring classes, the gentry were never photographed in their 'natural' surroundings. The surveyors decided that the actual interest here was the ancient architecture of the mansions, which they extended without difficulty to include other early buildings, including churches and bridges. They believed that photographs of all these structures would be useful, even in the near future. They intended to provide a record for evolutionists, antiquarians and educators, who would not only study the artefacts and appearances of different peoples in other times, but use such imagery to place themselves in relation to these others. Indeed, the unconscious and unformulated purpose of survey work was exactly that – to position the newly emergent, mobile and culturally active members of educated sections of the middle class against those whom they considered both socially inferior and superior to themselves. Crucially, the surveys, though they were haphazard in plan and execution, were deliberately linked to a strong historical sense, and a sense of regional and then national identity. The mobile photographing classes, armed with both stand- and hand-held cameras, took it upon themselves to write, record and see a particular history of England, a history from their point of view. Characteristically, in such writing and imagining there was no attempt systematically to record the lifestyles of their own class. The evidence of their existence and abilities was to be found, paradoxically, in their absence from the surveyed scene. Their power lay in producing the surveys, not in figuring in them, and the photograph reproduced here of a survey outing to Kinver in Staffordshire is the exception rather than the rule (Harrison 1892; Gower 1916; Foote 1987).

We can see this determination to record history in a project submitted by an occasional writer to one of the photographic journals in 1896, suggesting that photographers might attempt to make a comprehensive survey of life and character. I shall show that he was repeating only what had been said often before, and which members of photographic societies tried to organise into systematic form for years afterwards. What is interesting, because it is often encountered elsewhere, is the choice of language and subjects. The writer called for a continuous 'survey of life and

15. 'Outing to Kinver, Staffordshire', Warwickshire Photographic Survey, c.1890.

character' in these terms: 'Photograph (in natural surroundings, if possible) your baker, butcher, sweep, gardener, coachman, bootmaker, postman, newsboy, domestic, milkman etc. . . . If you are resident in the country, record the whole process of bread-making, from the tilling of the ground to the delivery of loaves. Carry your hand camera with you, and push the button at every itinerant tradesman and beggar.' In the world of record photography, everything was equivalent, everything, that is, which belonged to the same (and in this case lower) levels of society. The record photographers, like the writers who used the tropes of discovery rhetoric, could level the surface of the visible world to a qualitative sameness. Just as the service classes could be made equivalent to one another, so could the processes of the manufactory. The survey would show how the work-force was either content or could be written out of the scene altogether (in the manner of writing used by Major Verney and journalists describing work on factory floors). He suggested 'make a photographic survey of [the factory], from the bringing in of the raw material to the taking out of the finished article. Let no process, however seemingly insignificant, escape the

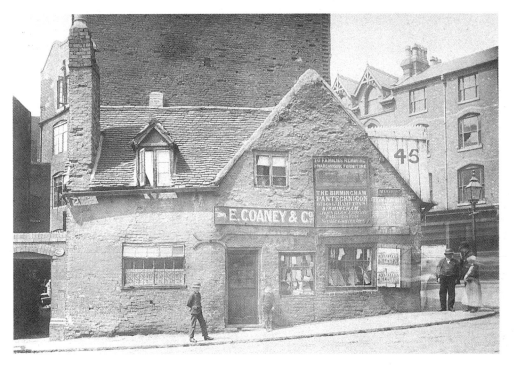

16. Harold Baker, 'Moor St, corner of Dale End, Birmingham', 1880.

searching eye of your camera' (Edwards 1896: 702).

I have already shown how the journalistic and photographic records of the manufactories were in fact carried out, and what were their ideological effects. In this case, photographers were expected to search out those who were utterly different from themselves. The author was advocating the merits of photography put to use – not for social reform or social engineering – but for the use of historians and ethnographers, the archaeologists of the future. The serious and accomplished amateurs, those who were organised into societies and did not consider themselves to be mere snapshooters, decided that photography would be useful for the emergent social sciences that were describing and delineating the undifferentiated masses and secure middle classes (a use seen in this photograph taken by Harold Baker for the Birmingham and Midland Institute Archaeological Section in 1880 of a street in Birmingham shortly before the area was redeveloped). The project to record was not unusual for its time, since photographers intended benefits to accrue to individuals and to the greater common good: theirs was another example of how middle-class capital could be allied with middle-class morality or duty (Thomson 1876–77; Browne 1886; Mallock 1887; Hill 1888; Layard 1888; Roberts 1888; Booth 1890; Anon. 1897a).

The moral dimension for photographers was made explicit in 1889 by the photographic journalist Cosmo Burton, who said that photographers were failing in their duty by not considering the use of the medium. This failure surprised and disappointed him since photographers were to be found everywhere. They went up in balloons, and down into catacombs, mines and sewers; they swarmed over the glaciers and peaks of the Alps, and eluded the guards of Buddhist temples; they 'penetrated forests'; they had even been at the bottom of the sea – 'in short, wherever man has penetrated'. These men (for he imagined them to be men) took untold numbers of pictures, but most of the photographs were not printed, or were printed in the inferior silver process which had a short life, unlike the 'permanent' processes of carbon and platinum. All this looking and photographing was serving no particular purpose, or only the unscientific purposes of every 'charm or fetish bought for money' (Burton 1889a: 668).

In place of random looking, Burton argued for looking with a purpose. He said the photographer was essential to every exploring party, 'whether in search of antiquities in Egypt, unknown types of man in Africa or America, new plants or animals or insects anywhere in the world' (Burton 1889a: 667). It was the 'whole duty of the photographer' to survey the world systematically, and then insert his 'permanent' records in albums so great that they would have to hold a supply of pictures 'far exceeding the capacity of any albums ever dreamt of' (Burton 1889b: 682). Everything was to be labelled with date, time, place, and details of the conditions. The emphasis was upon precision, permanence and fixity. 'Evolutionists of the future' would use these records to measure change, comparing their recent records with those preserved in the library.

Burton gave no details of how this enterprise might be organised. The 'plan' was so huge and ill-formed that it might even have seemed like a 'modest proposal', an ironic or comic assault on the plainly irritating 'ubiquitous' photographer. But there was no irony intended, and he suggested that the huge albums should be housed in a new national institution, to be known as the Royal Photographic Society (the present RPS received its 'Royal' title from Queen Victoria in 1894).

The notion of 'duty' arose because Burton's suggestion, though impractical as a centralised bureaucracy, derived from older ideas about total classification which had spread through the scientific community, and extended a European way of looking at the world. He imagined 'a library of great albums containing a record as complete as can be made … of the present state of the world', but he recognised this was 'not a small task'. To do it would completely surpass the resources of any one nation, and so he imagined that the foundation of the new Royal Photographic Society would be the start only in England. The idea and institution, like so many before them, would spread from England to every civilised country which would first catalogue itself, and then proceed to catalogue the remaining uncivilised countries, exactly those places where resources and 'prospects' were as yet undiscovered and unexploited.

Casting round for future uses of these vast, undreamt of albums, Burton was thrown back upon what current evolutionists might have liked to see if only photography had been available in earlier centuries or even fifty years before. He had four categories which were worth filling up: social class, working methods, flora and fauna, and topography. The one which interested him most, which he described at greatest length, was social class. He cited the Crofters' Commission which showed 'a passing interest in one class of poor people', which he thought would be 'most valuable documents a century hence'. He said, 'Nothing is surer than that the social relations of classes in this country will change profoundly in the not distant future, and after the change has come about records of the state of matters before will become valuable. Let it be remembered that though the poor are the majority, they are naturally inarticulate and die unrecorded' (Burton 1889a: 668).

To take this trouble over such unregarded subjects was in itself a validation of the journey, raising it above the level of touring to higher planes – giving 'voice' to the inarticulate and claiming moral worth in a disinterested survey for posterity's sake. Of course, Burton was only 'voicing' what was already an active campaign among others of the middle class. Many groups, for different reasons, were anxious to bring into the light and see for themselves (for some, preferably in photographs) the wretched conditions of the invisible and potentially dangerous underclasses (Tagg 1988: 117–52; Kemp 1990: 120–5).

The case for record and survey photography was different again, resting in beliefs about collecting, annotating and knowing (though of course all these beliefs were attached to class interests). In 1889, when Burton wrote his complaint, the survey movement was already under way. Reports of the plans for local photographic surveys in Sheffield and Manchester were published in the photographic press –

developing the methodologies of earlier scientific and historical surveys (Howarth 1889; 'Our Views' 1889). The year before, members of the Birkenhead Photographic Association declared their intention to organise a survey of part of Wirral, and believed themselves to be pioneers (Anon. 1888). They claimed primacy over the Birmingham Photographic Societies' plan for a comprehensive survey of the county of Warwick, which the geologist and educator, W. Jerome Harrison, had suggested in 1885 and which was announced in 1889 and begun the year after (Harrison 1889). While the argument over priority continued, the activists realised that the point was not who thought of it first, since photography from its inception had been used sporadically in depicting the natural sciences, topography, industry, and social states. The activists had practical problems to overcome. They had to define the geographical limits of their organisations, and the subjects they would photograph; they had to organise expeditions, house the resulting archive of pictures and make it available for study.

As Peter James has shown in his work on the record and survey movement at the end of the century, politics and personalities were decisive factors in its formation (James 1989). The personal ambitions and disappointments are worth noting because they show how a man from the middle class was vulnerable to others from the same group, whereas someone with wealth and political sense was able to take over the controversial projects and remain unscathed. W. Jerome Harrison, for instance, was primarily responsible for establishing the Warwickshire Photographic Survey at the Birmingham Photographic Society (BPS), but he had no particular authority, being only a member of the Society and subject to the rivalry and jealousy of other photographers of a similar station (P. James 1989: 54). Nonetheless, he had an idea of how Burton's vague plan might actually be realised. He recognised that some of the members would oppose the survey because an appeal to volunteers would mean the influx of professionals, and so spoil the status and atmosphere of the BPS as a gentlemen's club.

Harrison devised two tactics to persuade them. The first was to base his advocacy of survey work from 1885 in a longer historical perspective, making it seem that the idea had resulted from converging forces. Surveys had already been set up or suggested by other societies, in England and in Boston in the USA, and had for many years been the established practice among geologists (P. James 1989: 32–3). He himself had used photography in his geological work, and this was part of a wider recognition of its scientific uses, notably the newly formed British Association Committee for the Collection, Preservation and Systematic Registration of Photographs of Geological Interest (P. James 1989: 40).

Secondly, Harrison enlisted the support of Benjamin Stone, a wealthy industrialist and powerful civic figure who was well known to the Birmingham Society. Stone had been buying and commissioning photographs since the 1870s, and had amassed a somewhat random collection of 'history' photographs (dating from the early 1860s), which he sometimes exhibited or allowed members of the society to view in private (P. James 1989: 91). Stone believed photography was the 'science of truth', and should avoid art or sentiment (Anon. 1893: 246). Although not a member of the Society, he was elected its President in 1889, and in 1890 when the Warwickshire Photographic Survey began work, he became its Chairman. The plan for a complete record of a county may have appealed to Stone's sense of his own importance as a man of substance (he later donated thirty-eight volumes of press cuttings about his career to the Birmingham Free Library).

The Survey's task, laid out by Harrison, was to make a total and unbiased record illustrating the archaeology, architecture, landscape and scenery, ethnology, botany, geology and town life of the county, along with copies of old engravings and other relevant documents. Harrison was not daunted by the gigantism of the plan since it matched his passion for collecting data – he had a 'mania' for compiling bibliographies – which he thought were central to education. More revealingly, he also wrote about the possibility of 'light as a recording instrument of the past' (Harrison 1886b: 23). In this article, he went much further than saying that photographs transferred past scenes into the present. He suggested that the past (and consequently the present too) might always exist *in the light itself* (and so be recoverable in the future). He said there might be projected on to 'some exquisitely sensitive surface on the bounds of space' a perfect optical record of everything that existed in the world. Every action which was illuminated would be 'visible somewhere in space . . . and the vision permanently retained'. This permanent eye in the heavens might hold indelible records of life on earth – and more than that, these records might be used in evidence 'against which there could be no appeal'. Much more than Stone, Harrison seems to have had a profound belief in the primacy of sight and the possibility of everything being seen, with knowledge of it retained somewhere and so recoverable and usable. Rather like John Ingham, the submarine photographer, Harrison's ideas were in advance of the technical and theoretical machinery to make them work, though this fact does not diminish his visual imperialism, nor his expectations for the power of sight.

The differences between Harrison and Stone might have driven them to work in their own ways for the Survey, but they also contained the seeds of each man's severance from it. In 1892, encouraged by the success of the Warwickshire Survey (which by March that year consisted of 923 photographs – with a further 2,570 prints by 1896), and the large numbers of survey schemes among the photographic societies, Harrison argued for a National Photographic Record and Survey (P. James 1989: 51–3). Unfortunately for him, he did not envisage this happening within a loose federation of autonomous societies, but urged the unification of the country's photographic organisations. This idea of a 'concerted "photo-survey"' was rejected outright in the *BJP* as likely to be 'of debatable practical value when (if ever) finished' (Anon. 1892a: 306–7). Harrison used his pseudonym and his column in an American journal to counter-attack, but when his cover was revealed and he was vilified for his tactics in promoting his 'grand work', he felt he had been disgraced and resigned all connections with the Survey and the Birmingham Society (P. James 1989: 54-5).

Stone, on the other hand, went from strength to strength. In 1893, following the initial success of the Survey, six hundred of the photographs were exhibited in the Municipal Art Gallery; afterwards, Stone presented a thousand of his mounted prints to the Birmingham Free Library, where they would be accessible to the public. In the same year, and for his services to politics, he was knighted by Queen Victoria. At the same time, Stone was unhappy about the direction the Survey was taking. He wanted 'truth' in photography, whereas too many members of the BPS who were working on the Survey had become pictorialists, which meant they were concerned with the artistic and affective potential of their practice. This was too much for Stone, who wanted to resign as Chairman in 1893 (he was persuaded to stay on but rarely attended) (P. James 1989: 61).

Stone soon saw a greater opportunity for himself. In 1895 he had been elected a Member of Parliament, and since it was to be the Queen's Jubilee in 1897, he proposed the National Photographic Record Association, to be headed by himself (he instantly became famous as 'Sir Snapshot'). He modelled the NPRA on the Warwickshire Survey, though he never acknowledged it. The aim was to obtain records of all objects and scenes of interest in the British Isles, and to deposit them with explanatory notes, in the British Museum (see Anon. 1897b: 637; Anon. 1897c: 683). The NPRA amassed 4,478 prints by 1910, (over a quarter of them contributed by Stone himself), when he declared it closed, recommending that local societies continue the survey work. (Anon. 1910: 418). They were at last combining into the Federation of Record Societies, and Stone was appointed President, this time basing the scheme, without acknowledgement, on Harrison's proposals of 1906 for co-ordinated action among the various county survey groups (Harrison had died in 1908) (Harrison 1906).

The different careers of these men reveal something about station in society, and opportunism, but they mask an important consideration. The Warwickshire Photographic Survey plan, though an advance on Burton's wishes, could never be realised because the taxonomy of photography had been built around the pictorial and idyllic. There was no language of photography that matched the use of Latin naming or number in the natural sciences which theoretically could be extended to include any new example, and which was conventional and not subject to change by fashion or invention. Both the total survey and the notion of accuracy (in the sense of the measurable and repeatable) in record photography were impossible to achieve. Stone was caught in the widespread belief that photography could be 'scientific' if it stayed away from all the conventions of picture-making. On the contrary, photography in the Survey depended for its realisation on the existence and recognition of style. Photography could not be a pure equivalent to what Stone (mis)recognised as pure fact.

The Survey pictures had to be seen and 'written' just like any other view, but the surveyors tried to gloss over the impossible demand for a taxonomy of photography. There were two diversionary tactics in place by the time of the 1892 exhibition. Firstly, the surveyors claimed there was no contest between survey work and the standard types of exhibition photograph, 'either in art, quality or technique' (Keene 1892: 346). Secondly, they wrote something on the back of each photograph which was intended to determine its historical importance: they claimed the 'quantity of detail as to the object itself and the conditions under which it was photographed... would be of inestimable value to the archaeologist, and would enable an architect to reconstruct the original if it disappeared' (Keene 1892: 346).

Unfortunately, they were unable to protect themselves from a public which was used to looking at picturesque subjects, and which persisted in reading their

17. 'Outing to Tysoe', Warwickshire Photographic Survey, 1891.

supposedly new lexicon of subjects as more or less 'pretty', and not so very new: reviewers described 'a delightful jumble of old fonts, church porches, tombs, castles, halls, cottages, rivers, and lanes' showing 'a keen desire to produce pretty pictures' (Anon. 1892b). The tension between the 'historical' and what appeared to be either appealing or unexceptional pictures was unresolved, and was merely disregarded. Viewers found the pictures ordinary or attractive, and it was only once the show was over, when the images were put in store, that librarians and surveyors were able to see them function as records.

I have argued that writing and seeing landscape were linked. Nevertheless, the tone of the writing differed according to where it was to be read. For instance, a journalist might acknowledge the record purpose of the work but place less emphasis on this than on holiday fun. We find a version of this emphasis on photography and entertainment in a newspaper story of a Warwickshire Survey expedition in 1891 to Tysoe and Compton Wynyates, the mansion of the Earl of Northampton (see photographs of the WPS group and of the house which were taken on this outing). The anonymous author refused to allow survey photography to be taken solely on its own terms of worthy work for the sake of posterity. Instead, the journalist gently poked fun at the surveyors: he chose different images from soldiering and from romance, couching it all in the amused and comic tones which were common practice in accounts of holidays (which I discuss in chapter 3).

The journalist wrote that the Survey photographers 'besieged' the mansion.

18. 'Compton Wynyates', Warwickshire Photographic Survey, 1891.

Mindful of the Civil War battles fought in this spot, the journalist modernised the weaponry from muskets to machine guns: 'A score of men carrying satchels and tripods marched down upon the house from several points of the hill, fixed their stands like so many Maxim guns, to command it from every side, and then one heard the click-click that might betoken trigger work' (Anon. 1891).

Military language and photography had a long mutual history. In the early years of photography, during the period of the wet-plate when practice was difficult and most of the work of securing a negative had to be carried out in the 'field', the intrepid practitioners both mocked and celebrated themselves and their activities by speaking of successful 'campaigns'. They used the military term to suggest the logistic problems of wet-plate work and the sense of daring and bravado associated with venturing out among the curious though respectful lower classes. After the mass production of dry-plates from the 1880s, when the preparatory work was done in the factory and components were smaller, the whole apparatus could be carried on a bicycle rather than in a wagon, yet the terminology of assault or attack persisted (and was carried into cinema in the twentieth century – see Virilio 1989).

The journalist reformulated the work of the Survey in terms of a siege reminiscent of past times, but also decided it was a comic interlude typical of contemporary pleasures. He began his piece by referring to the programme of the Survey in the literally accurate but jocular phrase 'picnics for posterity's sake'. Unable to halt speculative builders and restorers 'chopping' the 'dainty old villages' into the ugly 'trim' and 'civilised' appearance of the big towns, the Survey was making a picture of contemporary Warwickshire for the benefit of 'future students and historians – and picnickers'. The sense of the journalist's amused distance continued in his description of the photographers behaving less like well-drilled surveyors than like a raggle-taggle army, likely to fire all their 'shot' before the main target was reached. Since 'photographers have their idiosyncracies, like other men', the leader had trouble keeping them together, with their cameras closed; he lost two of the party altogether. Eventually, when still only half-way there, the men's 'longing' to shoot could not be restrained, and they brought their cameras 'to bear on old-fashioned houses and a lilac fringed church'.

The journalist's choice of language is instructive. It is mocking, but affectionate, consigning the whole enterprise to the realm of harmless fun, with photographers of earnest rectitude enjoying the weather, the tea-rooms, the refreshments at the inns, the luncheons and each other's company. Whatever their scientific or historical dimensions, these excursions were nothing more or less than holiday 'jaunts'.

In addition to his observation on the social side of the trip, the journalist also undercut the pretension to objectivity by referring to the photographers in the language of sentiment. He even reduced that to its comic, juvenile form. As 'longing' suggests, some photographers were 'head over heels in love with churches', while others could not pass a road cross 'without a pang'. They all felt 'delight' and 'wants', which by the end of the day were satisfied by two hundred negatives, 'a useful and healthy outing'. The journalist hit upon the links between photography and longing, between photography and scenes which immediately pass away. If his main concern was to show in a light-hearted way how these so-called objective records were simply an excuse for middle-class people to escape into the country, he also touched on links between photography, place and desire – the longing for home, or nostalgia, with all its sense of loss in the midst of life (Doane and Hodges 1987).

These links were not explored by the anonymous journalist, nor by the surveyors, though in the few written records left by the surveyors themselves we can see that the genial or amused tone was not the journalist's alone. For instance, in some hand-written diary accounts, the photographer P. T. D. Deakin attests to the social pleasure of such excursions. He refers constantly to his companions, their bicycles, their meals and refreshments, and comic mishaps, emphasising the relaxing holiday mood of Easter weekends more than the serious business of survey work. In

Kineton in Warwickshire the Survey work seems to have been a 'search for the picturesque', and the photographer regretted that his picture of 'the Back premises of the Red Lion – a quaint old place', was less than it might have been because he took the picture just before 'the suitable figure for this turned up... in the shape of a modernized "Sam Weller" [who] began to black boots on the steps' (Deakin n.d.; see also Deakin 1896; 1900).

In such diary and newspaper accounts the bright experiences of holidaymaking are very much to the fore – cycling, racing, refreshment, the friendship of men. They allow us to see that the duty to survey according to the ideal 'scientific' approach of record work was unrealisable. The diaries, especially, betray the impurity of the scheme, the fact that it was always tied to the surveyors' own ideological perspectives on what was 'quaint' or 'historical'. We see that the claim to objectivity was only ever a part of the rhetoric of discovery. Surveyors demanded objectivity because they considered it to be central to educational 'improvement' (which they believed to be positive), and crucial to their desire to conserve the countryside against so-called 'improvement' by developers (which they saw as negative). They imagined the Survey, with its technology already in place, in the terms of John Ingham's submarine photography – something which had potential in many disciplines and was not merely of artistic interest to the few.

Yet the potential of survey work was ill-defined, and consigned to the catch-all of the 'historical'. The surveyors never considered themselves to be part of the historical scene. They remained outside 'history' in two senses: literally because they rarely included themselves in the pictures; metaphorically because they did not acknowledge that their sense of worth and duty was bound up in the work. Instead, they claimed the work was objective and that its use would come in the future, being the privilege of 'posterity'.

For everyone (including the manufacturers) who looked at the conventional landscape, it appeared to run like clockwork, though for aesthetic reasons rather than profit. This was an illusion which demanded a price, as I shall demonstrate in chapter 3 on class differentiation and anxiety in one of the least industrial spaces in England, the pleasure grounds of East Anglia. In chapter 2, I shall examine how travellers used cameras as 'clocks for seeing', though in ways different from record and industrial reverie. I shall consider voyagers to the heart of England, looking for Shakespeare in Warwickshire in the 1890s.

2

Shakespeare Land

SEARCHING FOR SHAKESPEARE

A T THE HEART of England were a tomb, a tourist trail and several sorts of ghost. The tomb was that of Shakespeare, in Holy Trinity Church, Stratford-upon-Avon. This was a place of 'pilgrimage' to travellers devoted to his works who went looking for the 'home and haunts' of the 'master'.

Searching for Shakespeare was hard work, and the results frequently disappointing. The closest tourists came to him was the burial place, and there they found a stock curse laid on them should they disturb it – 'Bleste be the man that spares these stones, and curst be he that moves my bones'. In the end, there was only this minatory tomb, a clutch of restored, picturesque or dilapidated sites, and the weight of ages. The journey to the heart of England, in search of Shakespeare, was always a journey towards loss and disappointment. For the visitor who saved Holy Trinity to the last, it ended in a graveyard.

If tourists took the trail seriously, and prepared themselves for the experience, the graveyard need not be absolutely disappointing. Tourists measured their success against certain expectations, which meant, for instance, that the graveyard need not be silent. The skilled tourist could turn it into the site of a rhetorical engagement with the past, conjuring up the voice of Shakespeare from beyond the grave. For these working tourists, a journey into Warwickshire revealed a heroic period of English history. Travellers (or viewers) who desired to sustain this idea would have to concentrate

19. W. Jerome Harrison, 'Cottages, Broom', Warwickshire Photographic Survey, c.1890.

upon literature and could use photography as a time-machine: they not only stood beside the photographer or travel writer but looked on scenes that Shakespeare himself was supposed to have seen.

Travelling beyond Stratford, pilgrims experienced the greatest biographical *frisson* at the cottage in Shottery, the home of Shakespeare's abandoned wife, Anne Hathaway. Or they visited places he had named, such as the villages of 'Drunken Bidford' and 'Beggerly Broom', finding they deserved his aspersions (see photograph of dilapidated cottages at Broom taken by W. Jerome Harrison for the WPS, above). Casting wider still for a key to the region, pilgrims used the naming of Shakespeare as the 'Swan of Avon'. Looking at the swans and the river, they could imagine that they were looking at Shakespeare himself; or, since swans and rivers were essentially unchanged, they could pretend they saw them through his eyes.

20. J. L. Williams, 'First glimpse of Kenilworth', from *The Home and Haunts of Shakespeare*, 1892.

Travellers could enjoy this reverie with a cursory knowledge of the plays, though there was opportunity for those who knew the literature to allow the language to overlay and effectively dim the contemporary scene. There were more Elizabethan ghosts at other sites, such as Warwick Castle and Kenilworth, linked to the Queen, her courtiers and their misalliances, and imagined for modern audiences in the novel *Kenilworth* by Sir Walter Scott (see the photographs of Kenilworth by James Leon Williams reproduced above and on page 27). Any visitor to these ruins, rivers and woodlands could thrill at the spirits of historical and dramatic characters, escaping from the present by the mingled routes of art, nature and antiquity.

This dream of pre-industrial times sat beside the industrial reverie which, as I argued in the previous chapter, made the factories and worked landscapes appear to be comfortable. The two dreams ran side by side, and both offered reassurance, but otherwise they were not the same. The reverie which involved imagining the factory to be empty of people was qualitatively different from the dream of olden times. Industrial reverie was a celebration of rationality and the reduction of labour to small parts which were either easily seen or invisible, but always under control. The relation of the dream to the factory was the imposition of order in the present.

The pre-industrial reverie, though it allowed the dreamer to take control, involved a search for a relation between past and present which depended on their absolute disruption. Since the actual past was erased, the pre-industrial dream made it available through artifice. It resurrected the past in terms of aesthetic pleasure, deciding that it was 'quaint'. The pre-industrial dream created a past which was available for consumption. The relation of this dream to the past was nostalgia, or desire for an impossible union.

It is not clear that the audiences for the industrial reverie and pre-industrial dream were entirely different, but the dreams of order and nostalgia were both responses to the transformations of monopoly capitalism which was the lived experience of all observers, travellers or tourists. Both dreams could be achieved only partially and at some cost. To make the dream-like journey into Shakespeare land required travellers to pretend that significant parts of Elizabethan England were recoverable, and that specific localities, emblems and words created the chance of contacting a special voice beyond the grave, a resemblance of the Bard himself.

Searching for Shakespeare took place within two general contexts – fear of failure and reassurance of success. At the same time that travellers worked to make contact with the past, they were warned of disappointment – so much so that desire and disappointment were the twin anxieties of the search in the centre of the country for its metaphorical heart. Tourists needed protection from the fear of not achieving the adored or desired object. That fearful circumstance could be forestalled by guidance on what to see. This led photographers and writers to compile lists of the country's beauty 'spots', also known as 'bits'. In 1884 the photographer Richard Keene said the list of characteristic English 'charms' could be found within 'five or six miles' of home. The store of subjects, Keene said, was in fact 'inexhaustible', and was repeated with variations the length and breadth of the country. It included abbeys or other ancient places; brooks, canals, lakes and rivers; birches and old oaks; ferns, foxgloves and ivy; crags, dingles and woods, if they were 'deep' and 'recessed'; 'cattle and rustics at work'; churchyards, gables, tombs, walls, water-mills and windmills (Keene 1884: 168-9).

Fifteen years later, the Reverend Holland thought a similar list was harder to find, but its discovery had increased in value from a 'store of subjects' to a 'photographic paradise'. The 'diligent seeker' would go in search of 'out-of-the-way villages', discovering places 'which seem to belong to past centuries' (Holland 1899: 795). He echoed Keene's list of flora, fauna, old buildings and light effects, but placed more emphasis on looking for places where it was still possible to be alone 'to walk and gaze and meditate and work' at making pictures. His aim was similar to Keene's – the recourse to beauty and nature.

In this chapter, I shall look further than these contexts to see how the relationship between photographs and subjects was organised beyond the cataloguing of nature. I shall discuss what photography had to offer tourists in their attempts to connect with the past. The connections were in some ways thin and unexamined, but at other levels they proposed imaginative entries into Elizabethan times by means of authoritative records of ancient sites, reassuring viewers that these places really existed now as then.

Though photography was intimately linked to the passage of time, to mutability and alienation, it also promised escape into permanence, with moments able to last for ever. Photography and tourism were the two means of time-travel which allowed tourists either to see the past or to journey to places which they believed to hold traces of earlier, unspoiled times. A third means of escape was literature, but only tourism recovered the authentic through direct experience of what the traveller conceived to be a mythology of 'the primitive, the folk, the peasant, and the working class [who] speak without self-consciousness, without criticism, and without affectation' (Stewart 1984: 16; cited in Frow 1991: 129).

Within the economy of tourism, it was only cameras which captured the desired objects in permanent and realistic pictures. Cameras were one of two types of contradictory instrument of time-travel. Each promised to assuage the disenchantment of the world, even though both simultaneously contributed to it. Firstly, the camera had been made in the high-speed environment of the factory, but promised to freeze time and end movement. It could perfectly record the authentic moments which were experienced (imaginatively) outside the ruined modern world, and which could now be brought back as evidence.

Secondly, trains offered fast transport to sites of authenticity. Of course, on arrival travellers hoped to find people who were as authentic as the site. This meant they would have to be totally unlike the visitors, unused to fast systems of transport or the activities of the leisured classes. Travellers hoped to find innocent people devoid of 'calculation or of interested self-awareness', who 'must therefore exist outside the circuit of commodity relations and exchange values'. Despite their desire to find people outside this circuit, travellers could only reach the quaint villages and photograph them by using transport and cameras, and so closing the circle of commodity relations. By arriving in a place, travellers themselves spoiled what they were looking for. Searching for the authentic could never be satisfied, and was 'one form of the basic contradiction of the tourist experience' (Frow 1991: 129).

Tourists ignored these contradictions and set about gathering proof that they had reached the desired destination. Guidebooks were the simplest ways to find the main sites of Shakespeare country, so by purchasing them tourists learned what to see and how to go about meeting their limited expectations. They could perform this work through relatively cheap publications, which showed places and offered historical or topographical facts.

Another method of displaying evidence, which was akin to the record work of the Warwickshire Photographic Survey, used photography and text in openly didactic ways. This work was rarer than everyday tourist pocket-books, and claimed a self-conscious role in forming the national collective memory. I shall look at this in *Shakespeare's Town and Times*, with 110 photographic illustrations produced by H. Snowden Ward and Catharine Weed Ward, and also in W. Jerome Harrison's *Shakespeare-Land*.

The third type of evidence came from the connection between photography and the passage of time. It was sentimental and nostalgic, and it dealt with a sense of loss in ways avoided by the pocket guides and by the Wards and Harrison. Its fullest expression was in the expensive folio edition by James Leon Williams, entitled *The Home and Haunts of Shakespeare*, with photogravures and reproductions of watercolours. The fact that Williams was an American writing primarily for his native audience added a significant twist to this work: he was more determined than the guides to use words and pictures to conjure up a sense of England's past to people who might never visit the country for themselves, and would have to enjoy it through imagination alone. Nevertheless, anxiety and disappointment constantly threatened to spoil the dream. Williams's work was a constant struggle against this eventuality, and he tried to overcome it in the density of his writing and the detail of his photogravures.

KNOWING WHAT TO SEE

No-one could expect to comprehend the whole of the midland counties, or even use the Avon as a touchstone or key to the poetry. Instead, tourists wanted the region made sensible for them – they wanted to have it brought to life and explained without their having to work too hard. The importance of satisfying tourists was evident in the continuous supply of guidebooks. In addition to entries in general tourists' guides such as Baedeker's, there were many penny handbooks and popular histories of Shakespeare, Stratford and its neighbourhood (Arbuthnot 1889; Fox 1890). It was possible to buy booklets which contained a series of photographs of the best-known views of Stratford (Pumphrey 1880); similar views by the firm of Frith & Co. were published by the East & West Junction Railway company in 1886 (*Shakespeare's Country*), and views by Francis Bedford were advertised in a guidebook of 1892 (Neil 1892).

These productions, along with postcards, reduced the region to its essence in a series of predictable shots: pictures were simply holiday souvenirs, with stock views repeated throughout the pamphlets, brochures and advertisements. They showed the places in Stratford and Shottery that the visitor should try to cover in a day's sightseeing: Shakespeare's birthplace, the Grammar School, the High Street, Holy Trinity and the tomb, the memorial statue and Anne Hathaway's cottage. Through these devices, tourists were already prepared to see 'actual objects *as if they are pictures, maps or panoramas of themselves*' (MacCannell 1976: 122). The guides, with their simple, illustrative use of drawings or photographs, promised tourists the certainty of an authentic relationship between themselves and the important site. This forestalled any anxiety they may have felt at reaching the end of the journey and then failing to recognise it. To paraphrase MacCannell, they could experience the precisely defined spot as a *typical* Elizabethan house; as the *very place* where the poet was born or buried; as the *authentic* place to hear the *actual* words he wrote; as the *original* school; as the *real* home of the *true* Anne Hathaway (MacCannell 1976: 14).

Uncertain tourists, who had not come prepared to find what they already knew, could check the actual place against markers sold on the spot. Taking in the sights, or carrying them home in the form of postcards, guidebooks or photographs bought or taken there and then, prevented tourists from experiencing the shame of 'not being tourist enough', from failing 'to see everything the way it "ought" to be seen'

21. J. Walter, 'Anne Hathaway's cottage, Shottery – back view', from *Shakespeare's Home and Rural Life*, 1874.

(MacCannell 1976: 10). The guides and pictures directed everyone on the trail towards the correct experience, resolving any anxiety they may have had about what to see. By using these pictures, tourists had the landscape of Shakespeare discovery laid out for them.

All these productions met the minimal requirements of tourists, which was to direct them in what to see. If they were photographers, they captured those images for themselves. They already knew the evidence they sought, and discovered it upon arrival. They later displayed this set of representations to confirm the original set and its relation to the real: as John Urry said, 'it ends up with travellers demonstrating that they really have been there by showing their version of the images that they had seen originally before they set off' (Urry 1990: 140).

Exactly the same experience was available in expensive folio productions. For example, James Walter's *Shakespeare's Home and Rural Life* (costing £2 12s 6d in 1874) was concerned with the literature and biography of the poet, and its approach was antiquarian. The photographs, finely produced heliotypes, were the standard ones of various town and country buildings, with the captions written into the plate in the style of ordinary tourist views of the day. All signs of modernity were excised, and if people were visible, they were unobtrusive and small in scale (seen in the photograph reproduced on page 71 of the back of Anne Hathaway's cottage). No attempt was made to incorporate the pictures into the text: they were merely presented as illustrations, without comment.

Neither Walter's book nor the cheaper guides mentioned so far acknowledged how photographs worked in relation to a sense of history – indeed it was outside their scope. They aimed to satisfy tourists' preconceptions of what to see and how to see it. Modern commodities were integral to their imaginative experience, which meant that the pre- or anti-modern world was impossible to enter. This in part explains the guidebooks' frequent warnings of disappointment, and those who took steps to avoid it were not immune. Disappointment awaited them wherever they went since it already belonged to them as moderns. Commenting on this, MacCannell writes:

> The solidarity of modernity, even as it incorporates fragments of primitive social life, the past and nature, elevates modernity over the past and nature. There is nothing wilful in this; it is automatic; it is a structure *sui generis*. Every nicely motivated effort to preserve nature, primitives and the past, and to represent them authentically contributes to an opposite tendency – the present is made more unified against its past, more in control of nature, less a product of history.
>
> (MacCannell 1976: 83)

For many tourists, the mirror of themselves that the guides provided may have been reassuring, and they may have been prepared to accept some disappointment on encountering the real thing if they overcame the anxiety of failing to see what was expected.

SEEKING THE AUTHENTIC

Of course, not everything worth seeing was Elizabethan. The tourist trail also took in the growth of the Shakespeare industry in the nineteenth century. The Memorial Theatre was opened in 1879, and in Queen Victoria's Jubilee year of 1887, an American philanthropist paid for the Memorial Fountain. It bore a quotation from the American author Washington Irving, whose *Sketch Book* had been a best-seller in 1815, and remained popular seventy-five years later: he had given thanks for 'the Bard who…gilded the dull realities of life with innocent illusions' (Irving 1890: 299).

Developing the Shakespeare trail was both reassuring and alarming. Tourists could take comfort in knowing they were in the right place, but they were in danger of being misled by false information into seeing or believing the wrong things, and therefore failing to be tourists. The quotation on the American Fountain was a timely reminder of the problem of illusions. In 1815, Irving had found plenty of examples of less innocent illusions in what was then a growing but unregulated Shakespeare industry. At Shakespeare's birthplace he had been shown 'relics' which his guide claimed were once owned by the poet himself – part of his poacher's gun, his tobacco-box, his stage sword and his chair. Freelancers preyed on the gullible, feeding their desire to believe in the presence of Shakespeare in surviving artefacts (Irving 1890: 281–2; Brown and Fearon 1939: 48–9, 125–6). Since the deceit cost Irving nothing, he said that he was 'a ready believer in relics, legends, and local anecdotes of goblins and great men'. He advised 'all travellers who travel for their gratification to be the same. What is it to us, whether these stories be true or false, so long as we can persuade ourselves into the belief of them, and enjoy all the charm of the reality?' (Irving 1890: 282–3).

This amused relationship with falsehood was too sophisticated for most tourists, who wanted something direct and without the need for ironic detachment or the work of suspending disbelief. From 1847 the Birthplace Trustees began to structure the Shakespeare industry to meet tourists' expectations of authenticity. The Trustees swept away the spurious 'relics', and set about buying other properties with Shakespearian connections. They administered the recently founded museum, the new memorials, and restored the architecture of the main Elizabethan sites (aided in 1891 by special powers granted by Act of Parliament). The Trustees' aim was to offer a historical landscape which was correct rather than deceitful. The regulated industry had to admit that the artefacts touted by fraudsters as genuinely Shakespeare's never existed, and replaced this desire for concrete evidence with pleasures that could easily be won through proximity and association with the actual sites. They advanced the cautious antiquarian's approach to the facts of Shakespeare's life in Stratford, facts which could be verified. They were aided by the simple, direct use of photographs proving the existence of Elizabethan England.

Rather than be fooled by false claims, tourists were content to accept fewer relics if they were authentic: an 'illusion' of Shakespeare-land was acceptable if whatever remained of the lost original stood in for what Walter Benjamin called its mystical 'aura'. Tourists wanted to close the distance between themselves and the imaginary, unique objects of the past. In order to achieve this they accepted losing 'the uniqueness of every reality by accepting its reproduction' (Benjamin 1973: 225). The tourists' quest for sites with aura meant that it was not enough for the Trust merely to *conserve* them; its main work was in satisfying the demand for authenticity, the production of sites which visitors could believe (or 'trust') were Elizabethan. If visitors could believe that what little remained was truly Elizabethan, they then felt free to augment the sparse remnants with thoughts of their own, or thoughts suggested in books which showed how Shakespeare was still available to the correctly tuned ear and eye.

Once the sites were clarified, and their errors dispelled, tourists could buy travel books which were equally clear in their display of the full Shakespearian story. At least, this was the position of the Wards in *Shakespeare's Town and Times*. They claimed to have found the proper balance between fact and fancy. The Wards wrote:

> Our task has been a simple one; – to write in plain words the tale of Shakespeare's life, to picture what remains to us of the scenes that Shakespeare saw. There are 'lives' more learned than anything we can attempt, and illustrations of Shakespeare's town more picturesque than anything we can make. But the pictures are too often fancies, the 'lives' too seldom distinguish between fact and theory…Our photograms may be useful in years to come, in reconciling the contradictions of more beautiful but less accurate representations.
>
> (Ward and Ward 1896: 7)

This claim was in itself a product and a measure of the positivism of the times – the belief in the accuracy and self-evidence of facts in both language and high-

22. A. Leeson, 'Picnic party on the Avon, 14 June 1890', Warwickshire Photographic Survey.

precision photographs. The Wards were simply making claims for the transparent nature of photographs: they believed the unexamined truth-value of photographic realism corresponded with the supposed objectivity of 'fact'. The indexical quality of photographs (standing in for the absent scene) meant they were as close to the sense of the 'Elizabethan' as the restored but actual buildings themselves.

So the Wards gave tourists the guidance they needed to believe in the photographs. They showed the sites which stimulated emotional responses – namely, the magical, semi-religious sites of Shakespeare worship – but they went further and made two important distinctions for their readers. Firstly, they warned against 'trippers': these were failed tourists, the sort of people who found it all too easy to visit Warwickshire and miss the Shakespearian adventure. Near Clopton Bridge in Stratford was a landing stage 'well supplied with picturesque and comfortable river craft'. Unfortunately, the place attracted those who were oblivious to the wonders of the town: it was, 'alas! the starting point of a somewhat ugly and incongruous steam launch, that provides cheap recreation for hilarious parties of trippers from the Black Country' (Ward and Ward 1896: 21). Tourists who wanted to sail the river should choose more 'comfortable' (and expensive) transportation and so avoid the masses (an avoidance illustrated here by the WPS photograph of a 'picnic party on the Avon' in 1890). Tourists could also avoid the masses, and prove their own worth as serious tourists, by visiting the mystic 'haunts' of Shakespeare safe in the knowledge that the trippers were on the steamboat.

The second type of guidance the Wards offered had to do with Shakespeare's and the Elizabethans' historical importance. It suggested an evolution culminating in the present condition of England, Britain and the Empire. According to the Wards, the special sites of 'The Church, the Guild Chapel, and the Grammar School, take us back in memory to times and manners of which we must know something if we are to fully understand the complex civilisation of to-day. Their records tell us better than any great city's record can tell, of the life and ways and thoughts of that sturdy yeoman class which moulded the English life as neither kings nor parliaments could mould it, and made Great Britain and her sons and daughters over-sea, the nations that they are' (Ward and Ward 1896: 27). This statement interpreted the sites along lines which were already widely believed about England and its heroic past. In 1841, Thomas Carlyle had written of Shakespeare in *On Heroes and Hero-Worship*, imagining him to be an 'indestructible…rallying-sign…over all the Nations of Englishmen', bringing 'all these together into virtually one Nation' (Carlyle 1900: 150). Since Carlyle's time, at least, sentiment and nostalgia for the lost home and haunts of Shakespeare was not primarily a search for the edenic, idealised origins of England in the form of a well-kept garden. It was a search for England in its heroic, innocent phase.

Although present times had unarguably evolved from the Elizabethan age, the two periods were completely different from each other. While the modern descendants of Elizabethan yeomen were still 'great', by the 1890s industry threatened to destroy the homeland. This led to a feeling that something had been lost in the transition from the glorious past into the contemporary world. In his portrait of *Merrie England*, published in 1894, Robert Blatchford looked beyond the increasingly wretched condition of the country over the previous twenty years to the 'greatness' of the 'England of Elizabeth', which 'excited the love, interest, and admiration of mankind'. The Elizabethans' 'splendid spiritual effort' would be remembered long after 'our coal, and our industrial operations depending on coal' were forgotten (Blatchford 1894: 28).

The guidebooks were so eager to make the connection between contemporary life and the Elizabethan period that they brushed aside the apparently strange, regressive pathway of evolution. Though largely an uncomplicated guide, the sheer accumulation of Elizabethan achievements meant that *Shakespeare's Town and Times* was another example of the general celebration of the heroic self-confidence of England in those days, a time which the Wards believed should be the source and

23. H. Snowden Ward and Catharine Weed Ward, 'The tumble-down stile', from *Shakespeare's Town and Times*, 1896.

inspiration for the present. The danger lay in allowing too many 'macadamised surfaces and steam road-rollers' to break the symbolic bonds with this heroic past (Ward and Ward 1896: 28).

Nothing destroyed these bonds more quickly than development, and the Wards condemned the so-called 'improver[s]' who had made 'sad havoc of the Shakespeare haunts' (Ward and Ward 1896: 7). In addition to the numerous photographs of unique sites, the Wards illustrated their book with a few pictures, such as 'The tumble-down stile', which showed people enjoying what remained of the general rustic scene. By the late 1870s, the landlords of Warwickshire had knocked down most of the area's 'quaint old cottages and their artistic surroundings', destroying the picturesque villages (Everitt 1882: 1). By the mid-1880s, the region looked derelict to the eyes of

Rose Kingsley, with 'dull, well-ordered' crops interspersed with wilderness, and with 'poor and squalid' people living in 'tumble-down old houses' (Kingsley 1885: 279). By 1898, the developers had also wrecked many of the older houses in Stratford:

> Each year brings about the destruction of a portion, if not the whole, of an ancient building, so that in the course of the next generation or two the greater part of the town will present a modern appearance...Stratford will lose the quaint old-world appearance so dear to artists and antiquarians, so highly appreciated by American and Colonial visitors.
>
> (Brassington 1898: 33)

To counter the spoilers, publicly-minded citizens formed numerous associations and societies in the 1890s to preserve 'the beautiful world' of England – for instance, the National Trust for Places of Historic Interest and Natural Beauty, the Commons and Footpaths Preservation Society and the Society for Checking the Abuses of Public Advertising (John Taylor 1990: 195, n. 39). The preservation of old England had national as well as commercial value, since it was 'absurd to talk of English freedom and prosperity and the greatness of our Imperial mission, if no regard be paid to the beauty of the landscape, to dignity and propriety in the common round' (cited in John Taylor 1990: 191). The only way to counter the arguments and actions of the developers was not through appeals to sentiment but by mobilising more powerful sectors of the establishment who could create laws protecting the countryside and do it in the name of national interest. Conservation became a patriotic duty. In 1903, when the local conservation groups drafted a proposal for Local Amenities Associations, they evoked a dense 'fabric' of interested parties which had 'its base in the village green and its apex in Westminster'. The Association had been proposed some years before, in 1898, by the Parliamentary Group for Concerted Action in Defence of the Picturesque and Romantic Elements in Our National Life (John Taylor 1990: 187). Hence in 1898 the framework was already established which made sense of the call to 'preserve the ancient characteristics of Stratford' as a 'sacred duty' and for the sake of 'commercial prosperity' which 'depends upon the maintenance of its ancient appearance' (Brassington 1898: 33).

We can see the mutual influence of magical sites, duty and a sense of history in W. Jerome Harrison's *Shakespeare-Land*, published in 1907 as the final part of the fourteenth and last volume of a complete 'Works'. The text throughout is factual and informative in the manner of guides, with the emphasis upon topography and descriptions of favourite sights. Ninety-one halftones illustrated the book, mostly of Harrison's own photographs taken over thirty years (many of them for the WPS) 'with a view to securing a faithful record and survey of Shakespeare-Land as it exists at the present day' (Harrison 1907: 269). What separated Harrison's use of photographs to illustrate history from the normal system of simple markers for tourists was his claim that photography proved the continuing existence of the past. Shakespeare's view of England was now verified by Harrison's survey technique.

Unlike the Wards, Harrison made no reference to class divisions or the place of Shakespeare in the present imperial state of the nation. He also steered away from nostalgia. He combined photographs with the topographic and historical information usually found in guidebooks into a different narrative. He wove the key sights and biographical details together with geographic facts and observations on the present decay of the region; he used record photographs to show the scene and authenticate his words. Since he was particularly interested in the local geology and botany, and wanted to demonstrate his claims for objective survey work, the first photograph was of a limestone quarry near Stratford.

As if to emphasis the scientific status of the pictures, Harrison called them 'figures'. He often mentioned them in the text, always emphasising that they showed the contemporary scene and sometimes referring to the different authority of Shakespeare. For instance, describing another one of his photographs of these cottages in Broom, he wrote, 'The cottages – many of them – are in a delightful state of disrepair. Slabs of limestone serve as garden fences: thatched roofs, dilapidated house-walls, patched and rebuilt bit by bit at intervals of a century or so, combine with the absence of an orthodox church and an inn to give a reason for [Shakespeare's] uncomplimentary title of "Beggarly Broom!"' (Harrison 1907: 254).

Harrison tried to make scenes of decay seem either picturesque or a permanent condition of the place, observed by Shakespeare himself and still apparent in the present records. The photograph of Broom seemed to directly 'figure' the decay of ages, appearing to be a summation of neglect, and was, as the photographer claimed, a 'delightful' example of both accuracy and art (see page 67).

Harrison used the same method of comparison in his photograph of 'The Master Blacksmith', writing, 'We are able to present a type of the Warwickshire working man of the present day – a type which has changed surprisingly little since Will Shakespeare wrote lovingly [of such characters]' (Harrison 1907: 240). The pictures were decidedly records of the contemporary scene, yet the photographer claimed the types of workers matched those who had lived centuries before. He did not discuss his claim, assuming that his readers shared his own beliefs about the fixed nature of social position in the countryside. As the American author Nathaniel Hawthorne had already noticed, though in a sarcastic rather than approving tone, the English were inured against change by their fixation on heredity. Hawthorne suggested that the English villager stayed put for centuries, and the 'stone threshold of his cottage is worn away with his hobnailed footsteps, shuffling over it from the reign of the first Plantagenet to that of Victoria' (Hawthorne 1890: 92).

The numerous conservation groups put political pressure on Parliament and local authorities to save the countryside, but they shared common ground with the serious, antiquarian tourist books, including those written by the Wards and Harrison. They were all concerned with demarcating the special sites by preserving them and by writing them into particular forms of history. The work of pressure groups and serious guidebooks was didactic, promoting a defined sense of national belonging and strength which could be properly traced into the deep past. This work was unsentimental, matter-of-fact and interventionist. The activists saw a task to be done, and believed it was possible. They set about creating resources to assuage the anxiety of tourists and were optimistic that they could save England for the future by recording and preserving it now. To this extent, the programme which writers, agitators and photographers set themselves was thoughtful, indifferent to sentiment, and uninterested in reflection or nostalgia. This programme of national conservation, with its antiseptic air of scientific distance, was akin to positivist social survey projects which doctors and town planners, for instance, had already developed to aid them in tracking disease and deprivation (Tagg 1988). The major difference, of course, was that sites visited by tourists did resonate with history, and conservationists or record photographers could not present this entirely as objective matter of fact.

CLOCKS FOR SEEING

Photographs were never simply markers of presence or continuation. Any of them could be used to suggest time passing, and the inexorable passage of life. James Leon Williams used photographs deliberately as signs of time in his *The Home and Haunts of Shakespeare*, published in 1892 and illustrated with 15 coloured plates of artists' interpretations of Warwickshire scenery, 45 photogravures and more than 150 other photographic illustrations. It was an expensive book ($37.50), but according to Williams's biographer, 12,000 were sold, and specially bound copies presented to Queen Victoria, Queen Alexandra, and King George V (Clapp 1925: 251).

Williams was an American dental surgeon who also practised in London. He spent four years taking the photographs and writing his book which was published simultaneously in England and America, but addressed an American audience (Clapp 1925: 250). Williams's ambitions were quite different from the unsentimental goals of Harrison and the authors of the guidebooks. He aimed self-consciously to use photography and language to describe the 'living links that bind the present to the past' (J. L. Williams 1892: 26).

Realism did not detain Williams for long from reverie. His passion was to weave text and pictures into versions of Elizabethan England. This idea of England as a palimpsest, a manuscript reused, with traces of the past not entirely erased by the present, was common enough. Photographers employed it with quite different aims in mind, such as the Wards imagining visitors 'on their light cycles' talking of how Shakespeare may have 'cantered' on country tracks where they 'glide' on metalled roads (Ward and Ward 1896: 28). The Wards used the idea that England bore traces of its past to make unfavourable comparisons between the present and the 'days of Good Queen Bess'. Indeed, according to the Wards, the changes were so great that it was 'difficult...to realise what Stratford and Warwickshire were when Shakespeare knew them'. They felt it was fanciful to attempt the comparisons, because they were trying to establish a relationship with the past which honoured it but made no pretence that it was still available. Williams, on the contrary, was 'striving to reproduce, and in imagination reënact, these scenes pictured in the records of a by-gone time' (J. L. Williams 1892: 80). He travelled the district looking for incidents or spots which would confirm his romance, proving that Shakespeare and England were continuously genteel. This perspective had been chosen by the English themselves, but what made Williams's project unusual, coming from an American, was the absence of criticism.

Compared to the guidebooks, *The Home and Haunts of Shakespeare* was also unusually centred on mutability and death, though this was heavily disguised by gentility. Photographs, Williams suggested, seemed to promise access not only to the immediate past, but to the deep past. This quality would be enjoyed more by future

24. J. L. Williams, 'At Shottery Brook', from *The Home and Haunts of Shakespeare*, 1892.

generations, born into a world of photography older than a lifespan. Even so, photographs taken in the 1890s, by showing buildings from centuries before, gave contemporary viewers access to the distant past. If a photograph pictured Elizabethan homes, it suggested a narrow tunnel to Elizabethan times. The realness of the photograph allowed the viewer to enjoy the illusion of travel in time, and allowed the two impulses of mortality and sentiment to act on each other. As Susan Sontag has written, 'the fascination that photographs exercise is a reminder of death, [but] it is also an invitation to sentimentality. Photographs turn the past into an object of tender regard, scrambling moral distinctions and disarming historical judgments by the generalized pathos of looking at time past' (Sontag 1977: 71). Sentiment and pathos entered the public realm as elegy or genteel grieving; the dead were elevated into a grand scheme of remembrance. Photographs of the past affirmed 'a continuity with the dead at the same time as it continuously reposition[ed] them at the heart of a narrative of the nation' (Frow 1991: 134).

In the ordinary fashion of tourist views, Williams adopted a comfortable

25. J. L. Williams, 'Waiting for the ferry', from *The Home and Haunts of Shakespeare*, 1892.

relationship with the past, assuming it to be coextensive with the present. His photographs of famous sites were taken to 'represent faithfully the characteristic features of Shakespeare's environment during his early years'. No effort was made to identify particular places with descriptive passages in Shakespeare's writings because, according to Williams, so much remained the same. He adopted a naive view of the English, and was determined to see them as he wished them to be: 'honest peasant folk go about their labors much as they did in the olden times. One's ears are greeted with many of the old tricks of speech, and one's eyes are occasionally delighted with the sight of ancient customs. The same flowers that charmed the poet's gaze spring up by hedgerow and stream and in the cottage gardens' (J. L. Williams 1892: 105–6) (see illustrations opposite and above 'At Shottery Brook' and 'Waiting for the ferry').

Williams's 'true pilgrims at the shrine of Shakespeare' would spend the day working themselves into the past. They might think they were wandering along 'the very path where Shakespeare's feet have often trod' (43), or imagine they saw what Shakespeare himself had seen, spying the ancient willow that 'grows ascaunt the brook

26. J. L. Williams, 'The old chair mender', from *The Home and Haunts of Shakespeare*, 1892.

...the self-same picture [which] may have attracted the poet's eye' (55). Spending time looking for traces of Shakespeare's past, using the poetry as an index or prompt, allowed the 'pilgrim' to see its 'colour', simply present in the ancient woodlands and old flower-gardens, audible in local dialect, and instantly available at Anne Hathaway's cottage, which on entry, 'takes us back three centuries at a single step' (44).

Williams was always on the look-out for parallels and links with the past. 'Every quaint and curious character', he wrote, 'is at once subjected to comparison with the personages in the great comedies and tragedies…A group of old women gossiping at a cottage door recalls such lines as these', or 'The old man resting on his barrow in the village street answers the questioner in nearly the precise words of the master' (80). He thought Shakespearian England could be seen in the unchanged rhythms of 'peasant' life. A song from one of the plays was 'instantly suggested' by 'a bevy of rosy-cheeked girls' (43). He later took a photograph of them (see 'At Shottery Brook' on page 82) 'filling their buckets at the old crossing', observing that their 'gayety [*sic*] has passed into that grave but not severe silence which is the characteristic mood of the English peasantry of to-day, from which, however, they are easily aroused to a sort of subdued geniality' (45).

Although Williams persisted with these comparisons, he fell prey to tourist anxiety. Firstly, there was the unpleasant imperative to mingle with 'the great army of sight-seers, with no other object in view than that of "doing" Europe in the shortest possible time' (43). More disturbing than the proximity of vulgar tourists was the gap between imagination and experience. The 'rustic scenes' which he saw around Stratford, and some of which he photographed (including 'The Old Chair Mender' reproduced on page 84), were unlike his conception of the art in Shakespeare's writing. He complained, 'There is always lacking something of the glamor and halo which surround everything when we look through his eyes.' The fact that 'we are not able thus to look upon such actual scenes as still exist' without something lacking, Williams argued, 'explains in part our sense of disappointment' (17). Shakespeare 'glorified' 'the common events of life', but Stratford itself was now 'disappointing', being 'modern and even commonplace', especially since at 'almost every spot within the town, you are unpleasantly conscious that the place is on exhibition' (49). Anyone looking for old customs such as a May Day festival would be disappointed, since those few remaining had degenerated into an excuse for begging. Rather than the largesse of harvest home the countryside rambler was more likely to find 'peasants trudging from village to village in search of work, resting beneath a wayside cross, or munching a bit of dry bread in an ale house' (87).

Williams used the words of Nathaniel Hawthorne, who had said 'The English should send us photographs of portions of the trunks of trees, the tangled and various products of a hedge, and a square foot of an old wall. They can hardly send us anything else so characteristic' to evoke the old country (J. L. Williams 1892: 105). However, he had no use for Hawthorne's sceptical view of the English. The contrast between the two travellers gives us a clearer sense of the conceptual and sentimental gap between an American tourist from the 1850s and another from the 1890s (see Tomsich 1971; Persons 1973; Lears 1981).

Only by narrowing his sights could Hawthorne see the 'charm' of England in its countryside. The 'charm' rested in the trees, hedges and ivy-grown walls, since England was characteristically small-scale and picturesque: it lacked grandeur in every area, including its sense of purpose. Unlike America, England was small-scale, satisfied with itself, and had no sense of the need for change (Hawthorne 1890: 152).

Nevertheless, Hawthorne felt obliged to visit Stratford, since this was 'one of the things that an American proposes to himself as necessarily and chiefly to be done, on coming to England'. He found the town 'tame and unpicturesque'. The river Avon was narrow and sluggish, loitering past the church where Shakespeare was buried 'as if it had been considering which way to flow ever since [he] used to paddle in it'. Moreover, most of the gravestones in the churchyard were modern. He seemed relieved to escape and sit down for a while, admire the forget-me-nots and watch his family eat oranges (Hawthorne 1941: 130, 134). Essentially, Hawthorne was unaffected by the precious site, and wanted his readers to know it.

Going through the motions of touring in Stratford, Hawthorne felt 'no emotion whatever' in Shakespeare's house, 'nor any quickening of the imagination'. The visit enabled him to form a 'vivid idea of [Shakespeare] as a flesh-and-blood man', but he was not sure this was 'desirable' since it destroyed the aura of the poet (Hawthorne 1941: 132). The closer he came to the material facts of Stratford or the poet, the greater was his distraction, and the more frequent were his unfavourable remarks on the picturesque nature of English scenery, and on the English character which was like John Bull – 'bulbous…heavy-witted, [and] material' (Hawthorne 1890: 101).

Hawthorne's most scathing remarks were directed at English history. According to him, English history never developed: instead, 'Life is there fossilized in its greenest leaf' into 'hoary antiquity'. The English enjoyed the 'monotony of sluggish ages, toiling in hereditary fields, listening to the parson's drone lengthened through centuries in the gray Norman church'. He imagined, and mocked, the English villager as eternal, a man whose life had remained unchanged for centuries, so that it became impossible and unnecessary to attempt to distinguish between generations which were always the same. He wrote, 'The man who died yesterday or ever so long ago walks the village street to-day, and chooses the same wife that he married a hundred years ago since,

27. J. L. Williams, 'When we were boys', from *The Home and Haunts of Shakespeare*, 1892.

and must be buried again to-morrow under the same kindred dust that has already covered him half a score of times' (92).

As well as disdaining the 'hardened forms' of English history, Hawthorne was exasperated by the 'diseased American appetite for English soil' – a longing for the same timelessness he disparaged. He observed in Americans 'a blind pathetic tendency to wander back again' to fulfil 'wild dreams' of inheritance, based on nothing more than 'an advertisement for lost heirs, cut out of a British newspaper'. Honest Republican brains were turned by 'rubbish' such as 'a seal with an uncertain crest, an old yellow letter or document in faded ink, the more scantily legible the better' (24–5).

If an American lived for a time in England, as Hawthorne did, then he would know that the 'stone-incrusted institutions of the mother-country' were like 'fetters' around 'her ankles, in the race and rivalry of improvement'. With this rivalry in mind, he wanted the English to lose the race, and he felt certain they would lose if they continued to be bound to the past: therefore he 'hated to see so much as a twig of ivy wrenched from an old wall in England' (93).

The difference between Hawthorne's and Williams's perspectives cannot be accounted for simply by the fact that Williams was one of those Republicans whose heads had been turned. Perhaps Williams's favourable perception of the country owed less to the development of the Shakespeare industry than to changes within his own society, which made England seem more secure than moribund. Genteel observers of the American scene would have found their views corresponded with his idea of England (Tomsich 1971; Persons 1973).

Yet he was expressly interested in mortality, and relished what tourists usually ignored, namely the anxiety of death. The purpose of photographs of tourist sites was to stave off disappointment, but more fundamentally photography established a relation to mortality. Williams saw that photography was most suggestive of time. He had used an old man as a model in several of his pictures, but returned to Stratford one year to learn the man had died. In order to see him again, he studied his 'counterfeit presentment' (J. L. Williams 1892: 54) in such photographs as 'When we were boys' (see illustration on page 89). In this act he recognised that cameras were what Roland Barthes calls 'clocks for seeing' in *Camera Lucida*, a meditation on photography, memory and death. Cameras, Barthes notes, are also like clocks because they are noisy, from 'the trigger of the lens, to the metallic shifting of the plates (when the camera still has such things)'. He writes 'I love these mechanical sounds in an almost voluptuous way, as if, in the Photograph, they were the very thing – and the only thing – to which my desire clings, their abrupt clicking breaking through the mortiferous layer of the Pose' (Barthes 1982: 15).

In addition, according to Barthes, the pose was like death because it was a kind of embalming, a 'micro-version of death' in which Barthes turned from subject to object, and into a 'specter'. The photographer's eye terrified him because of its ability to see, choose and fix the moment of his small death. As well as creating the face of (his) death in the picture, the act of photography also created the noise of 'Time' in the camera.

The camera puts an end to time, but photographs are perpetual reminders of its passing. When photographers or other viewers see the prints, everything in them is already over. Their eyes are always met with the prospect of time past, the portable graveyard of photography, what Susan Sontag has called 'the inventory of mortality'. Viewers always have the advantage of hindsight, and sometimes they have the advantage of knowing what the subjects of the pictures could only guess – their subsequent destinies. A 'touch of the finger' sufficed 'to invest a moment with posthumous irony' (Sontag 1977: 70).

The real subject of Williams's work, then, was a sense of loss, which he expressed in the form of polite, literary grieving. For instance, when the old man he photographed died, he took comfort in three registers of remembrance: a prayer for the man's soul in his text; the bequest he received of the smock the old man wore; and the photographs themselves – from which the 'genial old face beams out' (J. L. Williams 1892: 54). Williams's pleasure in proximity to Shakespeare was openly sad, or rather he affected the particular sadness of elegy, which he was able to relate to his photographs. As Sontag wrote nearly a hundred years later, 'Photography is an elegaic art, a twilight art...All photographs are *memento mori*. To take a photograph is to participate in another person's (or things) mortality, vulnerability, mutability' (Sontag 1977: 15). In Shakespeare's country, tourists went in search of sites which would place them mysteriously closer to the poet, and closer to the imagined nobility of Elizabethan times. On arrival, they discovered the places belonged decidedly to the past, leading from one ancient house to another, and finally to the tomb in the church. This actual experience of travel was matched by another, metaphoric journey: exemplified by photographs as *memento mori*, all journeys ended in the grave.

3

Travellers, tourists and trippers on the Norfolk Broads

CONFLICTS OF INTEREST

DESPITE THE promises of travel and advertising agents, tourists in England in the late nineteenth century never reached their holiday destination directly. Every journey and discovery was at the same time a process of evasion. Tourists were looking for something recognisable, and in order to find it they practised avoidance. As we have seen in relatively cheap guidebooks and expensive studies such as Williams's exegesis of Shakespeare country, tourists left out everything which threatened to spoil the picture, including undesirable groups of people. We saw how H. Snowden and Catharine Ward in Stratford were affronted by the ugly and incongruous steamboat, but the chief reason for their alarm was that, should they wish to row on the Avon, they might be forced into meeting working-class trippers. In all their long book on the local sights, and for all their concentration upon fact and reality, the Wards could not prevent themselves from admitting that other classes visited the spot, largely occupying different spaces, but occasionally coming into view. The brief comment about class, made in passing, was designed to prick their readers into a sudden awareness of difference, and remind them of the need sometimes to take evasive action.

The English understood the codes of behaviour which applied within groups, and between different social orders in the domestic or work place. These codes were less fixed when people were on holiday. Whole sections of newly mobile classes were

28. A. E. Coe, 'Photographer on the Broads', *c*.1890.

likely to meet more often in unpredictable circumstances. In this chapter, I shall look at these class collisions in East Anglia, which in the late 1880s was a region where the class lines were not as clearly drawn as they had become in other resorts.

The chief attraction of the Norfolk and Suffolk Broads and coastline, including the fishing port of Great Yarmouth, was not landscape but water sports. The region was popular for fishing, shooting, sailing and seaside holidays. It was now easy to reach by rail from London, where larger numbers of people had money to spare either for summer holidays or day-trips. But the numbers and social diversity of the new tourists meant that the middle classes, who paid for hunting rights, and were used to distant and uncomplicated relations with the locals, found their holiday-making changed into something much less welcome. Evasion was not always possible, no matter how much it was desired.

In this chapter I shall also examine the experience of P. H. Emerson, who for most of this century has been considered by photographic historians to be a forerunner

29. Payne Jennings, 'Artist at work', *c*.1890.

of modernism, someone whom Alfred Stieglitz admired as the first advocate of pure photography. In 1975 the American photographic historian Nancy Newhall called Emerson's *Naturalistic Photography* of 1889 the 'first great statement of pure photography', true to the qualities of the medium itself. She asserted it had the greatest impact on 'the young Stieglitz', who, 'apart from a few manipulative experiments', adhered to it all his life (Newhall 1975: 63) (see also page 105).

Apart from modernists claiming that Emerson was one of their own, it is usual and useful to place Emerson within the artistic concerns of his time (McConkey 1986). From the 1880s, artists such as B. W. Leader or Sir Frank Short often sought the marginal spaces of river estuaries at low tide, mud-flats, or barren ground. For the next quarter of a century, at least, serious art photographers also went in search of fashionably dull or 'dreary' landscapes, which were a sub-genre of the picturesque. Compositions were simple, with a few leafless trees cast in the fading light of winter or autumn, an empty sky, flat horizon and meadows, or the slow-moving

30. P. H. Emerson, 'The old ship', from *Wild Life on a Tidal Water*, 1890

and marshy Broads of East Anglia (see, for example, Payne Jennings's photograph 'Artist at work' on page 92, or Emerson's hulk rotting on the shoreline from *Wild Life on a Tidal Water* reproduced above).

My interest in Emerson is quite different from both these artistic contexts, and derives from his use of the aestheticising and distancing techniques of discovery rhetoric – though he used it with a difference. In contrast to the usual tourists' aim of keeping safe distances between themselves and the locals, Emerson actively sought their company. He did this for a number of reasons, some of them akin to the ideals of preservation of others of his class. At one level, he was concerned with the environmental state of the Broads; he recorded facts, dialects and everyday exchanges in the manner of anthropologists. He was open about his desire to preserve what he imagined to be the pre-industrial relation of owners and peasants. At a different level, I believe that Emerson's writings show that he needed to prove his masculine sexuality to himself. He expressed his desire for, and fear of, lower-class women. These characteristics were, of course, widespread among the upper and ruling classes (Pearsall 1971; Hudson 1972; Hiley 1979; Hull 1982; Mort 1987; Jacobus 1990; Showalter 1991).

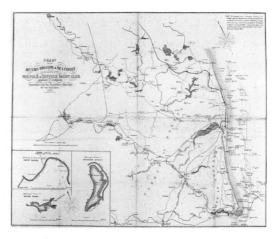

31. 'Chart of the rivers, broads & sea coast in the district of the Norfolk and Suffolk Yacht Club', 1879.

HOLIDAYS AND CLASS COLLISIONS

From 1886 to 1895, when P. H. Emerson was publishing photographs of what he called 'natives', the Broads and some parts of the coastline including Great Yarmouth became the popular holiday resorts of tourists from different classes. Each class was confined, to some degree, to its own world. For instance, the workers on day excursions from London stayed on the beach; the lower-middle classes ventured further up the coast or took short boating trips on the rivers and Broads; and the middle classes took longer holidays inland, at exclusive gaming reserves – social divisions which are, of course, not apparent in this orthodox map of the area (see above). The fear of class collision meant that the landscape was a place of exclusion and tension, factors deriving from the fascination and repulsion that the middle class felt for the lower classes. From the mid-1880s the different uses of photography became closely linked with these fears and fascinations.

In the early nineteenth century, before the invention of photography or mass tourism, the region was inhabited only by peasants and landowners. It was a network of slow-moving rivers which had flooded ancient peat workings to form a lowland region of marshes. In the 1880s, a writer recalled the East Anglia of the 1860s. He remembered it as a romantic wilderness, with the land half-submerged, and the water pools of oozy vegetation. Then the solitary reaches were inaccessible in most parts, except to the marshmen who worked along the waterways harvesting reeds. In the uncertain light of sunset, even the visitor of the 1880s would be overcome with a 'strange awe', believing the sight belonged to 'some older world than this nineteenth century of ours, with its crowded cities and busy people' (cited in Brittain 1891: 120–1). In its imaginary, idealised form, the region retained its earlier remoteness, remaining unspoiled.

This romanticism did not bear close scrutiny, since by the 1880s the region was neither wild nor exotic. In 1885 the historian Walter Rye dismissed as 'rubbish' the idea that the Broads were picturesque. Any stranger taken in by such publicity would be 'disgusted' with muddy rivers dragging through flat country, 'varied only by drainage-mills in various stages of dilapidation, and by telegraph-poles' (Rye 1885: 256). Undeterred, strangers came in mobs because they were attracted by the sailing, shooting and fishing. They were not looking for picturesque landscapes, and were only incidentally interested in taking photographs as holiday souvenirs. The arrival en masse of so many tourists in an area which only twenty years before had been exclusive upset the wealthier hunters (and the more serious amateur photographers with field cameras represented on page 91 by A. E. Coe's 'Photographer on the Broads'). They had become accustomed to treating the region as their private playground. Now tourists were spoiling 'the quiet and solitude' which were formerly the area's 'greatest charm' (Alfieri 1888: 216). By 1891 the idea that the region was a wilderness had become 'almost a joke': by then, 'every inch' had been visited by tens of thousands of tourists (Brittain 1891: 121).

Since the region was now overrun, tourists themselves became the objects of curiosity and annoyance to other tourists, and the guidebooks were full of distinctions which separated properly behaved, genteel holidaymakers from troublesome day-trippers from Yarmouth or Norwich. The experience of holidaymaking became the subject of discussion in the guides, in the press and in novels. Authors described its pleasures, its destructive powers, and the way it created new, awful class embarrassments. Though the categories were in practice ill-defined, the authors of novels and guides made clear distinctions between their readers who were travellers, or at least serious and responsible tourists, and those others who were troublesome tourists or, worst of all, mere day-trippers.

The differences between types of tourists led to class collisions. The fewest took place on the beach at Great Yarmouth, largely because this space had been taken over by the 'day-outers' from London, who flocked there at weekends and bank holidays.

In his *Tourist's Guide to the Rivers and Broads of Norfolk and Suffolk* (first published in 1882), the popular travel writer and photographer G. Christopher Davies, an exponent of responsible tourism, warned his readers against Yarmouth beach, which had been spoiled by the 'intolerable nuisance' of 'numerous young men visitors of the 'Arry type, who are styled Lambs, and herd together in noisy larks and outrageous dress' (Davies 1897: 53).

T. Coan, an occasional writer for the photographic press, also suggested that serious amateurs would avoid these holiday crowds. He vividly described life on the beach: trippers were entertained all day by 'hawkers, beggars, niggers, try-your-weight, blow-your-lungs, or extend-your-chest men' (Coan 1889: 403–4). There were stalls selling pickled mussels and fried fish, or sea-shells brought from miles away; German bands, hurdy-gurdies, donkeys, boatmen, and open-air singers dressed as bumpkins and banging sticks, inviting the audience to join in the chorus.

These trippers on the beach between the piers were virtually excluded from the world of photography. Coan wrote that such 'visitors' were 'varied', but they were not worthy subjects for photographers. Moreover, they did not have the means to practice the art or science of photography themselves. To the degree that photography existed at all at this level of society, its position was precarious. Trippers were served by only a handful of licensed beach photographers who found it difficult to make a living because they were heavily taxed by the town council, and their touts were such a nuisance that 'even now the people are very shy of this particular pleasure' (Coan 1889: 403–4). Coan believed that photography needed a more richly endowed space – the space of a different class – which lay beyond the piers, where the crowd grew 'marvellously less, more quiet and select', and further away still in the bays between Yarmouth and Cromer. These places had 'nice, clean little cottages at very reasonable prices', and were favoured by middle-class families who wanted a seaside holiday away from the 'bustle, mob, and noise' (Coan 1892: 7–8).

The Broads presented a different case. They were not so easily segregated as the coastline, and sailing there did not guarantee escape from gangs of youths. Most social comedy or conflict took place on the Broads, where different social groups bumped into each other and the older, more privileged and established tourists deeply resented it. Coan wrote the 'jolly young sparks bent on fishing, shooting, sailing and photographing' sailed up the rivers on cheap hired boats and clashed with businessmen who, with more time to relax and more money to spend, were trying to

Plate 1. John Kippin, 'Hidden, National Park, Northumberland', 1991.

Plate 2. Susan Trangmar, from 'Untitled Landscapes', 1986.

Plate 3. Chocolate box cover, n.d.

Plate 4. P. H. Emerson, 'Rowing home the schoof-stuff', *Life and Landscape on the Norfolk Broads*, 1887.

find peace and solitude in several weeks on the water (Coan 1889: 405).

Boating was a popular craze among many people from various sections of the middle class and more prosperous members of the working classes (Vine 1983). On land the professional middle classes expected to exclude their social inferiors from defined spaces or to meet them according to well-known rules of conduct, but they were confused and often angry at meeting the lower orders on water where the rules of conduct and the relative spaces were not so clearly defined. There were three common responses. One was to pretend that nothing had changed. An example is Anna Bowman Dodd's romance *On the Broads*, in which the beautiful heroine dines only with the gentry and meets no strangers other than her American paramour (A. B. Dodd 1896). Another response was to pretend that the sight of ''Arry and 'Arriet romping' about in boats and steam launches could be matched by upper-middle class sang-froid, as in Elizabeth Pennell's account of a month's boating on the Thames (Pennell 1891). The third response was to turn the confrontations into comic writing. This found an audience among the educated middle classes, and also among the less well educated but increasingly numerous white-collar workers, the clerks of suburbia (Carey 1992: 59). The fun of holiday novellas was largely based on comic incidents deriving from class differences. The most lasting testimony to this is Jerome K. Jerome's *Three Men in a Boat*, first published in 1889 and still in print. In the words of the modern Penguin edition, it tells the story of 'a hilarious voyage of mishaps up the Thames'. Its comedy draws on insults aimed at 'riverside roughs' or owners who blocked the tributaries; the boaters also laugh at themselves, and exploit the comic opportunities of the widespread but still mysterious hobby of photography (Jerome 1984: 64, 61, 68, 171; see also Jerome 1982 and 1989).

In another book in this genre, published in 1890 and set on the Norfolk Broads, the middle-class, university-educated and anonymous author described how he and a friend decided, with their wives, to go for a week's holiday on a wherry (once a working boat but now converted into a pleasure craft). Their other friends greeted the plan with 'a storm of ridicule and discouragement' because it was 'the latest Cockney tourist's trap' ('Blue Peter' 1890: 3). It cost ten guineas to hire a wherry for a week, which was expensive enough to keep the labouring cockneys on the Yarmouth beach, but not to discourage the better-off traders (see illustration on page 98). The well-bred couples, who still expected to have the place to themselves, were embarrassed to meet such cockneys, the embodiment of 'prosperous, cheerful vulgarity': these raucous

"THERE WAS THE CURIOUS LIKENESS BETWEEN THEM THAT
ONE OFTEN SEES IN PERSONS LONG MARRIED."

32. Drawing of cockney couple on board their wherry, from *Blue Peter*, 1890.

people sat on 'our' seats and littered the grass with the heads and tails of shrimps, ginger-beer bottles and scraps of bread. The middle-class couples were embarrassed when the cockneys tried to talk to them, and so they decided to ignore the intrusion; the couples took the first opportunity to sail away, but were humiliated when the cockneys jeered at them ('Blue Peter' 1890: 93–4).

Whereas this story made a joke of class differences, the guidebooks were disparaging about troublesome day-trippers from Yarmouth or Norwich. They assumed their readers, who were young men (a 'fault' tempered by their university education and work in professional offices), were bound to be well-behaved. While the guidebooks described the manly pursuits of fishing, shooting, sight-seeing and drinking, they incidentally reproved those who ruined the Broads. For instance, one of the 'unwritten laws' Davies recorded in his *Tourists' Guide* was that men should bathe early in the morning because 'Ladies are not expected to turn out before eight, but after that time are entitled to be free from any annoyance.' He suggested that his readers, when meeting 'young men who lounge in a nude state on boats while ladies are passing' should 'salute' them with dust shot, or thump their boat with the end of a pole. He added that of course only disreputable local youths would display themselves in this way. Davies's 'laws' indicate the annoyances of a holiday crowd. From the list of prohibitions we learn that trippers were firing pea-rifles and revolvers at birds and bottles; driving steam-launches at full speed past moored yachts to annoy their occupants who had just spread out their meal; ruining decks with nailed shoes; shouting insults and flinging scraps of fish at other tourists (Davies 1897: xv).

In response to the objections of well-heeled holidaymakers, landowners closed some of the waterways, and refused to allow anchorage, landing or fishing without permission. These restraints were aimed at rowdy youths, not at the more sedate, respectable and leisurely classes which contained the serious photographers, 'artists, naturalists, and other harmless water farers' (Doughty 1889: 33). Reporting on the crowds and prohibitions in an article on holiday haunts, the photographer and journalist Bernard Alfieri thought that landowners would not object to well-behaved hobbyists on the Broads. In a sentence that carefully separates the class of amateur photographers from the rest, he wrote that the property owners 'would hardly have the hardihood to put the amateur photographer on a level with the class of objectionable visitors who leave the refuse of their picnic parties behind them and throw ginger-beer bottles at the wild fowl' (Alfieri 1888: 217).

Alfieri gave Davies the credit for opening the region to tourists. The latter's *Handbook to the Broads of Norfolk and Suffolk* (1882) had gone through ten editions by 1887, and twenty-nine by the turn of the century. Perhaps we would not share Alfieri's conviction that Davies's book was so influential in producing tourists, given that the region was already attractive to hunters and yachters. Yet by the mid-1880s Alfieri saw pleasure craft sailing in an 'interminable procession', and he blamed Davies for appearing unconcerned about the status of photography or the importance of preserving the Broads for an artistic elite (Alfieri 1888: 216–7).

Alfieri's mistrust of tourists was shared by P. H. Emerson, who liked Dungeon Dike because it was narrow and difficult to approach, and so rarely visited by the 'ordinary tourist'. In contrast, he wrote that nearby Somerton Broad was 'a picturesque spot in midsummer', and thus had 'attracted a class to this district, who, with their loud-mouthed wranglings, accursed music-hall songs, cheap rifles, flimsy cameras, and servant girl flirtations, are detestable' (Emerson 1893: 244). Tourists, their paraphernalia and their rowdy behaviour, threatened the hitherto impregnable lifestyles of Alfieri and Emerson.

Emerson's contempt for tourists extended to the guidebooks written for them. He agreed with his friend and collaborator, T. F. Goodall, that guidebooks were useful as topography, but 'valueless' as art (Emerson and Goodall 1887: 80; Emerson 1887: 12). In his afterthoughts on *Naturalistic Photography* (1889), Emerson did not even mention Davies in his list of topographers. Doubtless this was because Davies (as the author of popular guidebooks) was so closely associated with tourism (Davies 1876).

33. G. Christopher Davies, 'River Wensum', from *Norfolk Broads and Rivers*, 1884.

Davies was simply middle-class while Emerson was upper-middle class; Davies was a working journalist whereas Emerson was a professional man with a private income. In order to secure his own class position, Davies separated himself from the locals by ridiculing their dialect, though he made no judgements on other holiday-makers. If the lake was full of 'Easter Monday holiday-parties', then that fact simply made the place 'merry' (Davies 1884: 172). The point of his books was to suggest a people 'blissfully content with the charming present' (Davies 1884: 60). He was more concerned with pleasure than conflict, and with the vagaries and comedy of holidays in boats, which derived from class difference but were never fully realised as embarrassment. He recorded the constant interruptions of schedules, near misses with other boats, blunders in hunting, and haphazard arrangements for photography. He made light work of the process of photography – he found it easy to find suitable subjects, and the actual job of taking the pictures fell to the crew. Whenever he saw a 'picturesque drainage windmill, a cottage in a group of trees, ancient ruins, yachts or wherries, making a pretty picture', he directed the skipper to run the yacht up to the bank, where the mundane work, as always, would be done by his employees. The mate would do the focusing and exposing, while the skipper ' "shoo'd" off the too curious bullocks and cows, or dispensed valuable advice'. Because Davies wanted to show his difference from the men he hired, he did not want to engage in anything technical. He employed others to sail the boat, and equally important, he stayed clear of the craft of photography. Having decided on nothing less than the view, and

34. 'Photographing under difficulties at Coldham Hall', 1885.

avoiding all else, he naturally 'had the plates developed when [he] got home' (Davies 1884: 38–9).

He was not at all troubled on discovering that most of them had been overexposed. His relation to photography was precisely that encouraged by the factory production of developing and printing. It aimed to create a market for those people who were wealthy enough to purchase photographic materials, and who could use them without any knowledge of the processes. For Davies, photography was only one amusement alongside others, to be enjoyed by people like himself on holiday. He could buy the equipment, and consume it with something of a show, but to take the craft seriously as art would have defeated its purpose (despite his protestations, he was in fact an accomplished photographer – see illustration on page 100). Rather than bother overmuch about the art of photography, amateurs were more likely to produce humour or sardonic asides, as in the above drawing of 'Photographing under difficulties at Coldham Hall' from an account of 'An Expedition to Brundall' in 1885.

This was very different from Emerson's position, recorded in his account in 'The Log of the "Lucy"', written in 1886. Speaking of his difficulty in seeing a landscape, he wrote, 'All the afternoon we studied the landscape, and even on reaching the outskirts of the village we were yet baffled. We felt a picture, but it was not till after three days' search that we found it' (Emerson and Goodall 1887: 1). Taking several days to find a landscape suggests not only an educated eye but the considerable resources in time and money that such sophistication requires. Emerson himself carried out the work of taking, developing and printing the photographs. It was an exclusive activity.

The purpose of this searching was made explicit in *Life and Landscape on the Norfolk Broads*, which he and Goodall worked on together (see colour plate 4). Goodall spoke of the possibility of art photography if the 'operator' had a 'genuine appreciation of the picturesque in landscape and figure' and 'cultivated artistic feelings'. He clearly separated the artist's gaze from the tourist's:

> As long as his ideas of pictorial art are confined in landscape to views in churches and ruins, rustic bridges and waterfalls, or topographical views of the haunts of tourists, taken from the guide-book point of view, and in figure to artificial compositions, reminding one of an amateur theatrical performance, so long will his work be destitute of artistic qualities, and, therefore, valueless; but if he brings to his work a genuine appreciation of the picturesque in landscape and figures, and a knowledge of how to place a subject on his plate as to convey his impression to others, he may produce most beautiful and meritorious results.
> (Emerson and Goodall 1887: 12-13; Emerson 1887: 79-80)

Goodall was not at all embarrassed by thinking that photographers were operators, so long as they were also cultivated. Distance and the finer feelings that could see a picturesque landscape were inseparable. Both derived from the Romantic sensibility, and were attached to the class of travellers. Goodall and Emerson were committed to the elaborate and specialised knowledge of art and science; using both meant they were not tourists but travellers – men with refined, artistic sensibilities and members of what Emerson called an 'anthropological aristocracy' (Emerson 1888b: 135).

These words clearly distinguish Emerson from Davies and other tourists in East Anglia. Other photographers and writers also used photography to define class positions, while always pretending it was an entertainment. However, in Emerson's case, much more was involved. He claimed that photography was the tool of disinterested social anthropologists, but actually he harnessed it to the project of class separation. He believed the rural hierarchy of landlords, farmers and landless labourers was not only natural within the social order of the historic countryside, but was indeed an evolutionary necessity. In *Pictures of East Anglian Life* he wrote, 'Hewers of wood and drawers of water there must always be, but why dull, unloved and uncared for? Equality there can never be; the stern law of heredity forbids that *in utero*. An anthropological aristocracy there must always be; the struggle for existence and survival of the fittest declares it' (Emerson 1888b: 135). He watched from the outside, always the social superior, and someone with an interest in the stability of the scene (he had been brought up on a sugar plantation in Cuba, which was the source of his private income – see Knights 1986).

Unfortunately for him, the old hierarchy which he supposed to have existed was breaking up. Businessmen left the cities for the countryside, and their greed destroyed the old social relations between farmers and labourers. Emerson was concerned by the dilution of the classes, and lamented what he believed to be the loosening of former bonds and allegiances. Nevertheless, his position as neither a marshman nor a farmer showed that class relationships on the Broads were more complex than he cared to admit. He occupied a modern position in the economy of the region, although it was a rare one: unlike the tourists whom he reviled, he was not on holiday from paid employment, nor simply hunting and yachting. In opposition to the pleasure-seekers, he set himself up to be a guardian of the old order, engaged in the cultural work of the 'anthropological aristocracy', and opposed to the influx of the lower-middle classes.

The lower-middle classes asserted their presence in the country in two related ways: they either passed through the Broads on holiday or, even worse, settled in newly-built suburbs or resorts. They brought with them the paraphernalia of modernity, which Emerson condemned in *Pictures of East Anglian Life* for being a gimcrack, superficial existence. He complained that 'the days of the old world life are numbered'. Soon farmers would face 'the noisy, fussy steam-launch', 'the stucco villa, fresh from the jerry-builder's hand', and 'all the snobbery of philistinism will blare at [them] from gaudily-painted gates' (Emerson 1888b: 81). His choices have to be understood within competing strategies for describing the land, guarding it against present intruders, and preserving it in pictures and texts for the future.

Emerson was most affronted when the 'natives' refused to remain in the idealised, pauper state, and showed that they had ideas of their own about how to dress and behave. Finding subjects for art was unexpectedly difficult: from the village grocer's shop 'The man came out in a hideous new hat, and the girl also was got up in the villagers' latest fashion. It was only after much talking and begging that they were persuaded to change and equip themselves in less pretentious manner, and then they were etched in silver for better, for worse' (Emerson 1886b: 1). In search of exotic 'specimens', he expected peasants to be profoundly unlike himself. When 'natives' began to look like the townspeople, taking on the materialist values of the despised, urban classes, he was evidently shocked. By abandoning the appearance of authentic country peasants for modern dress they had broken out of the distant time, untouched by history, where he had been used to placing them. Fashion could not exist in a society of caste and rank. When the 'natives' dressed in fashion, then the once clear signs of class (and class itself) had become confused. He begged them to dress in their everyday clothes, and not to change. When he fixed the peasants in time, he could demonstrate that the old values which supported him still existed. In the end he had his way, and recreated his ideal 'in silver'. In the end, aristocracy counted for more than anthropology.

While living on the Broads, Emerson had to draw three distinctions. Firstly, he separated himself from other middle-class fractions. Secondly, he insisted he was not a conventional member of his own class, but a bohemian looking for the exotic in regions of underdevelopment. Thirdly, he insisted on drawing close to the 'natives', while remaining utterly distinct from them. We can see all these factors at play in his distinction between 'fresh-air seekers' and 'Nature-lovers', between tourists and travellers. He considered himself to be 'a traveller, as is every seaman who lives aboard his boat' (Emerson 1890: 53). Only travellers, who spent long periods exploring the region, could live the bohemian and anthropological lives of artists among the 'natives'. He and Goodall became 'lake-dwellers', but their purpose was not to bridge the gulf which separated them from 'natives', but to preserve it, in fact to revel in it. They were delighted when their presence caused consternation among the villagers: when a peasant saw them 'she stopped her work, called another woman from a house, and they began chattering about the strangers...As we proceeded a boy in a field left his work and stared stolidly at us over the hedge, calling the attention of a carter boy' (Emerson 1893: 121-2). Emerson and Goodall had their awesome difference confirmed by the behaviour of the peasants, who received them as strange curiosities.

On one occasion, they sat on the deck of a houseboat and drank 'to the Arts in bumpers of claret'. During the afternoon, 'natives' came down to the marsh and watched them: 'they stared at us as if we, not they, were the "heathen", and when they went away, it was slowly and thoughtfully, as if considering what steps they should take to rid themselves and their Broads of the intruding lake-dwellers' (Emerson 1886b: 1). But the wealthy newcomers were here to stay, and intent upon preserving the distance between themselves and the 'pauper models', even while preserving them in photographs.

A certain ready-made distance from his subjects was granted by his superior station as a man of culture – a doctor, author, artist, and anthropologist. Preserving this distance was not always so easy, especially when sex was involved, as I shall argue shortly. Emerson constantly tested and proved his superiority against people whom he considered his social and spiritual inferiors, though he did this differently in photographs and prose. Most crucially, he took his photographs from a distance. For *Wild Life on a Tidal Water*, Emerson went to Yarmouth, the working-class seaside town and fishing port, and took many long shots of the harbour, docks and quayside. People were far away, in the middle distance, in profile, or completely turned away from the photographer. In a few cases – 'Decayed Fishermen', 'On the Baulks', and 'A Yarmouth Row' – the subjects looked towards him, but the distance between them was great, and not intended to be resolved through this process of observation. He kept his subjects in view, holding them up to the light, as it were, which allowed him to keep them away from himself.

For Emerson distance was a deliberate strategy, and light was its measure. Recognising this, we can reject the analysis in which photographic historians have continued to say that Emerson was chiefly interested by the qualities of form and light. For these writers, Emerson is always the same. He is an example that proves the history of photography within modernism – the severance from literature and painting, and the fulfilment of its own destiny (Newhall 1975; Bunnell 1989). Writing in this vein, Ellen Handy has argued that after his renunciation of art in photography in 1891, he continued to produce images but they 'became markedly more lyrical, precious and concerned with form for its own sake' (as in the picture from *Marsh Leaves* reproduced on page 109). At the same time, his writing 'altered out of all recognition' from that of the 1880s: the text of *Marsh Leaves* 'is a series of descriptive passages, small tales and observations utterly unlike their visual accompaniment in the frequency of grotesque incident, crude dialogue and cynical observation...The two sequences unfold simultaneously without genuine parallel or connection' (Handy 1989: 184). On the contrary, the written and visual text makes sense as a whole: neither form nor light were the subjects of the photographs, but each was used to create distance between viewer and viewed. The real subject of the pictures and the writing was the necessary gulf that lay between the worlds of aristocrats and 'natives'.

36. P. H. Emerson, 'Confessions', *Pictures from Life in Field and Fen*, 1887.

EMERSON AND WOMEN

Emerson's interest in landscapes had a great deal to do with his fears about the changes that were taking place among the social classes – among workers, farmers and landowners alike – which threatened to destroy what he imagined to be the clear lines separating them. In particular, these were the problem of tourists and what to do about them, and the problem created for middle-class men by their fear and fascination for the social orders surrounding them. These problems were not Emerson's alone, but were part of a long struggle between men vying with each other for status and the right to control the land, of which the right to represent it in images was only a part.

In pursuing control, Emerson was one (among many) who confused landscape with womanhood, gazing upon each and expecting to gain perceptual mastery over both. There was nothing exceptional in men of his time overtly comparing the two – as Emerson put it 'Une femme est au fond de chaque paysage!' (Emerson 1890: 84).

Marginal landscapes in undeveloped regions were places where 'high' class men, or men from the professional middle classes, could meet 'low' class men. Even more important, in these places 'high' class men could satisfy their desire for and fear of 'low' working-class women. It is important to remember that the opposition between high and low was not fixed, but relative: while Emerson believed himself to be always superior to 'natives', in his estimation country folk were themselves superior to tourists, developers, landlords or any other newcomers from the cities who spoiled the region and the country. Emerson found 'natives' superior because their existence confirmed his sense of class boundaries, while tourists and developers undermined the class separation that he considered was natural. Emerson placed this belief at the base of the strong nation. He said, 'when the land shall be built upon and enclosed, and the peasant is no more, then may old England go grovel before the world' (Emerson 1893: 27).

As we have seen, Emerson's interest in East Anglia lay in the great social distance that divided him from the 'natives'. This allowed him to enjoy an idealised love for them, particularly for women and girls. He took photographs of some 'native' girls and women at work, as we see in the examples from *Pictures from Life in Field and Fen* (on page 106) and from *Pictures of East Anglian Life* (see colour plate 5). However, there were not just 'native' women in Great Yarmouth, but also urban, working-class women on holiday. These attracted him, though he never photographed them. Instead, he explored the sexual excitements and dangers he experienced in Yarmouth in his prose. These descriptions of other women are so full, so vivid, so much like a view, that we can see how Emerson used them to add to his idea that local 'natives' were happy and decent, and fit to set against 'degenerate' people from the cities.

In his writing Emerson often expressed the contrast between the corrupting town and the pure countryside. He described the contrast in the language of class-bound, stereotypical sexual preferences, in which country girls were both strong and demure while town girls were 'sickly-looking' and 'tawdry'. In *On English Lagoons* he told the story of two children, and related the sickness or health of their spirits in terms of their bodies and their clothes. The 'country-bred child...turned her dear, calm eyes curiously upon us for a moment only...her dress swinging loosely and gracefully from her swelling hips – hers was the dignity and grace of strength'. In contrast, the 'town-bred girl' walked with 'hesitant, mincing steps'. Moreover, she was 'clad in a bright red dress, all puffed and puckered, fantastically distorted to hide her ill-developed little body'. He also saw their difference in what they held: the country girl carried 'a bunch of reed tassels', whereas the town girl had 'a velveteen bedezined doll, magnificent with tinsel'. The country girl stood for the innocent 'old England', which he came close to illustrating in his photograph 'Flowers of the mere' in *Idyls of the Norfolk Broads* (see colour plate 6). In contrast, the town girl stood for the 'cheap civilisation' of 'the city where degeneration awaits the race' (Emerson 1893: 26). Emerson associated the children's clothes and playthings with their moral strength or weakness.

In a comparable move deriving from the worth of commodities, Emerson and Goodall claimed moral strength through their use of difficult photographic processes – which signified art and science combined. Obviously, these skills separated them from tourist photographers. Both men attached moral worth to learning but also to some expensive, exclusive objects. Emerson believed that the status of individuals could be gauged by the things they owned or produced. He wrote that the order of rank for pictures was 'an oil painting, then a photogravure, and finally a good photograph… printed in platinotype' – a permanent and relatively expensive process (Emerson 1886a). Cheap goods, including cheap lithographs, photographs and illustrated books, offended Emerson. He went to great lengths to produce his own work in books of photogravures, and in limited editions of 500 to 700 copies or de-luxe editions of 50 to 150 copies (Newhall 1975: 262–3). To ensure the rarity and therefore exclusivity of these productions, Emerson destroyed the plates. He and Goodall believed that their control over artistic and scientific resources was the sign of their difference from serious amateurs. It empowered them to describe the 'natives' or 'specimens' of a region endangered by economic decline, internal social change, and the influx of temporary visitors who had urban, commercialised values and demands.

Emerson often expressed the contrast between town and countryside in terms of sexual conflict. Whereas Emerson regarded men to be naturally superior to women, he was pleased to see country women triumph over men from the town. He described what happened when 'native' girls on a towpath met young male tourists on a steamboat. He wrote, 'two stalwart country girls, gaily dressed' had to climb a stile near a steamboat full of 'rabble', who hooted and jeered at them. One of the girls,

36. P. H. Emerson, 'A corner of the farmyard', *Marsh Leaves*, 1895.

'superb in rage, planted herself firmly, and looking the mannikins full in the face, cried tauntingly, "Did you see what you were looking for?" They laughed stupidly, while the two girls strode off across the marshes to their father's little farm.' Emerson decided that it was the authenticity of the girls which had outfaced the 'browbeaten rabble' of young men from the city. Emerson the outsider, privileged to enjoy or scorn, was pleased, for once 'again were the city-bred discomfited' (Emerson 1893: 27).

Emerson stood in a whole series of possible relationships with the 'low' without ever losing the upper hand. He exemplifies the fraught fascination of his class with the lower classes. As Peter Stallybrass and Allon White argue in *The Politics and Poetics of Transgression*, there is a striking ambivalence towards the lower strata (of the body, of literature, of society, of place) since they are both reviled and desired. A recurrent pattern emerges in which 'the "top" attempts to reject and eliminate the "bottom" for reasons of prestige and status, only to discover, not only that it is in some way frequently dependent upon that low-Other...but also that the top *includes* that low symbolically, as a primary eroticized constituent of its own fantasy life' (Stallybrass and White 1986: 5).

There were many 'low' subjects which Emerson dwelt upon in his prose. He was better able to render his excitement in writing, which allowed him retrospectively to assert his superiority and control. In *On English Lagoons* he described the quayside at Lowestoft when the herring season was over, painting a picture that was not only lively but presented an economy with a sexual component. He wrote 'The quays were crowded with fishermen, with pockets full of money, and in and out amongst them glided tramps with sacks, collecting shot rubbish; German Jews selling concertinas; hawkers with nuts and oranges; and heavy eyed girls with fringes and shawls – all after Jack's money' (Emerson 1893: 136). Emerson was fascinated by these people, and did, in fact, approach them – especially women of other classes whom he found sexually alluring.

Emerson wanted to save working women from the men of their class. He achieved this most fully if the females were not human at all but boats, which he feminised and eroticised beyond their common designation in English as 'she'. In *On English Lagoons* he described how Norfolk wherries were 'converted' into pleasure craft: 'After having led boisterous and irregular lives, many of these strange craft don fresh dresses – become family house-boats, and settle down to respectable careers.' This was the common practice, but it was a reduction of the strange to the domestic, a progress that did not satisfy Emerson. Instead, his wherry, the 'Maid of the Mist', was never fully subjugated, always retaining a trace of 'her' original attraction though transformed to suit his needs. This wherry was 'one of a numerous class', and had fallen into the clutches of 'base' men such as 'old Tommy, the one-eyed winkle-seller', who turned her 'skin' 'rough' and 'spoiled' her 'complexion'. Emerson saw her 'beauty', and 'determined to possess her'; once purchased, he 'gave her over to the dressmakers', though he still found it 'irksome not to know the Maid's pedigree when [he had] to live with her' (Emerson 1893: 3–4). Her history among the lower orders was both fascinating and worrying.

What is significant here is Emerson's relationship to this sexualised boat, the role he gave himself as saviour of 'a pretty model' from a succession of men – the last disfigured – who 'used' her. His authority extended to an imaginary control over inanimate objects which he feminised and wrested from careless and unworthy men. Emerson's compulsion to save the boat for himself was driven more by his sense of class proprietorship than by anthropological enquiry or an artistic feeling for beauty.

As a writer, Emerson worked with the authority and eye of a photographer, controlling the elements of the scene, creating the landscape and the meanings of whatever he found there. We can see this at work in *Wild Life on a Tidal Water* in his description of the bizarre examination of a drowned woman, a day-tripper from London. A small crowd had gathered round her, and as a doctor Emerson went through them to attempt artificial respiration. He eventually pronounced the woman dead, but in his writing he invested her with purity, describing the routine loosening of her dress and bodice in sentimental terms, saying that he bared her 'white bosom over which the soft winds played'. Eventually, he 'gave her up and covered her pretty lips and face with my handkerchief. Then closing up her bodice to hide the dead, white bosom from the small crowd that had gathered round, I arose breathless with exertion' (Emerson 1890: 33) The knowledge of her, because she was dead, was supposed to be analytic, and may have appeared so to the crowd. But whereas she was breathless from drowning, Emerson's attempt to rescuscitate her made him breathless with exertion. In his writing he unconsciously revealed how the public examination became the source of his secret auto-eroticism.

Yet this knowledge was not taken from just any dead woman, but from a working-class tripper. Even here, or perhaps especially here, Emerson's sexual authority was class-bound. Some of its excitement rested in his power to translate her from a working-class tripper into a classical beauty with 'the figure of the Venus of Melos' (Emerson 1890: 33). The reference to Greek art made her dead body aesthetically pleasing, suggesting harmony and wholeness. This translation allowed him to fix her for ever in his image at the actual moment when she was dead but not decomposing. He saw her at the very moment she was perfect for him – at the moment when her animated body had been arrested in death, but before the decay of death had begun. As Elisabeth Bronfen writes, in describing the aesthetic pleasure an anatomist takes from a newly-dead, young female body, 'its beauty marks the purification and distance from two moments of insecurity – female sexuality and decay' (Bronfen 1992: 11). Emerson was able to cut through the crowd, open the drowned woman's dress, examine her freely, indeed to exert himself upon her body because she was lifeless, and her sexuality and class no longer presented any real danger.

Emerson wanted to get close to working-class women, but not too close; and he was particularly intimidated by women from the city. He never photographed any such women, though in his descriptions he exercised the same need to demonstrate his own mastery and control. What makes the descriptions so special, so unlike the photographs, is that in them he revealed how he gained the upper hand, and how he almost lost it.

This is precisely what happened during an encounter between Emerson and another lower-class woman from London that occurred while he was staying on a houseboat on Breydon Water, near Yarmouth in 1887. Emerson, seeking 'an adventure' on shore, rowed from the houseboat, and made his way to the promenade.

> All the girls of Norfolk seemed to be there...All sorts and conditions of men, and women too, were there – sweethearts, painted ladies, peacocks, 'gents', old couples, respectable families, rowdies, mashers, cads, and yachtsmen, all were there, butterflies and moths revolving around and around the lights of their imagination...I walked leisurely up and down the pier looking at the butterflies, it was growing late, and all the quiet people had gone home...Suddenly I stopped entranced; a tall dark girl, with a broad-brimmed soft beaver hat and black velvet cloak riveted my attention...I stopped, turned involuntarily, and gazed after her; she also turned and our eyes met.
>
> (Emerson 1890: 50–1)

This is important: the eyes must meet, and desire must be registered in a look, or a glance. At this point, Emerson gave up some of the mastery he had when he alone was doing the looking. Now the chase was on, and he was in some calculated danger.

> She had large dark eyes, eyes full of disappointment; – those eyes which promise much and give little, eyes symbolic of passion, but passionless as the jet on her cloak...Decorum bade us turn from one another, and I strolled on haunted by the turn of her head, by her shapely figure, and dignified bearing. I followed the crowd round the pier, but still saw her not. Suddenly a lady near me dropped her handkerchief, I picked it up [suddenly recognising] the shapely figure in the velvet cloak. She took the handkerchief, and said quietly, in a low voice, 'Sit down'.

Here Emerson interrupted his narrative with an aside, sitting beside her and at the same time asking himself 'Is this England?' He did not explain what he meant by this query, but perhaps what he considered to be un-English was the free access between

Plate 5. P. H. Emerson, 'Osier Peeling', *Pictures of East Anglian Life*, 1888.

Plate 6. P. H. Emerson, 'Flowers of the mere', *Idyls of the Norfolk Broads*, 1888.

Plate 7. Kodak brochure for Egypt.

Plate 8. Kodak brochure, 1932.

the classes, the ease of the pick-up and his own eager response to it. What Emerson described as un-English was potentially dangerous for him, so on putting that question to himself he also decided (as he soon revealed) to talk and act like a Yarmouth fisherman. This ploy allowed him to enter unknown territory with the protection of a local disguise. He continued

> She began to talk as if she had known me all her lifetime. She chatted of her tastes in reading, her love of dress...She told me her birthplace – she claimed five that evening. She spoke of her parents – they were numerous, and belonged to various grades of society. It was astonishing, this volubility. Poor empty-headed butterfly...I had longed for woman's society that night, but this splendid vacuity overpowered me. She gradually grew familiar, and began to ask favours. I knew what that meant. My empress, who came from the West End of London, as she naively informed me (I had simulated the Norfolk accent, and parochial knowledge), whose...ring of three diamonds...was worth a hundred guineas, this Lady, I say, asked me to stand her a dish o'cockles. I was not surprised.
>
> (Emerson 1890: 51–2)

Emerson took her to the cockle booth, and she tried to flash the ring in the gaslight, but 'that fatal light...stripped her of all her finery', revealing how poor she was, though 'her figure was still charming'. He remained interested in her, though he was more guarded now that the 'transfiguring' power of his 'imagination' had been corrected by the 'baleful' light of the cockle stall. He then took her, as she asked, to the 'Aquarium'. There 'she revelled in the artistes, she munched sweets, she drank brandies and sodas, she ogled the men and sniffed at the women, she asked me to lend her a sovereign, but this I did not...Suddenly she met "Jacky, a gent from the West End", magnificent with a scarlet tie and a horseshoe pin. They were civilised, I was a wildman from the sea, so I left them together, and fairly ran down to the quays, that scarlet tie and lacquered horseshoe haunting me' (52).

In this passage Emerson reveals a number of roles and bluffs brought on by the impossibility of an equal exchange between himself and this woman. Situating himself against the modernity of London life, he adopted an 'inferior' class role which concealed what he took to be his actual superiority. At the same time, according to Emerson, this woman who felt superior to him and was seeking to dupe him was actually inferior and was herself duped. A contemporary reviewer of *Wild Life* wrote that Emerson gave the impression of being 'manly' and 'cynical' (cited in Emerson 1893: advertisement facing p. 298). Certainly he put himself in a position to observe this woman, pity her, and after the initial excitement remain unthreatened by her. But in order to re-establish himself as an anthropologist, the aristocrat needed to turn himself inside out, to pretend to be ignorant of metropolitan ways, so he could watch her safe inside the disguise of a local fisherman. In this the function of the imagination was crucial. The sexual allure of the woman began and ended in Emerson's mind; it was his own thoughts that had presented the greatest challenge and danger. In other words, as long as he had a system for controlling his imagination, he was never truly in danger. By masquerading to her in the form of an ignorant fisherman, and assuring himself that he was an anthropologist, he was in control. He was unwilling to leave her so long as she ate sweets, ogled, sniffed and called him 'ducky'. He left her only when the 'gent' turned up, and then he ran away from them both, because control deserted him. What seems to have concerned him most, what he admits haunted him, was the man's cheap tie-pin. That punctured whatever remained of the sexual interest in the scene. At this moment Emerson was clearly overcome with the cheapness of it all, signalled in the vulgar adornment of the 'gent'. The scarlet tie was an aggressively masculine appendage, and Emerson's flight suggests that the triangle was too complex in terms of class and gender hierarchies for him to want to go on pretending to be inferior.

Soon after this incident, Emerson went back to the houseboat for a process of actual and symbolic self-restoration. We learn of the healing powers of the boat in his description of a dream. The dream mixes together several of his fears, beginning with the divide between town and country, but transferring this on to the difference between men and women. Describing the dream in *Marsh Leaves*, he wrote:

> I found that the more the people lived in house-clusters the more monstrous and feeble were they, and as I sailed on, in my dream, I found that those were happiest and best who chose to live in the fields, for such became men even though they had been as women in the houses. But I too was becoming womanish in the town, and very quickly, for I had begun to talk of dress, and to love to see what every dirty worm who wriggled more than his neighbour did, and I loved strong drink, and could not eat like a man; just as my disease broke out, I was snatched back to my ship, and became whole.
>
> (Emerson 1895: 55)

The ship was the safe place where he went when the nightmare became overwhelming, when he was no longer in control of his body and his fear of sexuality seemed to be expressed by his fear of turning into a woman.

During the incident with the dark-haired woman, Emerson was in control of himself until the moment when she introduced him to Jacky with the scarlet tie and fancy pin. Jacky's arrival created fears in Emerson's own mind, fears that were unexpressed directly – though they led to his flight from the scene – but which revealed themselves later in the dream. He had been prepared to disguise himself to gain some advantage, but this voluntary breaking of bounds could lead to confusion. He was afraid that he might become womanish, be an inferior man to Jacky, and so be diseased. When gender and class ambiguities threatened him, he ran away and rowed back to the bosom of the boat. He was determined not to succumb to any dissolution of his sense of himself as a man, and so showed a fear and a need that seems to have been commonplace at the end of the century. As Elaine Showalter argues in her work on sexual anxiety, by the turn-of-the-century a post-Darwinian 'sexual science' testified to the evolutionary differences between men and women. It was the sexual borderline between the masculine and feminine which represented 'the dangerous vanishing point of sexual difference': 'What was most alarming...was that sexuality and sex roles might no longer be contained within the neat and permanent borderlines of gender categories...Where, men asked themselves, were they placed on the scale of masculinity? Were they dangerously close to the borderline?' (Showalter 1991: 9). Emerson proved his style of masculinity by continuously asserting his attraction to women, while continuously protecting himself from what he also considered to be their potential for contamination, dilution, and disease. Furthermore, his style of masculinity was utterly different from Jacky's, and because in that particular context he had been unable to assert himself without revealing his masquerade, he fled the scene of potential disaster. For Emerson, it was the masquerade which had to be preserved, since his interest lay in sexuality as signification rather than in its practice.

Emerson's style of masculinity was safe in Norfolk among the 'natives'. His style was anxious and polite, adoring even, in regard to 'native' women – quite unlike his relations with 'native' men, which seem to have carried no ambiguities or threats. From his own testimony, he had a straightforward relationship with all the lower-class men in his employ, which he based largely on his superior insights into motivation and character. At the same time, the friendship with Goodall was never the subject of remark, and was taken for granted to be an artistic collaboration. He was pleased to have found in East Anglia a region that satisfied his need for clear lines between the worlds of men and women, and between owners and the landless labourers. He worked to dispel the threat posed by the encroaching classes which threatened to dissolve the once clear view. Yet, at the same time that he approved and fought to sustain the former stability of class, he also tested himself against the dangers from the evident instability of the region. Looking at the flood of trippers from London, he deliberately placed himself in the way of temptation to prove his ability to resist.

With the cockney woman Emerson had expected to avoid a social error, but on meeting Jacky and running away he seems to have come closer than expected to a psychological disaster. His dream revealed that he almost failed to maintain the distinction between himself and the object of his desire, which had to be kept at a distance because it was also the object of his revulsion. The incident with the cockney woman was buried inside a chapter in *Wild Life*, but the next time Emerson's imagination ran away with him and he became fatefully involved with a woman, the event took a whole chapter to describe. Its title ('Lady in White') recalls the already famous sensation novel of 1860 by Wilkie Collins, *The Woman in White*. Emerson made his admirer more acceptable by calling her a 'lady', but satisfied his desire for the forbidden or exotic by admitting that he failed to 'diagnose who and what she was'. She was 'either a fast aristocrat or a clever adventuress', but he could not tell which – certainly 'respectable middle-class maidens would not have called her a lady' (Emerson 1890: 81).

He first saw the anonymous 'Lady in White' in daytime. In characteristic fashion, Emerson's description of her relied on objects as points of recognition. He associated her sexual attraction with her parasol and straw hat – which he called 'coquettish'. As a necessary complement to this excitement, he decided the whole 'picture' of her was 'fresh, elegant, and charming'. Straightaway the inventory of objects was replaced by the engagement of eyes. She glanced at Emerson over her book and, as they exchanged looks, she blushed and 'we both knew we shall meet, speak, and perhaps love, so quick is the telegraphy between two minds' (80).

They eventually met when Emerson 'rescued' her 'little nephew', after he had been nipped by a crab. He thought that her head was sensible and clear, yet her temperament was passionate. At lunchtime, after they parted, Emerson walked on the beach, observing clerks and their sweethearts 'clasped in all sorts of positions beneath the shelter of the boats', beach photographers 'busy immortalising 'Arry and 'Arriet', a phrenologist and a charlatan corn-doctor. He followed a well-dressed crowd on to the pier, where there was 'a higher class of vulgarity' in the form of a band, and the lady in white came to meet him there. She was 'like a sea-shell fresh from the water; and we were soon lost in the crowd of laughing promenaders' (Emerson 1890: 81–4).

Emerson almost ends the description of their first, day-long encounter in this fade from view, a literary escape from sexual encounters. However, he finally closes the scene with his significant remark in French, quoted earlier–'Une femme est au fond de chaque paysage!' The choice of language was an obvious deflection or cover for his desire: it suggested his way of always seeing landscape in sexual terms, a secret which he could only divulge through a rhetorical convention.

Because Emerson had erected this conventional screen, one book reviewer said the 'Lady in White' was 'a misty and half defined love story', reflected so dimly 'that it can only be compared to a mental photo-etching' (cited in Emerson 1893: advertisement facing p. 298). Another reviewer wrote that in this 'episode of romance' Emerson 'tantalises us with an explicit account of the meeting, and leaves the sequel in mystery' (cited in Emerson 1893: 2).

In fact, the sequel was less than mysterious. The 'Lady in White' made three more appearances in the book, twice in the form of letters which she sent to Emerson. Each letter used nature to refer to personal feelings, which in both cases were sad: it seems Emerson was rejecting her. The first letter recalled how in springtime buds 'arrive like love in the human heart', but 'the sun, like happiness, does not always shine, and the buds wilt' (Emerson 1890: 93); the second letter asked whether she, like autumn leaves 'once courted and warmed by the loving sun' was to be cast aside and forgotten? She asked, 'am I right or wrong?' with Emerson only adding coyly 'That is all I may tell' (118). Even so, the relationship had not ended, quite. She came to look at Goodall's finished painting of Great Yarmouth from Breydon: he liked her 'sane' criticism, and took her to dinner, and they 'walked together by the sea' (120). Her sexuality, her somewhat indeterminate class, her unconventional mind and passionate nature had briefly captivated Emerson. He never expressed his own feelings in this affair, only using her letters to chart her pain, always keeping that reserve befitting (and serving) a gentleman at moments of emotional crisis.

The perfect realism of the first encounter and the misty romance of the second were two contrasting 'passages of sentiment' which were 'cunningly set amid the strongest and sturdiest bits of word painting', and which were 'manly always and refreshingly cynical'. Though his head might turn, or be turned by, the two beauties, and though he might express certain longings, his manliness and cynicism in telling the stories meant he always appeared to be master of himself, and, in his account, in control of the two women. Whatever the disturbance caused by the dark woman, it was resolved in a psychic victory over the 'Lady in White'. With her, he never felt contaminated by womanliness. On the contrary, because she was only ever a 'delicate flower', he was confirmed as the keeper of a 'wild garden' (Emerson 1890: 120). Since there was no place for her – since she was of no ascertainable class – she offered no threat. She ameliorated her feelings by writing of them in the conventional language of flowers. In contrast, Emerson never told of his feelings directly, choosing instead to turn boats into women and women into Woman, an idealisation without flesh or desiring of her own. Emerson was most comfortable with the idea of Woman: she was compliant, undemanding, distant, most like the drowned Venus of Melos. At the same time, she allowed him to lust without fear or shame. In *On English Lagoons* he told the story of an old man who pointed out an island and said it was 'where the ladies bathe in summer'. Emerson thought of a picture which held 'the beautiful figures of lovely women, the greenery of summer, and all the poetry of the open air'. He continued, 'I long looked at the island; it seemed sacred' (Emerson 1893: 188). The sacred island was perfect: no gentleman would violate its peace, and in return, no earthly woman would interrupt his dream.

The landscape was not an innocent place, at least not for Emerson. He had a personal, class, and psychosexual need to maintain the distance and difference between himself and his subjects. Photography allowed him to sustain and govern this distance. When we follow Emerson into the landscape, we see that it was a complexly social and gendered space, and his practice as a photographer was much more complex than capturing aesthetically pleasing or even anthropological views.

Considering Emerson's work to be the product of someone troubled by changes in East Anglia is quite different from the reading preferred by many of his contemporaries and early modernists. They concentrated on Emerson's claims in *Naturalistic Photography* for the artistic quality of 'pure photography', and though Emerson repudiated his claim, this judgement was not accepted by those who were determined to raise the medium to the status of art. Differentiating themselves from scientists and social record photographers, they established photography as a means of personal expression, in the manner of recent art movements or contemporary *fin de siècle* styles (Naef 1978; John Taylor 1978; Harker 1979; Weaver 1989a). In the first quarter of the twentieth century, the cause for photography as art was further developed within modernism, with a continuing belief in creativity matched by the emphasis on the specific qualities of the medium itself (Holme 1905; Child Bayley 1906; Guest 1907; A. J. Anderson 1910). Seen in the context of modernism, Emerson has been appropriated as a forerunner, though the proto-modernist 1890s left Emerson behind. As Aaron Scharf said, the irony of Emerson is that he prepared the ground for modernist practice, yet was unable to capitalise on it himself (Scharf 1986: 31).

The few commentators who write about Emerson's interest in natural history and ethnography eventually place him among artists, and continue to evaluate his work as self-expressive. For instance, Ellen Handy makes some observations on the social implications of his photography, in so far as it was committed to neither 'the pastoral mode nor the idyllic...but the georgic', but she does not pursue this line of enquiry (Handy 1989: 184). Instead, she conforms to the modernist perspective, in which the subject of Emerson's work is formalism and his own sensibility. She decides that by 1890, when Emerson published *Wild Life*, his interest in 'a beautiful clear light' was 'as much the subject of [his photographs] as anything else' (Handy 1989: 191). By this time, he had retreated from picturing people in landscapes, and this continued in his later books, *On English Lagoons* (1893) and *Marsh Leaves* (1895). She concludes that 'his exploration of East Anglia led him from a local survey finally into himself' (193). Caught between the binary oppositions of art and science, Emerson became 'tranquil' only when 'subjectivity overtook theoretical argument' – and, by implication, social involvement (195). Despite this dominant reading, by looking again at Emerson's writing, and by placing this in the class and gender politics of his time, what the retroactive ideals of modernism have turned into a narrow path of pure, formal photography suddenly becomes a much wider and more difficult route.

4

'England' as a reliable make

THE AFTERMATH OF WAR

SINCE WE are about to leap forward from the 1890s into the period 1925–42, without covering the intervening years, a few remarks about the effects of the Great War will help to show what the photographic industry retained from the earlier period, and how it changed. The industry had been relatively late in adopting the speedy production methods of the factory system, but speed or velocity was now an integral part of modernity, and critical to survival and victory in the Great War. The velocity of machines and machine-production in the factories which promised and delivered so many goods before the war was not discredited by its capacity for destruction. On the contrary, the destructive element of velocity – delivering death through long-range guns – was a benefit of the means of production and delivery. This was true not only of armaments and transport but also of the photographic industry. After a slow start, from 1916 the armed forces systematically gathered 'intelligence' from ground and aerial photography, moving it to the centre of the military-industrial complex. After the war, photography continued to be used in reconnaissance and propaganda at home and overseas. Whatever the war destroyed, it was not the photographic industry.

In the age of mass production, when cameras and films began to be produced in bulk in factories during the 1880s, the great promise of the photographic industry was reliability. This emphasis on certainty was the main selling point of Kodak from 1888,

37. Cover of *Amateur Photographer*, 16 May 1934. Original in colour.

when the company aimed its box cameras (already loaded with film to be processed at its factory) at a mass market centred on the idealised family and its holidays. Located in the family, the subjects of popular photography were the hearth, the nursery, the annual holidays in the country or at the seaside.

During the Great War, when outdoor photography by amateurs was largely forbidden, photography in the home became even more popular. In addition, the break-up of families led to an increasing demand that they be remembered in pictures. The sentimental attachment to domestic, family life was a refuge from military life and the increasingly apparent harsh realities of war. Once the war had ended, enthusiasm for the tough, masculine life of the military was discredited, and no longer considered to be central to national life. Instead, cosy family life became the focus for rebuilding the unity and sense of purpose of the nation. In this chapter I intend to show how the factor of reliability converged with the way 'Englishness' was refashioned after the war.

Between the world wars, because of improvements in the technology of cameras and the latitude of film, this policy of marketing photography to be central to home life, and certain to retain happy memories, gained a new impetus. In this period the idea of 'England' was reformed to match middle-class aspirations for a more domestic and dependable way of life than had been fostered in the preparations for and propaganda of war.

I shall discuss how the new-style 'feminine' England received widespread promotion in guidebooks, and how the pre-war 'invention' of the 'Kodak girl' to promote that company's products came into its own once 'Englishness' was aligned with a 'feminine' sense of certainty and unstuffy youthfulness, exemplified in the popularity of hiking among women (represented by the cover of *Amateur Photographer* of 1934 – see page 121).

I shall look at how Kodak, more than its British competitors, pursued nation-wide campaigns appealing to the middle class through popular snapshooting, promising its members a relaxed and permanent world of reliable memories. Alison Light, in her book on femininity, literature and conservatism between the wars, has said that 'any use of the term [middle-class] must ideally stretch from the typist to the teacher, include the "beautician" as well as the civil servant, the florist and the lady doctor, the library assistant and the suburban housewife, and the manifold differences between them' (Light 1991: 12). Many of these occupations were not secure or professional, and so fall into the category of lower-middle class. Between the wars, this section of society began to tour England and take photographs in greater numbers than ever before.

Finally, I shall discuss how the ideas that both England and photography were mutually supportive 'reliable makes' coincided with the ways in which the British Empire was promoted as unified. In turn, selling the unity of Empire was complemented by the way photography was promoted as a universal language (the Kodak brochure for Egypt was one of many aimed at British colonies and protectorates – see colour plate 7). Photographs of the Empire were used to conceal any potentially disturbing sense of difference. The diverse activities of touring in England, selling photography, taking part in competitions, looking at the Empire and spreading the idea that photography was a universal language were joined together in the inter-war search in the leisure trade for whatever was stable and secure.

FEMININE ENGLAND

Alison Light argues that between 1920 and 1940 Englishness was redefined, especially through a realignment of sexual identities, in reaction to the excesses of national pride based on heightened active masculinity and passive femininity. She says the period saw

St. Cross, Winchester, where
the weary traveller may
still ask and receive a crust
of bread and a cup of beer.

HOW easy it is in this England to step aside into some small
pool of history, to be lapped awhile in the healing peace of a
rich still-living past. For this people — more perhaps than any
other — carries tradition and old usage into its daily life . . . in places
as in habits, in great things as in small. Thus do you have an ale such
as Worthington remaining unchanged through the centuries — because
it is brewed in a manner so long ago found worthy of continuance.

38. 'St Cross, Winchester', from *This England*, 1937.

'a move away from formerly heroic and officially masculine public rhetorics of
national destiny [of 'Great Britain'] to an Englishness at once less imperial and more
inward-looking, more domestic and more private – and, in terms of pre-war standards,
more "feminine" ' (Light 1991: 8). This replaced one of the more notable casualties of
the war – the heroic stamp of masculinity. Front-line soldiers often experienced
normative masculinity as a bluff and were unable to sustain it. They fell prey to 'shell-
shock', taking on a range of hysterical disorders which before the war had mostly been
diseases of women (Leed 1979: 163; Showalter 1987: 167–94). During the war, the
bluff of masculine power became increasingly apparent, since the 'will to fight' was
coupled with fear, disorientation and passivity ending in war neuroses or 'shell-shock'
(Fussell 1975; Leed 1979: 163–92). This failure of masculine nerve and loss of
confidence in masculinity created the potential for the peacetime emphasis of home
and the family. The former virtues of the private sphere of middle-class life took on a

new public and national significance. The English at home or abroad defined themselves in the terms of sentiment and fond memory, what Alison Light calls 'throttled emotion' or conservative nationalism – 'a politics which eschews politicking; a system of beliefs and values without systemisation; an organic and inevitable way to be' (Light 1991: 212). Such sentiment was widely used in advertising. For example, in 1937 Worthington breweries sold beer and Englishness as traditional and evident in 'some small pool of history…lapped awhile in the healing peace of a rich still-living past' (see illustration on page 123).

However, as Light argues, many men found this peace to be 'lower-class and effeminate' (Light 1991: 7). Writers such as E. M. Forster, W. H. Auden, D. H. Lawrence, George Orwell, Graham Greene and Evelyn Waugh, 'drawn from across the social spectrum but from within a notional high culture', lamented the domestication of national life and went abroad. They travelled to escape an England which they felt was safe and smug.

But the 'femininity' of the inter-war years was not a continuation of the submissive (and so disastrous) complement to the heroic masculinity destroyed in the war. While the women of the middle classes were seen to adopt the stiff upper lip which had been the model of an imperial masculinity, that idiom could at the same time become a new kind of Englishness, with a new-style 'femininity' in control. It was a 'feminine achievement' using reticence and detachment, and a 'tone of irony towards the emotions' (Light 1991: 161); it 'feminised' the idea of the nation as a whole, 'giving us a private and retiring people, pipe-smoking "little men" with their quietly competent partners, a nation of gardeners and housewives' (211). These people enjoyed the idea that English landscape was a perpetual bower (represented opposite in a photograph of ramblers from the *Amateur Photographer* of 1927).

The steady production of images of Englishness in a 'female tone of voice' of reliability, representing the middle class, was as much a product of modern retailing as the masculine adventure rhetoric of the Victorians. 'Feminine England' became a new centre for the idea of a stable national history. The modernity of this culture was seen in the 'spawning' of commercial fiction, with popular books by Ivy Compton-Burnett or Agatha Christie, for instance, mechanically reproduced for years on end for the enlarged middle classes. 'Englishness' was steadily produced according to the specifications of a 'reliable make'. Novelists generated books 'as someone might produce ball-bearings', each fiction bearing a 'trademark' which stressed the '*sameness*

39. 'The Ramblers', *Amateur Photographer*, 21 December 1927.

of the formula', with plots unfolding in unchanged, pre-war landscapes, country houses and steadfast relations among the classes – a conservative England suiting the modern taste for reliability (59). This newly constructed Englishness was widespread. As Light says, 'the English began to see images of themselves and of their cultural behaviour...at "the pictures" and in magazine photography as never before' (215). This Englishness appeared on the radio and at the cinema. It appeared in illustrated newspapers, in weekly magazines such as *Weekly Illustrated* (founded in 1934), and in monthly journals such as *Vogue, Lilliput* (founded in 1936) and *Picture Post* (founded in 1938). The photographer Bill Brandt, for instance, worked on photo-stories for *Picture Post* in 1939, showing what purported to be the daily lives of women in service industries, as in 'Nippy: the Story of Her Day' (4 March), 'A Barmaid's Day' (8 April), and 'The Perfect Parlourmaid' (29 July) (for a full list of Brandt's commercial assignments see Jeffrey 1993: 176–89). This feminised England appeared everywhere to be the same, its trademark being whatever was decent and dependable.

The photographic industry was in step with inter-war conservatism. Photography already had a base in the family, but now that common-sense beliefs about what mattered in life were more firmly anchored than ever to the private and individual, the trade was well placed to take advantage of the new circumstances. Bearing in mind the idea that Englishness had become 'feminine', dependable and a 'reliable make', I shall now look at how touring in England was promoted in guidebooks.

TRADEMARK 'ENGLISH LANDSCAPE'

Comparing pre- and post-war attitudes to landscape, the greatest disparity in perception derives from different middle-class groups who began to believe they had a stake in the countryside as a national asset, even though they did not own the land (Lowerson 1980). These groups were exploring England, and buying guidebooks which rendered the country accessible and enduring, an 'England' as clearly defined as any trademark.

The rise of a mobile and demanding tourist industry put pressure on those who had become used to having the countryside to themselves. Before the war, the landscape had been restricted in its appeal to relatively wealthy and educated groups. In 1909, C. F. G. Masterman had identified the 'beauty of the English landscape' as the 'landlords's country...given up to opulence and ease' (Masterman 1960: 157). It was a 'vast accumulation of acres', with 'great avenues leading to residences which lack no comfort, broad parks, stretches of private land, sparsely cultivated, but convenient for hunting, shooting, and a kind of stately splendour'. Meanwhile, 'In England alone, among all the modern countries, the English [people] are imprisoned between hedges, and driven along rights of way' (156-7).

As I noted in my comments on holidays on the Norfolk Broads in the 1890s, the middle-class English on holiday seemed less concerned about being kept to highways than that their class 'herd-instinct' should not be disturbed. Their 'abundant' way of life was safe if they never met the wrong sort of people. It was better that resorts were 'exclusive', and many tourists chose their holidays on this basis. The worst that could happen in exclusive resorts was that they might become crowded, since local councils

SHOWING THE BRAVE EFFORT OF A POSTER-ARTIST TO DO JUSTICE, IN THE LIMITED SPACE AT HIS DISPOSAL, TO THE VARIOUS ATTRACTIONS ADVERTISED BY THE MUNICIPALITY AND SPORTS COMMITTEE OF MIXINGHAM-ON-SEA.

'MIXINGHAM-ON-SEA', 1912

40. 'Mixingham-on-Sea', *Punch*, 1912.

and entrepreneurs recognised the benefits of attracting paying guests.

In a cartoon published in *Punch* in 1912 (and reproduced above), the 'poster-artist' tried to do justice to the 'various attractions advertised by the municipality and sports committee of Mixingham-on-Sea'. He drew the beachhead crowded with people, the sea full of boats, and the air full of aeroplanes. The crowd was spliced together, comfortably playing numerous middle-class sports, including tennis, croquet, and hockey in the same 'limited space'. Looking into this scene, viewers had their gaze returned only by a singing clown in the middle distance, and two infants in the foreground – three people whose opinions carried no weight. The rest of the crowd expressed itself in frantic activity, and though the point of the joke was to make Mixingham appear ludicrous to the outsider, there was no denying that within the world of the cartoon every active person was happy and occupied (Pimlott 1947: 255).

The cartoonist avoided the problem of class conflict by ensuring that the overlapping games were played by people of similar social status: no working-class sports were played on the beach, which was also empty of all signs of difference. The pier, which may have held more carnivalesque amusements, was pushed to the back of the drawing, far away but not altogether forgotten. Apart from this, and the appearance of a charabanc or coach, the cartoon world was a place where middle-class people of like mind met and enjoyed themselves. The only problem was that there were suddenly so many of them, and all in the same place.

In the same way that the cartoonist made the world of Mixingham peaceful, by

41. J. Dixon-Scott, 'Summer in a Cotswold lane, Gloucestershire', from *English Counties*, 1937.

ensuring that games were played by people of similar social status, guidebooks used photography to stress social and environmental harmony. We can see this in the publications of the Homeland Association, which were aimed at both relatively secure and aspiring members of the middle class. The Association began publishing guides to (mostly southern) English towns, villages and seaside resorts in the 1890s; it flourished between the wars (with a rare venture into Scotland in 1925), and continued into the late 1940s. It was 'founded in 1896 with the view to collecting and publishing accurate descriptions of the towns and countryside of Great Britain, the Motherland of our Empire...Its desire is to help our fellow countrymen to travel in, to appreciate intelligently, and to study their own country and its story, in other words to encourage knowledge of, and love for, our native Britain' (Anon. 1926: frontispiece). The Association also produced *Handy Guides* and 'useful books of a more ambitious character on Architecture, Ecclesiology, and British Antiquities'.

Before the Great War the Homeland Association promised to resolve the problems of 'where to live'. Readers found advice on the 'choicest' areas around London, with maps, price guides and photographs of houses, and with advertisements from railway companies extolling the 'charming residential districts in the garden of England' (Prescott Row 1911–14). The information was practical: it included the cost of living, along with other 'handy' hints to householders and gardeners, including where to stay and what to see for 'tourists, visitors and would-be residents'.

After the war the Homeland Association continued to appeal to the relatively

Plate 9. P. G. Hennell, 'Children in a residential nursery', from *British Women go to War*, 1943.

Plate 10. Martin Parr, 'An amateur photographer at "A Celebration of Photography", Lacock Abbey, Wiltshire, July 1989'.

secure middle class. In the early 1930s it published *This Homeland of Ours* in three volumes, two of them dedicated to southern and northern England, and one to central and eastern England and Wales. The books were a compendium of middle-class interests, continuing to extol the abundant, stable life and commitment to an integrated nation which the middle class enjoyed in the Edwardian period: it comprised essays on the 'fair Heritage British men and women possess', bibliographies of literary connections with place, and numerous advertisements for housing agents, hotels, laundries and golf courses (Spenser Allberry 1932–34).

Many of the post-war Homeland books or pamphlets were not so clearly aimed at those who wished to sustain an Edwardian lifestyle. They were less concerned with housing than with collecting together views and scenery which stood for England. These pamphlets were heavily illustrated with pictures which repeated the resonant sites of the region or town – the abbeys, castles, churches, village greens and war memorials – usually with wide views across open country, with few people in sight, and undramatic lighting (see photograph reproduced opposite). The countryside was expansive, with open roads enticing the touring classes. Many of these photographs were taken by Herbert Felton, Will F. Taylor, and J. Dixon-Scott (see for instance Anon. 1928a; Cockett 1928; Anon. 1929), whose trademark was a distant, uninflected gaze which invited 'a sort of unfocussed dreaming' (Jeffrey 1983: 62). Like other guidebooks produced between the wars, these Homeland productions stamped 'England' with an overall, definite and dependable character (see illustration of a guidebook cover and frontispiece on page 130). The country was a 'white-walled garden', and the new residential estates for commuters were 'charming'; the country was 'read' in terms of its ancient and modern literary heritage – Bunyan, Kipling and Hilaire Belloc (Tweedie 1927; Hodgson 1928; Anon. 1928b). The scenery, though sometimes a 'wilderness' as in Hampshire's New Forest (Tweedie 1927), was rendered 'fair' and 'native' by 'History, Traditions, Antiquities and Literary Associations' held in common (Spenser Allberry 1932–34).

The middle-class commodification and domestication of the English landscape extended to the production of a wealth of guidebooks. The middle and lower-middle classes were doing most of the countryside travelling and photographing. They could enjoy the illusion of ownership through other inexpensive guides which were published in large numbers from the late 1920s, following H. V. Morton's *In Search of England* (1927). According to Alex Potts, many of these books were 'distinguished

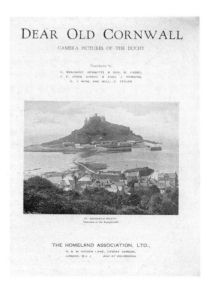

42. Cover and frontispiece from *Dear Old Cornwall*, *The Homeland Illustrated*, Homeland Association, 1926.

by the introduction of high-quality visual illustration – reproductions of the best modern photographs picturing the characteristic features of English country scenery' (Potts 1989: 166). Central to their success was photography and print technology.

While photography had been a marginal activity in the late Victorian period, limited to certain elite sectors of the middle classes both as a practice and in the form of reproductions in their books and magazines, in the post-war period it became the common coin and ordinary experience of millions in relatively cheap snapshooting, and in a cheap book trade full of half-tone reproductions. The countryside was made available in pictures, so that when tourists went in search of what they had already seen, they found exactly what they were looking for, and either bought postcards of the favoured sites or took their own photographs.

The reassurance of the 'beautiful England' experience was sought by what Potts calls 'the large sectors of the middle classes who were not that well off and certainly had no cause at all to feel in a relation of ownership to the country'. He writes that discovering the beauties of the countryside became an obsession among a not-so-privileged middle class who on many counts felt marginal, but who wished to possess a sense of themselves at home which outweighed their insecurity in terms of social place. They sought countryside images that promoted 'a little-England jingoism', celebrating 'an English essence, enduring safe and beautiful, a home, a haven, and at

43. J. Dixon Scott, 'Cottesmore village, Rutlandshire', from *English Counties*, 1937.

the same time England's glory...(Potts 1989: 162–4). For them, too, 'Beautiful England' was a reliable make, and a standard.

Even as this was being established it was gradually changing. Dixon-Scott set aside the usual picturesque views in favour of blank, airless scenes, as we see in this picture of 'Cottesmore village' in Rutland from his *English Counties* of 1937 (see Ford 1935; Clunn 1936; Dixon-Scott 1937). It seems the mixture reflects a change in ways of seeing the countryside: older ways of seeing were placed alongside more modern, restrained or reticent ones, indicating the unsettled state of landscape, travel and topographic books.

Dixon-Scott's views were often taken across wide expanses of land. He sometimes included farmers working with horse and plough, but the growth of industrialised agriculture and consequent changes to fields and forests led to a more organised appearance to the countryside. This encouraged a type of writing and looking which dwelt on the garden of England appearing to be an orderly place and all the richer for it. Alex Potts believes that the stereotypes of chequer-board fields and old buildings nestling in comfortable hollows represented in calendars, advertisements, films and guidebooks are 'largely the creation of the period, and not, as is often imagined, the end product of a long tradition of English landscape depiction'. As proof of this, he says that in Morton's *In Search of England* 'the new visual stereotypes have not as yet quite settled down', showing 'slightly shabby' picturesque scenes rather than 'the image of a cultivated garden of England landscape that eventually takes over as the visual emblem of Englishness' (Potts 1989: 166–7). In fact, the new-look fields did not disrupt the canon, which otherwise remained full of picturesque subjects and treatments. The 'shabby' picturesque, however, was transformed into a tidied version when country cottages were claimed by the middle classes and 'restored', which meant 'improving' them, bringing them up to the new owners' standards.

The touring guides that were rushed into print in the 1930s were part of a long history of books popular since the previous century among middle-class holiday-makers who went 'in search of' England. The interest in topography widened as the class itself had widened, but still this material was not designed to reach everyone. The guides focused upon history, topography and antiquarian interest, demonstrated the virtue of self-improvement and advocated the beauty, or legacy of England. Again, as we saw in guides to Norfolk, they continued to address their readers as people 'in the know', people of like mind and sensibilities. They enabled travellers to go on looking down at tourists, while seaside trippers did not figure at all, since they were scarcely attentive to the historic resonance of the country. Snobbery and the desire for a pure class experience of the country still drove the conservation movement, with an intensity and hostility fuelled by knowing that the pre-war privileges were lost for ever. A newspaper article in 1933 argued that 'the only way to save the countryside for democracy is to keep democracy out of the countryside' (cited in Jeans 1990: 259). For the author of this report, the cheap books and photographs were a sign of ground lost to the wrong sort of people. For those who bought them, the same books were a sign of group identity, a badge of respectability and seriousness.

'Democracy', then, was double-edged. Citizens who enjoyed its freedoms were caught in complicated tensions, many of them arising from the success of the tourist trade. Developers were beginning to spoil the countryside. They had put up advertising hoardings, built petrol stations, tea-shops, pylons, and bungalows, among other monstrosities, which compelled C. Williams Ellis to compare developments to an octopus that held England in its grip and whose tentacles were destroying it (Williams Ellis 1928). Access and mobility ruined the very places that people wished to visit. Tourists had to buy postcards of streets and gardens that no longer existed at 'cash chemists' – exactly the sort of shops which promoted tourism and advanced the spoiling. Williams Ellis blamed the destruction of the countryside on tourists, and used

44. 'Treasure trove – a home-counties bridleway', from Clough Williams Ellis, *Britain and the Beast*, 1938.

photography in *Britain and the Beast* to illustrate his point. Picnickers left behind them a 'treasure trove' of rubbish on a 'Home-Counties bridleway', though he felt the greater fault lay in the tourist trade's unregulated exploitation of amenities (Williams Ellis 1938: plate facing p. 204 – see illustration above).

Arguments about countryside planning increased between the wars. Different middle-class voices were raised in protest against planning, or approbation of it, despite the overarching themes of 'beauty' and 'legacy' (Sheail 1981). There was disagreement over how to balance the rights of traders and tourists with the need to protect the sites as national assets. The arguments disrupted the idea that England was a single place, producing what Philip Dodd in *The Art of Travel* calls the acknowledgement of 'England*s* rather than England' (P. Dodd 1982: 128). He contrasts the 'confident exploitation of place' enjoyed by Edwardians with the difficulties which were experienced by 1930s travellers. He suggests that the later travellers enjoyed none of the advantages of their predecessors' central position: 'what distinguishes 1930s travel books is not any particular stance but the variety and complexity of stance'. He identifies four conventions within travel writing, all of them concerned with what Charles Madge, an instigator of the Mass-Observation project, called 'the anthropological study of our civilisation' (see next chapter for a discussion of Mass-Observation) (Dodd 1982: 128). Two of the stances are very like the travel writing of the nineteenth century and earlier, in which authors observed their subjects and did not join them, or used them in order to determine their view of themselves. Dodd recognises these stances (respectively) in Edwin Muir's *Scottish Journey* (1935), where the author remained distant from his subject, and in Graham Greene's *Journey Without Maps* (1936), where 'Africa is less the property of those who live there than of the European writers who have made it theirs' (Dodd 1982: 130–1).

According to Dodd, the other two stances are less stable. In *English Journey* (1934), J. B. Priestley's analysis of England in terms of class conflict 'co-exists with an account of a "real enduring England" '. He held contradictory beliefs, confident of a ' "traditional" England of shared valuations', and doubtful 'that a single standpoint can accommodate the various class experiences of England in the 1930s' (Dodd 1982: 129). Finally, Dodd says that in *The Road To Wigan Pier* (1937) Orwell adopted the stance of the 'explorer' venturing into 'unknown England', though 'the objects of scrutiny are not passive before the observer's gaze but have a life which can challenge and chasten that gaze' (Dodd 1982: 132). Even so, the working-class gaze did not deflect Orwell: the genre of travel writing was so much a middle-class point of view that they could not easily rework it from within. As Dodd says, for Orwell to have 'shown the working class active in its own making, [he] would need to have chosen some literary form other than the travel book' (136) (see next chapter for a discussion of *The Road To Wigan Pier*).

Each stance permitted and conditioned various meanings which were conventional in travel writing, from the outsider who 'masters' the scene in various ways to the author who shares with the reader feelings of instability, alienation or inadequacy. In class terms, none of these stances gave away any advantage. In all of them, the authors contrived to maintain their positions. The mixture of certainty and doubt that we find in the literary 'art' of travel writing we also see in travel books with photographs. The main difference between the 'literary' books and the guidebooks with pictures is the degree to which authors became exposed to investigation, their stances open to question in ways not experienced by authors of guidebooks. Writers were more likely to admit anxiety than the authors of guidebooks, in which everything was seen to be comfortable in photographs. Yet they both fulfilled similar ideological functions, sustaining the middle class against its opponents. The difference between the literary and the guidebook method of production was that one was intended to show artistic authorship while the other was a trademark, a repetition, a reliable make. The guides and topographic books confined themselves to repeating the certainties of favoured sites, meeting the expectations of tourists, and promising a defence against unwelcome intruders on the scene, whether they were actual bodies from another class, or the destruction wrought by passing time. In each case, the guides and pictures set out to restore the readers' faith in a personal and national stability which could be gained through owning objects and repeating signs. They have been overlooked in books on travelling and tourism because they are so apparently artless, so ordinary, which is the most transparent sign of all.

The conservative stamp of the guidebooks was also used to sell amateur photography. The markets overlapped, as did the same concerns and anxieties to which they appealed. Class position always had to be maintained, and unease or even fear of losing place was matched by the unease of losing time. This sense of impermanence in everyday life was one of the mainstays of the photographic industry. During the war, the industry had made a virtue out of its ability to produce the illusion that time was fixed in photographs. By apparently stopping the passage of time, the photograph could keep a dead relative in the family. As *memento mori*, photographs appealed to sentiment and memory, and offered a sense of stability in contrast to a changing world. After the war, and in contrast to the flux of everyday life, the trade continued to promise stability by fixing time in photographs. Just as important, it tried to convince the secure middle class and the nervous sectors of the lower-middle class, those whose sense of themselves were maintained with difficulty, that they could gain status through the astute purchase of affordable luxuries.

Through its development in wartime applications the technology of photography became more reliable, with film able to cope with greater extremes of light and dark, and increasingly cheap cameras made more robust and 'foolproof'. These developments allowed the photographic trade to aim at a different type of user. The trade now addressed less wealthy consumers in a period of recession, and so the language used to advertise photography emphasised reliability, thrift and economy. In addition, the elaborate and exclusive language used by art photographers of the 1890s was superseded in advertisements by a mode of address aimed specifically at an expanded, younger and less expert audience. The photographic trade continued to cater for wealthier middle-class amateurs, and set out to capture those lower-middle-class people who had less money and less social status, but enough to spend on holidays and other, family memories.

KODAK WORLD

George Eastman, the founder of Kodak, had long been clear about his aim to dominate world photographic trade. In 1894 he said: 'The manifest destiny of the Eastman Kodak Company is to be the largest manufacturer of photographic materials in the world or else to go to pot' (Jenkins 1975: 1). He achieved his success by buying virtually all patents relating to roll film, buying and stripping companies which threatened his own, and imposing restrictions on dealers. These tactics led to legal action in the USA and in Britain, but had no lasting or damaging effects upon his business (D. Collins 1990: 82, 148–50, 158–9). In a cartoon printed on the cover of an American photographic magazine in 1907, the Eastman Kodak Company was pictured as a bulldog with the bones of ruined competitors scattered about, the 'meat' which this 'caesar' had fed on to become so great (*Photographer* 1907).

In the early 1880s, falling profits in his dry-plate works had forced Eastman to make innovations, replacing glass with roll film (Jenkins 1975: 12). To his surprise, the majority of existing photographers who were already using plates did not switch to film. He realised that 'in order to make a large business we would have to reach the general public and create a new class of patrons' (Jenkins 1975: 13). He knew that anyone who invented an article 'which the public needs' must present it to them, since 'as a rule the public has to be educated to its own needs'. The invention must be 'thrust down their throats and held there by some enthusiastic, imaginative person whose object is, of course, to make money' (Collins 1990: 148). The subjects he wanted to hold down for this sort of treatment were the inexpert amateurs who wanted nothing to do with the technical side of photography, and who could be persuaded to engage with it as practitioners only if they found it affordable and effortless.

Eastman founded Kodak Limited in 1898 by reorganising the Eastman Photographic Materials Company, based in London, and the American Eastman Kodak Company. The company expanded, and by 1902 had opened retail and wholesale outlets in Belgium, Holland, Austria and Hungary (Collins 1990: 94). Before the war, it used the British Empire to set up Kodak Houses in Canada, India and South Africa, and bought up the main manufacturing company in Australia (Willis 1988: 127). It built a large administrative centre and showroom in central London in 1911, all of which provided the base for Eastman's aim of world-wide commercial domination. In 1927 the company added an eighth floor to its London showroom, which then housed nearly fifty departments supplying its products to the British Isles, and goods 'to almost every corner of the earth' (*Kodak Trade Circular* 1928: 22–4). By 1936 advertisements boasted that Kodak 'Photographs the world!' with eight factories in seven countries (five of them in Europe), and suppliers in forty-nine others (*BJP Almanac* 1936: advertisements 16–17). Kodak needed the extensive bureaucracy of production and distribution to 'keep faith' with consumers by being 'constant' and 'consistent', qualities of uniformity which it guaranteed 'every day, year in and year out, in every country throughout the world' (*AP* ads 1927; *Punch* 6 August 1930). As part of the promise of an eternal present for its customers, Kodak declared that it was always and everywhere the same.

Kodak was the trademark: it stood for durability and reliability, and matched these qualities with the virtue of thrift. The idea was to provide an infallible camera with equally dependable film, and sell the promise of infallible and dependable memories. Kodak was not alone in marketing this idea. The British company Houghton's sold 'Ensign speedy roll film' as 'faster, safer, brighter' (*Daily Sketch* 19 July 1925), and the German company Agfa promised 'success' with holiday snapshots (*Daily Mirror* 2 July 1931). Despite this competition, Kodak was first in the field of roll film and, aiming to create a new market, it traded on its film being 'dependable' over a longer period and advertised more widely than other companies. Advertising in monopoly capitalism is vital, since it encourages loyalty to the brand name which, in the view of consumers, cannot be replaced by a close substitute (Baran and Sweezy 1968: 121).

Kodak joined its brand name and the promise of reliability with an older idealisation. Its advertisements used illustrations centred on an untroubled, middle-class family. In selling itself through such a family and its ways of feeling, Kodak directed its appeal to a particular segment of the middle class, and by advertising widely in many different types of publications it aimed to reach aspiring members of less secure sectors of the middle class. Of course, Kodak's emphasis on the ideal family did not determine how people actually used photography. Kodak advertising may have been pervasive, but in the end consumers' use of products was not determined by Kodak. Purchasers used film in ways which may have had nothing to do with families or holidays, and they may have intended that their pictures should never enter a semi-public or stabilised narrative like the family album, instead producing photographs (such as erotic or pornographic shots for private circulation) which fell outside public or polite discourses. Kodak had no need to identify these individuals, or groups of individuals, or even acknowledge their existence, since the main ideological work was in the promise of 'sure shots', pictures which would come out. The essence of Kodak was certainty, and that preceded and transcended any other use consumers made of the products. Their memories were not as predictable or as standard as the dependable film in the yellow carton, but the material which was placed in the realm of shared memories in family albums or their equivalent, for the pleasure of family and friends, was stable over generations (Hirsch 1981; Spence and Holland 1991). The small differences were the sign of consumers' individuality as families and members of families – or not – but the point of convergence was the authority of the idea of the reliable make.

From April to September 1922 Kodak 'covered the country' with a thousand advertisements in a hundred newspapers and magazines (*Kodak Trade Circular* 1922). In 1922 illustrated advertisements with lengthy captions appeared in the expensive shilling weeklies such as the *Tatler* (22 May), the *Bystander* (5 July) and the *Sphere* (8 July) and in cheap 2*d* papers such as *John O' London's Weekly* (12 August). They appeared in expensive daily papers such as *The Times* (13 May – price 3½*d*), and cheap ones such as the *Daily News* (27 June, price 1*d*). They appeared in local newspapers throughout the British Isles. At the same time that it was paying for national coverage, Kodak appealed to dealers to pay for their own local publicity (*Kodak Trade Circular* 1923: 8).

Advertising was just as heavy in 1925 (*Kodak Trade Circular* 1925: 56–9). Illustrated advertisements were commonplace in the expensive titles, but also appeared in the cheap dailies (*Daily Sketch* 17 June; *Daily Mirror* 3 April; *Daily Mail* 19 May). In addition, Kodak used simpler, verbal promises in the cheap dailies, with boxes carrying plain-text advertisements which said 'Kodak film "never lets you down" ', since it was always 'dependable' in its standardised 'yellow carton' (see, for instance, *Sunday News* 21 June).

Throughout the inter-war period, the advertisements emphasised certainty. They differed only slightly from publication to publication, suggesting that amateur snapshooters existed at all levels of society. In the shilling weeklies, the drawings were sometimes printed in two colours, and often took a whole page. There was no possibility of colour in the newspapers, but the advertisements were printed large: they took nearly a quarter page in the broadsheet *Daily Telegraph* (2 April 1925), and three-quarters in the smaller-format *Daily Sketch* (17 June 1925) and *Daily Mirror* (3 April 1925). The scenes were the same across the titles, with aspirational appeals to join 'the car and the "Kodak" ' in the *Sketch*, and seaside imagery in the expensive magazines. There was a greater variety of pictures in the illustrated journals, but otherwise it was always the middle class who were shown on holiday in the countryside, or at the seaside. The middle class always formed the decent middle-of-the-road family, exactly the people who would take and enjoy 'happy little snapshots'. The keynotes were aspiration, trust and identification. The advertisements did not attempt to create a single or 'actual' family, since the structural position of members of the family mattered more than specific identities: the positions of mother, father, daughter and so on were fixed relative to each other, but were standardised for the readership, so they could readily identify with one or more of them. This made the family into the source of components in which parts were interchangeable, just like any other domestic consumer unit. But at the same time the Kodak family was unique, since each memory (which was given objective and permanent form in the photograph) was special to that family. So the consumer bought sameness in the reliable make, and difference in the shape of personal mementos. Simultaneous sameness and difference, just like the simultaneous appeal to the anxiety of time passing and reassurance that time could be made to stand still, were (and remain) central principles in the capitalist marketplace.

The advertisements showed photography to be a communal affair, with women having as much say in the production of memories as men. Though most photographers were men, in advertisements it was usually the 'Kodak girl' who held the camera and decided to capture happy family events. Kodak had always used images and photographs of young women to advertise its products, but the 'Kodak girl' in her distinctive striped dress first appeared in Britain in 1910 (Coe 1977: 33). Between the wars, 'she' was the one in the family who seemed to be most concerned with memories and fleeting moments. Though 'she' always appeared in the advertisements, the copy was not usually framed in 'her' voice. There were exceptions to this practice, seen in the image reproduced on the next page. The advertisement is in the form of a letter from a 'Kodak girl' to her 'Dear old Dad', whom she implored to leave the 'stuffy office' for a holiday in Bridgecombe. This was an imaginary fishing village which was shown to be old-fashioned and free of trippers, exactly the place of

45. Kodak advertisement from *Punch*, 3 August 1921.

46. Kodak advertisement from *Punch*, Summer number 1921.

his dreams (*Punch* 3 August 1921). The advertisement caught perfectly the modern horror of being 'stuffy', a word which conjured up 'both the horse-hair sofas and the moral airlessness of that late Victorian world'. What mattered now was an 'airy' manner: breeziness and youth were 'the measure of modernity, a carelessness and vitality of being which could be cultivated...by the older generation too' (Light 1991: 69). In the illustration we see that the photography-minded daughter appears to be the essence of modern womanhood – standing by herself, armed with a camera and, in the manner of all viewers of landscape, 'she' occupies the commanding heights of the quayside to look down on the beach scene below.

Kodak advertisements rarely acknowledged that men used cameras. In one version (reproduced above) which did identify the husband and father as the photographer, the purpose was to allow him to join the younger set. In the advertisement we see the mother (a 'Kodak girl') and daughter returning from the beach. When 'Father' catches the 'happy little scene' with his Kodak, 'Mother' says 'he is getting younger instead of older' (*Punch* 1921 Summer Number). Kodak advertised that it knew the secret of youth. As we see across several examples, Kodak gave a different twist to the theme of time-travel. Kodak cameras not only turned back the clock, keeping 'the happy scenes...alive for ever' (*Punch* 13 July 1921), but they also prevented sights from running away like water through the fingers (see page opposite). They transformed sights into a refreshing drink 'on dry and dusty days' (*Punch* 30

Click! went the 'Kodak'

*Don't let sights like these
run like water through your fingers.
Catch them with a 'Kodak,' so that on dry
and dusty days you may
drink again.*

Click! went the 'Kodak'

*Thrifty little 'Kodak'—
storing up sunshine—bottling
the wine of life—
keeping youth
young!*

47. Kodak advertisement from *Punch*, 30 May 1928.
48. Kodak advertisement from *Punch*, 10 July 1929.

May 1928). The secret of eternal youth was to store the 'wine of life' in pictures. In another advertisement, Kodak promised an endless deferment of age; the Kodak camera was described as 'storing up sunshine – bottling the wine of life – keeping youth young!' (*Punch* 10 July 1929).

The Kodak world was unchanging, a quality the fantasy of advertising copy transferred on to the lives of its inhabitants and promised its consumers. The advertisements listed potential subjects, should photographers need reminding of the telling moments in their lives. They included 'memories of the children at play, the river, the country, the sea, and of those with whom you shared these long summer days!' (*Punch* 14 May 1924). The copy addressed the tourist directly – 'You will see England!' – which meant visiting 'places far from the main roads and railways – the quiet old-world villages with their ancient churches and flower-decked gardens' (*Punch* 29 July 1925). Readers were told to 'take a "Kodak" with you and bring home your own pictures – pictures eloquent of the loveliness and the strength and the age of Britain' (*Punch* 13 July 1927). Whether the view was old England or the family at play, the purpose of photography was to stop time, ensuring that nothing in the picture became any older. Families without cameras would rue the passage of time: the only regret uttered by anyone in Kodak advertisements was that last year's holiday (when the children were that much younger) had passed unrecorded for the lack of a Kodak camera (*Punch* Summer Number 1921).

49. Kodak advertisement from *Punch*, 2 July 1930.
50. Kodak International Competition, World Awards brochure, 1931.

Kodak gave several assurances: an eternal happy moment; the illusion of unravelling time; reliable film; and a machine which worked itself. This last promise was enshrined in Eastman's earliest slogan 'You press the button, we do the rest'. After the war it changed subtly: all 'you' had to do was simply 'Let your "Kodak" tell the story' (*Punch* 18 June 1924). 'Your' task was to abdicate responsibility to Kodak, and 'let your Kodak retain the memory of the scenes that please you' (*Punch* 23 July 1919). By 1930 the age of intelligent machines had finally arrived, with Kodak film so dependable that 'it makes allowances for your little mistakes' (*Punch* 2 July 1930 – see illustration above). Kodak would not only save its customers' memories but would stand in for them and overcome their tendency to error *in the camera*. Kodak of itself could do the telling *on behalf of* its customers.

The Kodak world was free from anxiety. In 1925, to underline this carefree attitude, the company devised a contest which was actually more like a lottery, involving no element of skill. In this respect, it matched the way Kodak sold itself as effortless, and something in which everyone could easily become involved. Kodak invited British consumers to 'estimate' the number of hand cameras in use in Britain that summer. The winning number (3,165,847) did not represent the actual number of cameras, but the average of the total number sent in by 'contestants'. The prize-winners were those contestants *closest to the average* (*The Camera* 1925: 301). The decision to award the prize to the average of guesses rather than the actual number of

142

cameras was significant: Kodak stood for a self-sufficient average world, that of the unassuming little men and their partners, and shifted this world to the heart of what it meant to be British.

Between the wars, the lower-middle-class market was overlooked by many British photographic companies, which continued to make glass plate negatives, and thus to target the relatively secure middle class. These companies went on appealing to a generalised patriotism, as in the Imperial Dry Plate's call to 'Buy British!' to 'Keep Britain Busy' (*The Camera* 1926). Stemming from the experience in the Great War, when it was patriotic to use only British goods, they continued to appeal to the national spirit of customers, and held competitions for all-British photographic goods (*AP* 1922a: 48; 1922b: 548). Unfortunately for them, the British companies failed to target and pursue those people who constituted the largest market – the amateur snapshooters. The period 1929–38 was the 'golden age' for amateurs: competitions were part of the newspaper circulation war, and companies from pet food manufacturers to railways used to advertise photographic competitions in the daily press to encourage sales of their products. Consumers could save coupons from packets of Private Seal cigarettes and obtain 'free' Ensign cameras (*News of the World*, 26 July 1931), while Kodak cameras were 'free' with coupons collected with Black Cat cigarettes (*News of the World*, 12 July 1931). National and local newspapers, as well as weekly and monthly magazines, commonly offered cash prizes from £1 to £250 for pictures by amateurs (see *AP* 1929: 26; 1932: 41; 1935b: 144; 1938: 27).

The biggest competition of the period was held by Kodak from May to August 1931. It was '*strictly for amateurs*' – a code for no plate negatives – and offered prize money totalling $100,000 (£20,000). As if to demonstrate Kodak's global domination, the competition had an elaborate, world-wide structure, involving 89 countries divided into 47 'contest districts' (*Annual Report* 1931: 15). In Britain the competition was heavily promoted in illustrated advertisements in the popular press during the summer (see *Daily Mirror, Daily Mail, Daily Sketch*). Once again, amateurs were told they had to do very little, except use Kodak cameras and films, and increase their chances by sending in as many pictures as possible. No-one had to decide where to place their pictures, because the 'Prize Contest Office' would put them in one of six classes (children, scenes, occupations, interiors, portraits and animals). The competition required 'No technical skill', since 'subject interest only will count' (*AP* ads 1931: 2).

In all, Kodak received over three million entries, but it was intended from the

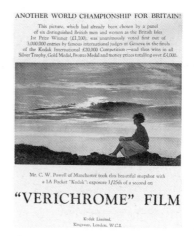

51. 'Pictures taken on "Verichrome" ', *The Kodak Magazine*, 1931.

52. Kodak advertisement for 'Verichrome', *Amateur Photographer*, 16 December 1931.

first that one picture should scoop the pool of £3,300 and various trophies. This photograph would earn £1,100 and a bronze medal for winning its 'class' and then beating the other sections in its 'district'. By coming top in the International Competition it would win £2,200, a gold medal and a silver trophy. As we see in the illustration on page 142, all these prizes were awarded to Charles Powell, an amateur photographer and 'young textile designer' from Manchester, for a snapshot of his fiancee silhouetted against the sunset (taken on the Isle of Man, and used for years afterwards in Manx tourist publicity).

Powell was the ideal Kodak consumer. He read the *Kodak Magazine*, which in June that year had published photographs to show how the company's new Verichrome film produced 'a silhouette against the sunset, with edges sharp and clear of any spreading of the brilliant highlights' (*Kodak Magazine* 1931: 102–3 – see illustration above). The name of the film suggested that Kodak had made it even easier to depend on the company to create an image that would enhance memories. The film was very true to the chromatic scale, and extremely reliable in adverse lighting conditions, faithfully capturing scenes which would defeat other films. Both film and competition were promoted heavily in the press, with suggestions that entrants should use the new 'master film–the faster film' (see *AP* ads from May to August 1931; see *AP* 1931a–d). The judges, who were theatre and sports celebrities, chose the winners on 'general appeal', or 'the interest they aroused' and not on the basis of any technical

Plate 11. Martin Parr, 'Peak District', 1989.

Plate 12. Paul Reas, 'Constable country', 1993.

knowledge, but it was convenient for Kodak, to say the least, that the winner had used Verichrome. His picture was then used to advertise the product (*AP* ads 1931: 2 – see illustration on page 144).

Kodak engineered the competition so that amateur snapshooting would turn elitist culture on its head by awarding princely sums of money to the popular and the everyday (because the prize money was in dollars, Powell received over £4,000, and was financially secure). The prize photograph also came close to popular ideas about what constituted a proper picture, something which was (according to one of the judges' remarks) as good as a painting (Kodak 1931). The competition was grandiose in its organisation, but domestic in its ambitions. It proved the apotheosis of the lower-middle class, clearly seen in the reliable, true-to-life, and yet magical world of Kodak.

PHOTOGRAPHY AS A 'UNIVERSAL' LANGUAGE

Ideas about English landscape, touring guides, and Kodak film drew on expectations of sameness and certainty – the attributes of a positive kind of femininity. If these ideas were critical to the self-image of the English between the wars, they were reinforced by looking abroad and finding the same values reflected back. The central idea of the 'reliable make' was 'Made in England', but there was nothing incongruous in adopting foreign goods, such as Kodak film, which set the standard for the world. The English approved of goods that were standardised, and intended to sell the same degree of certainty themselves. They proved their success in exporting the stamp of surety by finding that it flourished in the British Empire. The twinned ideas of femininity and reliability moved not only to the centre of 'Englishness' but were central to what Alison Light has called 'the domestication of the imperial idea between the wars, and the elaboration of imperial fantasies within different kinds of national, private, and indeed feminine contexts' (Light 1991: 211). The Empire (in Agatha Christie's novels) was no longer the site of adventure and conquest, but had simply become 'abroad', remaining 'exotic whilst at the same time being reassuringly familiarised' (90). Travel books, photographs, and photographic advertising rediscovered the Empire, as the guidebooks had rediscovered England, to be full of delight and variety in scenery and holiday experiences. At the same time, none of the spectacle of Empire was threatening or required special heroic adventurers to bring it back home. Anyone could go and see it, just as anyone could take photographs.

This structure of feeling matched the idea that photography was a supposedly natural and 'universal' language. Photography was believed to be a 'common language' which made sense throughout the world, dissolving the linguistic and cultural barriers between people. The 'universal' language of photography and the reorganisation of Englishness around the hearth and home combined to present a view of England and the Empire which was stable, and, by 1939, worth fighting for again.

Though the segregation of cultures was maintained overseas and preferred in England, advertising and travel photographs signified a world united. This notion, of course, supported the idea of a world market. These were crucial years in the promotion of Empire, which was a humanistic idea useful in the market-place, and exploited effectively as a source of new economic strength in a period of increasing world economic difficulty (MacKenzie 1984; MacKenzie 1986; Mangan 1990; Greenhalgh 1988; Opie 1985).

John MacKenzie has argued that popular imperialism found expression in exhibitions, broadcasting, school texts, popular juvenile literature and the ephemera issued by commercial companies, all of which continued to convey an imperial message of immutable order in ways little changed from their pre-war guise. MacKenzie writes 'an implicit imperialism, partly economic, partly moral, underlay most propagandist and entertainment out-put in the 1920s and 1930s. In 1940 George Orwell was able to write that he easily felt a positive surge of patriotism, for "that long drilling which the middle class go through had done its work". Orwell went on to consider the extent to which the middle class had also successfully drilled the rest of the population' (MacKenzie 1984: 11).

For 'drilling' to be effective, it had to correspond to everyday assumptions. One of these was the pretence that differences between England and the Empire were dissolved by the universal appeal of photography. This was expressed in its simplest form by suggesting that photographs, the English language and the Empire complemented each other. They were to be found throughout the world and united it. We can see this shift towards familiarity in the way the *Amateur Photographer* encouraged photographers to view the landscape. In 1909 its editor, F. J. Mortimer, organised an exhibition by 'colonials' which became an annual fixture, continuing, save for 1917–19, until 1946 (*AP* 1909: 36). The exhibition was modelled on photographic competitions in Britain and attached to the established photographic

53. 'The empire of the camera', *Amateur Photographer*, 20 March 1911.

institutions. The *AP* invited readers living in any part of the Empire and Dominions to submit photographs. The entries were judged, and the winners and others exhibited in London (initially at the Little Gallery in the offices of the *AP* and, from 1920, at the Royal Photographic Society, London). Individuals could win a silver or bronze plaque or a certificate, and there was a special award for the best collective entry by an 'Overseas Club'. Competitors could also choose to have their photographs submitted to the juries of the London Salon and the Royal Photographic Society (*AP* 1935a: 316).

Readers living in any part of the Empire and Dominions were invited to submit, and many of their exhibited photographs were reproduced not only in the annual 'Empire Number' but throughout the year. As the magazine claimed in 1911, the empire of the camera was universal (*AP* 1911: 267 – see illustration above). The magazine became the main channel for such ideas in the photographic press, consciously aiming to 'spread the cult of the camera, both at home and abroad' (*AP* 1912: 147). Though hopes for seizing German trade in the Great War came to nothing, the enlarged Empire after 1918 offered a great opportunity for expansion: 'the elements of Empire have become more closely knit than ever before in the pursuits

54. 'Empire number', *Amateur Photographer*, 8 March 1910.

of peace…The empire of the camera is world-wide [and the *AP* is] the connecting link between English-speaking photographers in every corner of the globe' (*AP* 1921: 201). During the Empire Exhibition held at Wembley in 1924, the magazine continued to stress its part in promoting photography world-wide. 'The cult of the camera', it claimed in an editorial, 'is not only universal in its application, [but] is more extensively and successfully practised in the British Empire than anywhere else in the world' (*AP* 1924: 425).

Before the Great War, photographs often made play with the authority of the British armed forces. A graphic headline the *AP* used in 1910 showed a camera lens and a length of film attached to a spool: on the 'film' is drawn a panoramic view of the Royal Navy in convoy, with the sun on the horizon bearing the logo of the magazine. Not only does the sun never set on the Empire, but the *AP* is similarly ever-present, which is its attraction to advertisers (*AP* 1910a: 219 – see illustration above). In this image, the eye and arms of the Empire are supervisory and controlling. This imperialist image survived the war, and was recycled in 1921, the year which saw a 'crescendo of jingoism in Britain' (Light 1991: 83).

In 1910, the magazine also initiated a graphic device which was not dropped until 1933 (see *AP* 1910b: 41; 1933: 298 – see illustration opposite). While still emphasising the centrality of Britain, this drawing stresses harmony under the flag and obedience to the crown. The Union flag in the background unites art, trade and the Crown. The central figure is a symbolic woman, doubling as Britannia and the female 'Spirit of Photography'. She is looking at prints handed to her by four men: three of them are standing, wearing a bush-hat or pith helmets, which marks them out as colonists; one figure kneels, and he is marked as a Sikh. The only 'native' on display is from India, testifying to what Bill Schwarz has called 'the inescapable centrality of India for the self-image of the English' (Schwarz 1987: 149).

55. Graphic device used from 1910 to 1933 to accompany reports of 'colonial and overseas' competitions in the *Amateur Photographer*.

The coexistence of these drawings of the convoy and the examination of prints indicates what Schwarz described as a 'cultural map profoundly organised by racial, class and gender boundaries', a map of complex colonial relations (Schwarz 1987: 149). The English governing classes tried to resolve these relations by writing themselves into the landscape, as when Sir Edward Lutyens built New Delhi from scratch between 1913 and 1930. They also brought their solution back to England, writing their colonial experience into the English landscape, as when Lutyens built modern country houses 'for the retired imperial functionaries' in Surrey and Sussex. Given the active interweaving of the histories of English colonials and India, Schwarz argues it was 'little wonder that *A Passage to India* was conceived and written in Weybridge' (149).

In a parallel development, the middle class used photography to picture the Empire in the 'universal' language of the centre. They brought the Empire back to England disguised as something already familiar. The myth that photography was a universal language erased the excesses of the colonial system. The *AP*'s reproductions of 'colonial' work from 1909–46 normalised commerce and travel as comfortable.

56. Z. D. Barni, 'Sunrise', *Amateur Photographer*, 6 April 1938.

Although the economies of the imperial satellites were 'drastically transformed by the pressures exerted from the aggressive centers of finance and trade', photographs could make scenes of the colonial economy look harmonious (Sekula 1984: 80). They could exclude all sense of difference, other than that required by the newly domesticated tourist experience. The photographs demonstrated the tourists' need to discover 'unspoiled' beauty. We see this, for example, in picturesque photographs of palms taken in India (Barni 1938), or a junk 'Homeward Bound' to Hong Kong (Chak 1938 – see illustrations above and opposite).

Indigenous peoples were shown to be exotic, proud and beautiful, satisfying tourists' demands for signs of authentic culture (Kharegat 1932). The white settlers, when in evidence, enjoyed the material benefits of governors and guardians (Burman 1933). In the Kodak brochure (see colour plate 8) the photographer appears to be a white space, a gap which none the less casts a shadow across his female companion. Both are very different from what they have come to see, and the white space is fully felt as presence. Entirely in keeping, the history of settlement was never seen, and the new state appeared fully-fledged, contented and modern – the work of heroic pioneers

57. L. C. Chak, 'Homeward Bound', *Amateur Photographer*, 1 June 1938.

(Stening 1914; Bostock 1923). Apparently with no history of settlement, no representations of 'prospecting' and no scenes of displacement, the colonial state in photographs seems ready-made and self-perpetuating. They represent a radical emptying of the category of production.

The peaceful world imagined by the financial centres was an orderly international market in which economic bonds became sentimental ties, and in which 'the overt racism appropriate to earlier forms of colonial enterprise' was 'supplanted by the "humanization of the other" so central to the discourse of neo-colonialism' (Sekula 1984: 95). In the favoured depiction of the British Empire, the mechanisms of oppression were invisible; history was over in the remote regions. This was evident in the photographs which were submitted to London from the peripheries. News from abroad fitted neatly with the news which was preferred at home, where there was also no visible oppression, only a smooth surface reflecting back the desired values, and pronouncing the end of conflict. The basis for success on a global scale (in the practice of photography and in the imaginations of viewers) was the capacity to resolve problems, stop time and declare the world to be at one with itself.

5

Documentary raids and rebuffs

Observers

IN THE PREVIOUS chapter we looked at places where 'England' was established as a 'reliable make'. In this chapter we shall look away from the rural scene towards the cities, and at how observers gathered information in regions where the idea of England was *not* a reliable and dependable make. The idea of 'Beautiful Britain' had no purchase in what the National Government called the 'distressed areas', places in south Wales, Cumberland, Durham, Northumberland and the west of Scotland where the working class had held turbulent demonstrations against unemployment. The observer-travellers under review here visited the northern industrial areas of England, or the working-class East End of London.

The landscape of the working class was more than an emblem of economic slump. It signalled that the term 'Beautiful Britain' was incomplete if not hopelessly inadequate as a description of the whole island. The story of the urban wastelands could not be told in the language that celebrated rural life. The storytellers needed to use different techniques of discovery from simply travelling the roads to the resorts and into the countryside. This was the moment of 'documentary', in which (largely middle-class) eyewitness accounts and apparently factual photography brought to light the living spaces of the urban working class.

Documentary photographers, though they may have occasionally felt uncomfortable at coming close to their objects (see Humphrey Spender's testimony

58. Humphrey Spender, untitled photograph of children in the street, Bolton, 1937–38.

page 158), were in a quite different relation to them than tourists in holiday resorts. Whereas tourists had some contact with and dependency on the locals, and some desires or expectations of the locality, documentary photographers were more fully independent of the people and region. This released them from the awful anxieties always attached to tourism. While tourists could fail by not seeing or feeling in the prescribed fashion, documentarists gained their authority from the widespread belief in the truth-value of simply 'being there' and 'seeing for yourself'. A relative innocence in the 1930s about the conditions of mediation and the currency of imagery meant that both film and photography were still believed to be the source of raw, unmediated sights. This apparently innocent use of photography by one class in observing another was maintained despite the fact that the images were ordered according to middle-class preoccupations. Once middle-class explorers and observers had gathered their information, they withdrew and disseminated their findings mainly through books by named 'authors', journalism supported by photographs and documentary films in which slum dwellers or workers were the curious objects of study by their social 'superiors' (Sussex 1976; Colls and Dodd 1985).

In this chapter the object of study is not the urban scene in itself but the way socially superior explorers and observers conducted themselves. I shall look at what methods they used and what types of information they brought back. I shall examine how photographs were used as evidence of working-class life in three key texts. The first is the project of Mass-Observation which 'was established by a small group of upper-middle class intellectuals and artists, but grew to involve...observers from all social classes and from all over the country' (Editorial 1978: 1). Mass-Observation set out to give the masses a voice. It invited ordinary people to report on their daily lives in diaries; it recruited a team of observers to watch, listen and document all types of ordinary behaviour; it involved poets, writers and artists to complement what it took to be the objective records of observers. Though most of Mass-Observation's records are written, the photographer Humphrey Spender took pictures of the inhabitants of Bolton. Secondly, I shall discuss George Orwell's *The Road to Wigan Pier*, the original edition of which, published by the Left Book Club, carried many photographs of deprivation. Finally, I shall look at Bill Brandt's book of plates called *The English at Home* (1936).

In some senses, each of these projects and their photographic components were failures at the time. Brandt's book was a commercial failure and has never been republished in its original form (though Brandt's current status has made it a collectors' item). In contrast, Orwell's book was commercially successful (Crick 1980: 311), but was regarded by Victor Gollancz and the other editors of the Club to be flawed as a factual account of working life and a distortion of Left politics. Gollancz therefore changed the book by writing a foreword and introducing news agency photographs into the text. Since Left debates of the 1930s have less currency than Orwell's status as an author, this book also has never been republished in its original format. The popular Penguin edition remains shorn of Gollancz's introduction, and the photographs were restored only in 1989. This change to the book has obscured a critical moment in the history and practice of documentary.

The work of Mass-Observation was yet another kind of failure. At the time of its formation in 1937 it was a prototype for the audience research industry. The project is unique, though, for its mania for collecting data in a surreal and random fashion rather than in accordance with known methods in statistics or social science

(Chaney and Pickering 1986: 39). The greatest failure of Mass-Observation was in its first phase: it never succeeded in its grand intentions to bring a greater awareness of democracy to the people of the country through 'an anthropology of ourselves' (cited in Jeffery 1978: 2). But along with Orwell's and Brandt's books, Mass-Observation's failure was only partial, since it underwent several more successful phases. It was employed by the Government in the Second World War to measure home-front morale, and later it became a market research company. Finally, the records, reports and diary entries which were gathered from 1937–49 have now become a historic archive housed at the University of Sussex. The raw material is becoming increasingly available to scholars, generating articles and scholarly analysis of the history and methodology (Stanley 1990).

The work of Mass-Observation, Orwell and Brandt provides the material for the chapter on the gambits of investigation – chiefly the ways observers oversaw and overheard the objects of their enquiry while they themselves tried to remain silent and invisible. None of the three texts discussed here were completely successful in the role of the 'unobserved observer', as we shall see, and none of them were judged then or subsequently on this level alone. Each text presents other problems: Orwell's book was at the centre of an ideological struggle over factual truth against literary invention; and Brandt's book embraced the fictive nature of his project, scarcely attending to any of the reformist or anthropological interests of the English explorers.

Whereas Orwell and Brandt set out to write or compile books, Mass-Observation, on the other hand, aimed to gather an archive which has required considerable expenditure of time and money over decades to house and interpret. With so many observers and competing methods of survey and record, with bases in Bolton and London, and with powerful and often divided leaders or co-ordinators, the project was always unwieldy. Its aim in Bolton, declared in 1937, was objectively to 'amass material, without unduly prejudging or pre-selecting from the total number of available facts. All this material, all the reports from our observers, carefully filed, will be a reference library accessible to every genuine research worker' (Editorial 1978: 1). Its aim in London was to invite a 'National Panel' of diarists to volunteer subjective 'Day Surveys' of their thoughts and actions on the twelfth day of each month. From 1937–45 a maximum of 2,847 observers had sent in at least one response, though the number of regular observers was only 1,095 (Summerfield 1985: 441). Yet by 1938 the mass of words was such that after only a year the reports already amounted to over two million words. Charles Madge (the sociologist who, along with the anthropologist Tom Harrisson, was one of the key founding members of Mass-Observation) stopped the Day Surveys (except for special occasions like Bank Holidays) because information continued to gather at a pace that outran the organisation's ability to process it (Calder and Sheridan 1984: 73). The volume of documents has remained a problem for subsequent curators (Sheridan 1991: 1; Summerfield 1985: 439). Mass-Observation's plan for a complete record was similar to the hopes of the photographic survey movements of the late nineteenth century, and like the earlier surveyors' attempts to divide 'record' photography from art, it tried to sustain a gap between its objective work in Bolton and its subjective work in the National Panel. We shall now look in turn at the techniques of the observers.

MASS-OBSERVATION AND ITS 'RUSES SO TO SPEAK'

Certain key figures and figurations recur in each of the texts, especially publishers and documentary modes of expression. For instance, in 1936 Victor Gollancz of the Left Book Club was willing to finance Tom Harrisson in his 'impressionistic social survey' of Bolton 'based on his work as a lorry driver and in the cotton mills' (Mellor 1978: 4). Harrisson was born outside England, and his early life was 'shaped by the Imperial tradition of exploration and administration' (Mellor 1978: 4). He was educated at Harrow, became an ornithologist and anthropologist, mixed with the poor of the East End of London, and spent five years in and around South-East Asia before returning to England to 'explore the peculiarities of the English' (Jeffery 1978: 20). Like Orwell, he realised that to find exotic strangers to study he needed to travel no further than a few miles to the east of central London, or north to 'the wilds' of Lancashire: 'In particular, my experience living among cannibals in the New Hebrides...taught me the many points in common between these wild-looking, fuzzy-haired, black, smelly people and our own, so when I came back from that expedition, I determined to apply the same methods here in Britain' (cited in Jeffery 1978: 20).

These converging interests between anthropology and social documentary were publicised in the *New Statesman*, beginning in December 1936 with an article which asked for an 'anthropological study of our own situation' (cited in Jeffery 1978: 2). The request had been brought on by the Abdication Crisis: this affair concerned the historic duty of King Edward VIII to the State and the Established Church which were thrown into disarray by his desire to marry the twice divorced Mrs Wallis Simpson but not make her his Queen and, (should they have children), resign all claims to the Throne on their behalf. This brought on a constitutional crisis, all the more sudden and alarming because the affair had been kept out of the newspapers by agreement among their owners. The King's subjects were uninformed until the last moment, in a country which claimed to be democratic. The mixture of law, rumour and sex meant that the crisis was a suitable subject for anthropological enquiry.

In response to the suggestion in the *New Statesman*, Charles Madge (then known as a South African poet and *Daily Mirror* reporter) wrote a letter to the journal saying that a group of artists, writers and film-makers had already formed Mass-Observation to develop an 'anthropology of ourselves'. In the same issue of the journal, Tom Harrisson had published a poem about cannibals – and he contacted Madge to discuss the similarities of their work. In January 1937, little more than a month before Gollancz published Orwell's *The Road to Wigan Pier*, Mass-Observation was formally announced in another letter signed by Harrisson, Madge and the documentary film-maker Humphrey Jennings.

Mass-Observation's strategy in Bolton was based on what the eye could see. The first technique was to watch and act like 'cameras without distortion' (Madge and Harrisson 1938: 66). The second technique was to invite subjects to explain what they were doing, though this was not necessary if it was intrusive. Finally, the 'facts' had to be written down and filed away 'without unduly prejudging or pre-selecting from the total number' (Editorial 1978: 1). The raw data, gathered by the innocent eye, consisted of notes, diaries, reports, and photographs. Altogether it comprised verbal and visual trophies of what the working class looked like. The observers gathered information in unobtrusive glances, noting or photographing the scene. Whatever they discovered, they would take away with them and weave into their reports. Describing the best room in a pub one observer wrote 'Tiled fireplace – over mantle mirror – adverts', and he listed them in 'photographic' detail (Picton 1978: 2).

The observers' need to *view* the field resulted in another particular tactic. To gain knowledge, Tom Harrisson encouraged them to be silent, to make themselves dumb in the alien centres they explored in order to pick up snippets of authentic conversation. The voluntary dumbing of all Mass-Observation's observers in Bolton was supposed to allow an 'objective' study of life in a typical northern industrial town to emerge through the convergence of innocent eyes and objects of study. Harrisson said 'The ideal instrument for the job is an ear-plug. *See* what people are doing. *Afterwards*, ask them what they think they are doing, if you like' (Picton 1978: 2). According to Harrisson, 'On this data science will one day build new hypotheses and theories' (Editorial 1978: 1).

Sometimes a temporary silencing of the observers' own voices was necessary because their accents were a sign of their class 'drilling'. Photographer Humphrey Spender, like Orwell, wrote that he was sometimes afraid to speak to the inhabitants of Bolton because he was unable to disguise his upper-class origins. Speaking would have dislodged his anonymity, invited suspicion, and changed the social chemistry of the scene before his subjects fell into unselfconscious revelation (Spender 1982: 16). The voluntary dumbing of observers in Bolton supposedly allowed the authentic lives of the workers to be seen and noted in an objective fashion (through the pretence that observers could expunge their own subjectivities). The observers watched their subjects, taking from them involuntary confessions. They perceived these to be the booty of class information which more than anything else confirmed their authority as explorers.

Besides 'objectively' listening to and watching the working class of Bolton, Mass-Observation also enlisted volunteer diarists, self-selecting 'subjective cameras' coming mostly from the middle- and lower-middle classes and making up a National Panel. In this case, Mass-Observation worked to enable the newly voluble classes of non-professional writers or speakers to be read and heard, to signify at some higher 'national' level in the publication of books. Harrisson and Madge edited information from the diaries into the fragmented, cross-cut prose of *May 12* (1937), or co-ordinated it in *Britain* (1939). Their roles as editors were less important to the success of the project than the diarists' accepting the challenge to write as part of a collective enterprise. Along with their acceptance went Mass-Observation's duty to preserve and possibly to use the diaries in publications. Hence the diarists broke their silence for the promise of a voice. The books showed these volunteers had indeed confessed themselves, emerging into the light from what Orwell in another context called England's 'shadowy caste-system' (Orwell 1937: 154).

Photography was marginal to Mass-Observation. As part of the lexicon of discovery, it appeared to lack a grammar, or to be useful only as the visual equivalent of a simple sentence, joining things together. Other than this, it was fraught with difficulties: pictures were hard to obtain for practical reasons; they were too expensive for Mass-Observation to print them in books; they were apparently more open to interpretation than factual lists; they were only illustrations to the main published work, which was drawn from the written accounts; in the early days they were the work of Spender working by himself, and so were unsupported by similar types of records. Despite this, Harrisson in meetings was constantly issuing lists of possible subjects to photograph, so much that, as Spender says, 'we didn't really do enough. There should have been five photographers working, not one' (Smith and Picton 1978: 6). The inadequate coverage of subjects, felt by both Spender and Harrisson at the time, meant that photography occupied an uncertain position within an organisation which was deeply fractured in other ways, with personality clashes and disagreements over methods (Jeffery 1978; Stanley 1990). But the uncertainty attached to photography reveals much about the explorers' methods and preoccupations.

Spender was already a well-known press photographer, and in 1935 became the *Daily Mirror*'s 'Lensman' (Spender 1982: 11). Sometimes, as with factory work, he would get permission to take photographs, knowing that managers would be wary of his work in case any of it might be used 'in evidence against' them. None the less, he disliked constructing the picture, and getting permission seemed to destroy the spontaneity of the shot. Consequently he 'was more interested in secret photography' (Spender 1982: 20). Harrisson, who knew of Spender through personal contacts, persuaded him to work in Bolton for nothing. Reminiscing in 1978, Spender thought he remembered staying for about twenty weeks in all, staying for five days to about three weeks in occasional expeditions (Smith and Picton 1978: 6). In 1982, he remembered making about half a dozen visits, of not more than a week each time (Spender 1982: 20). He took photographs at Harrisson's request, but 'without anything except the vaguest plans for their possible use, they remained virtually unknown and unused during four decades' (Spender 1982: 8).

This photography which remained secret for so long began in secrecy. It started with a double concealment – Spender was already the anonymous 'Lensman', and now he tried to be not so much nameless as invisible. Using his experience with miniature cameras, he concealed one under his coat and pretended he was not a photographer at all (sometimes catching his coat in the photograph, and inadvertently inscribing himself and his methods in the picture, as we see in the untitled image from the 'Street Life' section of his book *Worktown People* (see page 157). In addition, he was

59. Humphrey Spender, 'Library reading room', Bolton, 1937–38.

working in a renamed place – 'Worktown' was the pseudonym for Bolton. Everything now involved roundabout manoeuvres – false names, secret identities, remaining foreign in a foreign land and evading detection.

A sequence of events beginning with instructions from Harrisson characterises Spender's espionage-like routine. After discussing possible topics, Spender would venture out into Bolton with Harrisson's 'voice ringing in [his] ears', telling him to notice such details as the different ways people hold teacups. Harrisson would ask, for example, 'what do they do with their little fingers, are they sticking them out indicating they are socially superior?' This sort of detailed instruction (in which, incidentally, Harrisson showed himself oblivious to upper-middle class prejudice against the genteel habits of the lower-middle class) was enough to inspire Spender to take photographs (Spender 1982: 17). Instructions were followed by Spender's raid to bring back booty, which was then examined for clues. The pictures, however, seemed inconclusive: those taken indoors in poor light failed to show 'the kinds of interior that Tom Harrisson would imagine were going to illustrate the ordinary life of

60. Humphrey Spender, untitled photograph of street and mill in Bolton, 1937–38.

people', or they 'caricatured' the truth, as when Harrisson accused him of making 'serious' headmistresses look comic or freakish (Spender 1982: 17). So the cycle would begin again with Harrisson's exhortations and Spender sent on forays to collect more evidence, often looking from the side, as in 'Library reading room' (on page 160).

Spender went out to photograph according to instructions, but could not directly approach his subjects. He did not dare enter people's houses because they would change from being their 'normal' selves, and Harrisson was 'preoccupied with the likelihood of influencing, disturbing, the details of people's habitual behaviour, and literally giving a false picture' (Spender 1982: 20). Spender had to adopt 'ruses so to speak' (Spender 1982: 19). The most critical was to deflect his potential subjects' curious and suspicious gazes, to prevent them looking at him by becoming 'part of the landscape', perhaps standing in the shadows, as in the picture reproduced above of one of the mills where the woman appears to have been unaware of him.

If he was a stranger in a place where people knew each other, such as a pub, he would immediately be 'a focus of interest'. To overcome their stares, rather than defy them, he would fiddle with his camera and use any trickery or deceit to pretend he was not taking photographs until they forgot him, and continued with whatever they were doing. Becoming part of the landscape might take time, requiring the 'patient method', where he settled down for an hour or more before producing the camera (Spender 1982: 19).

Spender found spying difficult and unpleasant. It was potentially embarrassing and he knew his foreignness set him apart. He did not dress or speak like Bolton people, and sometimes he could not understand what they said to him. He recalled 'the whole landscape, the townscape, was severe and made me apprehensive...I always come back to the factor that I was constantly being faced with – the class distinction, the fact that I was someone from another planet, intruding on another kind of life' (Spender 1982: 16).

The final act occurred when Spender returned with his cull. Then Harrisson would 'literally search the whole surface of a collection of photographs for information, about small details – the number of rings that people were wearing on their fingers, whether they were wearing horn-rimmed glasses, how many people had beards...how many people had cloth caps in a football crowd. It was factual data, of every kind, that he wanted from photographs' (Spender 1982: 20). After the initial looking and enumerating, Harrisson seemed to have no idea what to do with the photographs. The excitement lay in collecting. He was obsessed with data, collecting 'as much raw material of all kinds as possible, and he saw the photographs as part of that: in a sense, the main thing was that they were there'. Over the years, Spender writes, Harrisson came to view the photographs 'from time to time, and he was always very enthusiastic. He had a standard thing to say: "One day these will be fantastic, they will be of great use. At the moment we haven't enough money to produce a book, but it's very important to keep them" ' (Spender 1982: 21).

The photographs were largely unusable at the time and often could not be interpreted. The material Spender gathered was so diverse, or seemingly inconsequential, that neither he nor Harrisson knew how to record it. The photographer was unable to make sufficient notes at the scene to provide captions later, and in some cases the location was forgotten even in the short time it took to print the negative. Spender, Harrisson and others would have to try to locate the places from memory. So here were social explorers armed with a method and a machine which prised *something* away from the objects of study, but the exact nature

61. Humphrey Spender, untitled photograph of hostile man in a pub, Bolton, 1937–38.

and use of that thing was a mystery. The photographs had been taken in line with observational practices which apparently produced certain types of knowledge in abundance – especially knowledge concerning relationships, movement, narrative structure. In this respect photographs were disappointing: the reader could never be sure, unless told of the whole circumstance by the photographer, whether a man holding up his hand in the 'vaults' of an unidentified pub was a sign of greeting or warning: in the above example, the gesture was in fact a threat and an order to 'get out' (Smith and Picton 1978: 7). Allowing for the technical difficulties of poor light and so on, the promise of knowledge in the photograph was uncertain, more open to ambiguity than even a verbal account of the same scene.

What Harrisson and Madge, especially, intended was that the voluntary dumbing of explorers would be temporary. The verbal records were carried away and some of them re-presented in the form of books, so that the explorers and their subjects, to some extent, demonstrated their eloquence to audiences of readers. Thus the spoils of the journey signified not only whatever was found in that place, but reflected on the skill and foresight of the explorers themselves. The only type of spoil to fail to give credit to the observers was the cache of photographs. It seemed altogether more intractable to read and publish, since there was no framework for seeing the work of the inquisitive photographer as similar in status to the work of writers. So the 'information' of the photographs piled up and was forgotten. The observers had not intended this amnesia. Nor could they have guessed that some forty years and more would pass before certain voices would be heard again, or their imprints seen for the first time in the 1970s with the rediscovery of Mass-Observation, the increased status for documentary photography as authored work, and the elevation of Spender as an art photographer before differently educated audiences of viewers.

PHOTOGRAPHS AS INTERRUPTIONS AND PROOF

For Orwell, travelling from England to Burma was a journey to the outside only in the sense of confronting foreigners at the edge of Empire. Otherwise, the journey was an ordinary imperial trip, with eyes already accustomed to the sights and customs of strangers long before arrival. The journey was always along the inside of his world, a journey intended to reveal not the stranger's strangeness but the foreigners' familiarity. Travelling, Orwell discovered what he already knew to be true: 'the whites were up and the blacks were down' (Orwell 1937: 180).

On leaving Burma for England in 1927, Orwell brought back first-hand knowledge of the difference between 'oppressors' and the 'oppressed'. Fully conscious of the sharpness of difference, he wanted to expiate his 'bad conscience' by joining the oppressed 'against the tyrants'. He realised that the journey he needed to make was not across the surface of empire, because there he would go on policing the blacks or the poor whites for the boss class. He had 'to submerge' himself, 'to get right down among the oppressed', escaping 'not merely from imperialism but from every form of man's dominion over man' (Orwell 1937: 179–80). The result was that he became more class-conscious than before. As a member of 'a shabby-genteel family' Orwell felt he was 'in much the same position as a family of "poor whites" living in a street where everyone else is a negro. In such circumstances you have got to cling to your gentility because it is the only thing you have; and meanwhile you are hated for your stuck-up-ness and for the accent and manners which stamp you as one of the boss class' (Orwell 1937: 154–7).

Back in England, he 'realised that there was no need to go as far as Burma to find tyranny and exploitation. Here in England, down under one's feet, were the submerged working class, suffering miseries which in their different way were as bad as any an oriental ever knows. The word "unemployment" was on everyone's lips' (Orwell 1937: 180–1). Orwell went to the coal-mining areas of Lancashire and Yorkshire, partly because he wanted to see 'what mass-unemployment is like at its worst, partly in order to see the most typical section of the English working class at close quarters' (Orwell 1937: 153). This was the only way of deciding whether 'things at present are tolerable or intolerable'.

In order to develop 'a definite attitude on the terribly difficult issue of class', Orwell undertook some famous downward journeys – either to live among the 'down and outs' in Paris and London who were figuratively 'the lowest of the low', or literally, 'travelling' in a mine – which meant walking (bent double) in subterranean passages to the coal-face (Orwell 1937: 25–30). The aim of these new journeys of submergence was to empathise and understand for himself what these others already were.[1] He never intended to become like them, but continued to embrace difference, sometimes cursing it but always using it in the end as the way to escape from whatever low levels he reached. Of his time living with the working class, he wrote that 'though I was among them…I was not one of them, and they knew it even better than I did. However much you like them, however interesting you find their conversation, there is always that accursed itch of class difference, like the pea under the princess's mattress' (Orwell 1937: 188).

Stamped as a member of the boss class, but excluded from it in England as a member of the 'shabby-genteel', Orwell had no position in the London 'town' or county lives of his social superiors. Similarly, he had no place among the workers he had been taught to fear but had come to admire. His journeys were a solution – not to the problem of class but to the problem of his position. He set out to retrieve enough to discomfort the centres of the upper-middle class and to negotiate for himself an identity among the intellectuals of the south of England. In other words, he chose a displacement which was not off the map, but a journey of exile restoring him to the literary centre. This journey was also difficult and uncertain. However, it was not the intention of his editor, Victor Gollancz, that Orwell should write a literary book. In this section we shall see how photographs signalled the clash of intentions over Orwell's *The Road to Wigan Pier*.

In January 1936 Gollancz commissioned Orwell to write about 'working men in poverty and unemployment'. Consequently the author spent two months in the North, living with working people in Wigan, Barnsley and Sheffield (Crick 1980: 278–9). Then he wrote it up as *The Road to Wigan Pier*. On sending the manuscript to his agent on 15 December 1936, Orwell thought it was 'too fragmentary and, on the surface, not very left-wing', so (as Crick says) 'the chances of Gollancz including it in the already highly successful Left Book Club were small' (Crick 1980: 279).

Receiving the book the same day, Gollancz was disturbed to find that it fell into two halves – the first being a description of Wigan and the second consisting of attacks on other Left writers and middle-class socialists (Orwell 1937: 214). Despite his reservations, Gollancz hoped to make it a Left Book Club choice, and invited Orwell to come in to discuss the idea. Within a week Orwell left England to fight in Spain, leaving the negotiations to his literary agents. Gollancz tried to persuade the agents to publish the book in two versions – with Parts One and Two appearing together in a small public edition in hardback, while the large paperback edition of the Left Book Club would contain only the first half on Wigan (Crick 1980: 309). They refused to agree to this. Gollancz set about altering the text so that he could publish it whole without compromising the Left Book Club. The specific ways in which he altered Orwell's book resulted from what he and his other editors believed to be accurate documentary expression rather than any feeling that it was marked by overblown writing and diatribe.

The Road to Wigan Pier was not a careful and sophisticated political analysis. It was wide open to criticism from reviewers for generalising Left 'mentality' without mentioning facts or figures, the Labour Party or the Trades Union Congress (TUC), for ignorance of socialist theory, and for stressing the squalor of the lodging house to the exclusion of 'the humanity of even the most poverty-stricken working-class homes' (Crick 1980: 343). As co-editor Harold Laski complained that it ignored 'all that is implied in the urgent reality of class antagonisms. It refuses to confront the grave problem of the state. It has no sense of the historic movement of the economic process. At bottom, in fact, it is an emotional plea for socialism addressed to comfortable people' (Laski 1937: 276).

To force the book into the mould of the Club, Gollancz decided to write an introduction which distanced himself, Laski and Strachey from what he called the

62. Anonymous photograph of 'Coal searchers', from George Orwell, *The Road to Wigan Pier*, 1937.

'highly provocative' details and general argument of the book (Orwell 1937: xiv). Gollancz also instructed his deputy chairman Norman Collins to find some photographs, which he intended to insert in the text. This second intrusion, without permission from Orwell, would take advantage of the convention that photographs were straightforward documentary proof. Collins wrote to the secretary of the Housing Centre in London saying 'Mr. George Orwell has written a new book (which we are making a future choice of the Left Book club) dealing with life in the distressed areas. Any photographic material of this kind which you could let us have – either slum interiors or exteriors – would therefore serve a most useful purpose. We are going to make the book fully documentary, both as regards the text and as regards the pictures, and the finished work will probably contain some forty-eight plates' (Taylor 1983: 31).

In fact, thirty-three photographs were printed on thirty-two plates. Drawn from various photographic agencies serving the newspaper industry, they showed slum conditions and mining in various parts of Wales, Durham, and the London districts of Stepney, Poplar, Limehouse and Bethnal Green. None of them show places which Orwell talked about, though (as in 'coal searchers' reproduced above) they illustrate activities he described.

There were no pictures from Wigan and surrounding areas at all. This omission was probably fortuitous rather than deliberate policy, given the speed with which the publishers were working. Only Ethel Mannin, writing in the Independent Labour

Party's *New Leader*, noted that the photographs were of slums in South Wales and London, but apparently she was not concerned that Orwell never talked about these places in his text. To the contrary, the generalised notion of seeing-is-believing showed that 'appalling housing conditions' were spread across the country, giving Orwell's remarks more general validity (Mannin 1937: 5).

Introducing photographs seems to have had the desired effect on reviewers and readers of the Left Book Club edition. When the unheated, somewhat remote pictures of journeyman reporters were sewn into the book, they changed its tenor, and made it more factual. A reviewer noted that 'photographic "documentaries"' saved the text, countering the 'incantation' of the prose with proof (Miles 1937: 726). At least six reviewers stated that the factual accuracy of the account was established by photographs (see Calder-Marshall 1937: 382; Goldring 1937: 505).

One anonymous reviewer in the *Times Literary Supplement* thought that Orwell himself had 'provided photographs as well as words, since it would be difficult to imagine such places, without visual help to one's imagination' (Anon 1937: 238). Photographs could do nothing to save Orwell's political arguments, but as records they placed two limits on the prose. They prevented it from being only an emotional plea, and they were also the measure of Orwell's literary invention. They drained the too-bright colour from 'vivid' prose (stigmatised as the author's personal interpretations), and strengthened the reality of deprivation by being so banal, ordinary, transparent and apparently empty of style.

The 'factual' authority of newspaper photographs, anchoring stories in a visible reality, was the context for Gollancz's decision to insert them in this descriptive text, moving it towards the authority associated with documentary. Intruding documentary into the book, however, turned it into a medley of conflicting 'voices'. While Orwell talked of Lancashire and Yorkshire, the photographs reproduced views of Wales and London; while Orwell attacked the Left, it distanced itself from Orwell through the foreword and the photographs. The Left interrupted the authorial voice, and disturbed the credibility of its witness. This interruption was significant, not to say momentous, and yet it was polite. The foreword was circumspect, and the photographs helped to extend the polemic to other distressed areas. Nevertheless, by the addition of the journalistic photographs, there could be no doubt that the value of Orwell's text was supposed to signify no more than 'accurately observed information'.

Gollancz's use of journalistic photographs could not illustrate Orwell's sense of personal displacement, his attempt to 'submerge' himself and so expiate his guilt at being one of the oppressors. This would only be possible, he wrote in *The Road to Wigan Pier*, if he could abandon class. He saw that 'to get outside the class-racket I have got to suppress not merely my private snobbishness, but most of my other tastes and prejudices as well. I have got to alter myself so completely that at the end I should hardly be recognisable as the same person' (Orwell 1937: 198). This was not only a difficult process, he wrote, but might still not end class conflict. On the contrary, when 'we set out to greet our proletarian brothers [we might find that they] are not asking for our greetings, they are asking us to commit suicide. When the bourgeois sees it in that form he takes to flight, and if his flight is rapid enough it may carry him to Fascism' (Orwell 1937: 201).

The Road to Wigan Pier was published in the spring of 1937. In the autumn of the same year Gollancz published another book on the condition of Britain, closely modelled on Orwell's book. Written by Wal Hannington, it was called *The Problem of the Distressed Areas*. The book contained a short preface, this time by Laski. Here, as in Gollancz's introduction to *The Road to Wigan Pier*, he distanced the Left Book Club editors from the communist views of the author. Even so, there was a difference between Hannington and Orwell: the communist must be taken seriously because he 'has literally lived with and for the unemployed ever since the close of the war. Whatever be our differences from the political views he holds, there are few people in this country who know their problems so intimately as he does' (Hannington 1937: 9). Whereas Orwell had avoided 'facts and figures', Hannington gave fully documented evidence from parliamentary reports, official government statistics and Fabian Research Bureau papers on the effects of malnutrition, for instance, and the implementation of the Means Test for state benefits. Hannington's authenticity was unquestioned since the written text was so dense with factual as well as eyewitness proof that the photographs simply added their weight, rather than largely supplying the truth-value of the text as had been the case in *The Road to Wigan Pier*.

Hannington had already published one social documentary book with photographs, *Unemployed Struggles 1919–1936*, with forty-two photographs, mostly of civil strife. Hannington himself chose the pictures for *Distressed Areas*, and owned the copyright. The book used thirty-two photographic plates to support his text, which dealt with (among other things) the causes of the slump, the 'slave camps' (Ministry of Labour Instructional Centres), the policy of transferring individuals and

63. Wal Hannington, 'Charge! Hyde Park during 1932 hunger march', from *The Problem of the Distressed Areas*, 1937.

families from the distressed areas, the resettlement of industrial workers on the land as smallholders, and the danger of fascism among the unemployed. The pictures included shots of slums, derelict steelworks, miners at the coal-face, men at the Labour Exchanges, crowds of men and women queuing for jobs, and a charge by mounted police in Hyde Park during a Hunger March in 1932 (reproduced above). Apart from this picture and three others (the visit of King Edward VIII to the derelict steel works of Dowlais, the disaster at Gresford where 265 men were entombed, and a slum clearance in Camberwell) none of the rest could be dated accurately. The photographs of slums, camps and the unemployed were general examples of what Hannington described in his text. Nevertheless, he succeeded in closing the gap between his experience and the photographs. They seemed to support each other. In addition, his text was full of facts and instances which did not fly in the face of the political and economic theorists. The political message of the book was of fundamental importance. Strachey and others had demonstrated in general theory the breakdown of capitalism: the Distressed Areas of Britain were the living proof. *The Problem of the Distressed Areas* and *The Road to Wigan Pier*, as they were published by the Left Book Club, were intended to encourage political action. Hannington's book was more fully realised than Orwell's because it was determinedly factual and firmly rooted in the particular crisis of the Distressed Areas. Despite this, Hannington's book faded more quickly from public view precisely because it was a polemic deriving its power from the convergence of a political crisis with the moment of documentary 'fact'. These concerns and Hannington's work all receded into historical time. In the long run,

Orwell's book fared better. Like Mass-Observation, though in a different key, Orwell tried to efface himself before the working class in order to bring back the truth about their situation. He then wrote his discoveries and himself into the established framework of literary journeys of exploration.

THE ENGLISH AT HOME

So far, in the work of Mass-Observation and Orwell, we have seen two strategies for the traveller – strategies for infiltrating the working classes and returning with seemingly objective knowledge of them won by turning the research field into a confessional for overheard remarks and overseen acts. Beliefs about truth, with the power of cultural myth, supported both approaches. The photojournalistic truth-value used to change Orwell's book was based on the myths of the eyewitness, and of the photograph as a transparent window on the world. In a similar vein, Mass-Observation used Spender as an 'unobserved observer', a basis for gathering truth by using a hidden miniature camera. In this system, truth would arise of its own accord as long as the actions of the stranger were kept secret. In both strategies, the authors pretended to absent themselves in order to gather more authentic information for later use in books. Orwell's publishers thought his text could not stand on its own. It was only returned to its original form (dropping the editor's introduction and the photographs) once the Left Book Club and their concerns were past. Spender's text emerged as the work of an author at an even later date from its inception, since it was not intended to be such at the moment of production, had no preferred original form, and had not been deliberately suppressed so much as hidden by other data which it was easier to read.

Photojournalism was the pre-text in both cases. In each case it was differently perceived. On the one hand, photojournalism anchored Orwell's account to the truth-values already established in the newspaper industry. On the other hand, Mass-Observation was committed to investigation of these values, and sought to replace mystifying journalism with anthropology, taking the data from a supposedly neutral ground of eavesdropping and spying. Stepping outside the realm of documentary realism which was practised and understood by the press, Spender's text immediately entered obscurity. There was no simple or methodical way to read his photographs, and so they fell into a limbo. They emerged only when the immediate historic project

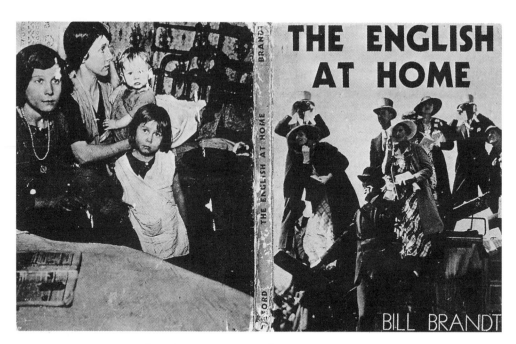

64. Bill Brandt, front and back covers of *The English at Home*, 1936.

of Mass-Observation was past, and the photographs could serve in the context of the 1970s' rediscovery and revision of 1930s documentary realism.

The third strategy for the traveller was adopted by Bill Brandt in *The English at Home*. Brandt was neither a secret observer nor an eyewitness, but someone who stood at the thresholds of different classes, taking and inventing photographs, and weaving them into a narrative of Englishness more intricate than is suggested by the rich/poor contrast of the front and back covers (see illustration above). Since narration rather than fact was the driving force, the threshold strategy did not decentre the author. Indeed, his position was the key to reading the book. However, when the book was published in 1936 the importance of the photographer as narrator went unnoticed; instead the book was misrecognised as documentary. As we have seen with Orwell, authorship presented problems in documentary, and Brandt's book also suffered from the tension between photographs as facts and authors as storytellers.

The English at Home only achieved its status within Brandt's *oeuvre* once the cultural production of the 1930s was revalued in the photo-historical discourse of the late 1970s. Only then was Brandt's position as the leading British art photographer of the period secured in a series of exhibitions and publications of his work, though this was much extended and refined by Mark Haworth-Booth's and David Mellor's seminal *Bill Brandt – Behind the Camera* of 1985, and by Ian Jeffrey's *Bill Brandt, Photographs 1928–1983* of 1993 (see Turner 1975; Mellor 1981; Haworth-Booth 1984; Haworth-Booth and Mellor 1985; Jeffrey 1993).

Brandt was a threshold figure in English society because, unlike Orwell and Spender who were from the upper-middle class, he was a foreigner (born of an English father and German mother, but living for much of his young life in Germany, Switzerland and France). Whereas the other travellers were caught in the resurgence of social concern within their native country and in the traditions of exploration which sent them out of the capital into the distressed areas, Brandt was a stranger first and foremost. Whereas the point of reference for the other travellers was the metropolis, which they left behind, much of Brandt's work in *The English at Home* depended upon his having access through his family to wealthy houses, journeying to those marvellous places, the hearths of Mayfair. Set down in them, he drew not from the culture of his family but from the wider field of art and photographic developments in Europe already established by the late 1930s, and which he brought to London. He found Surrealism suited his temperament, and rejected the new realism of German photography with its penchant for 'extraordinary angles' or for photographs of the unfamiliar, 'such as a close-up of the heart of a cabbage' (Brandt 1948: 11–13). Brandt's aim was to begin with the familiar but transcend it. His journey was intended to continuously fashion himself as an outsider, a stranger who prized and sustained his ability to view England 'as familiar and yet strange': in 1948 he said 'It is part of the photographer's job to *see* more intensely than most people do. He must have and keep in him something of the receptiveness of the child who looks at the world for the first time or of the traveller who enters a strange country' (Brandt 1948: 11, 14).

This explanation, even if it had been available to his publishers and audience in 1936, may not have dislodged them from their preoccupation with documentary realism. For instance, in 1934 the art publisher Anton Zwemmer turned down *The English at Home* because he thought the opening picture of a gull in the fog over the Thames was a 'fake, a collage' of two separate prints. For Zwemmer, as for most publishers of topographic books and consumers in the 1930s, the value of photography depended on its veracity or documentary truth-value (Haworth-Booth and Mellor 1985: 12).

The book was quickly accepted by the publishers Batsford who also misrecognised it. Batsford saw *The English at Home* as another travel book, and they thought it was 'the answer' to a German rival's series covering 'works of art and architecture and separate towns and cities' (Haworth-Booth and Mellor 1985: 12). They packaged it as a companion to Paul Cohen-Kortheim's travel book *The Spirit of London* (1935), introduced by the journalist Raymond Mortimer who was also invited to introduce Brandt's work.

Unlike the publishers, Mortimer recognised the book for what it was: the work of someone who remained a stranger to England. Most people who travelled abroad knew what it was like to return home and find it strange, but they never sustained this feeling. In his introduction, Mortimer wrote that a 'hundred details which are peculiar to England' were easy to see after an absence; only then would 'you [catch] a surprising vision of your country' for an hour or two, seeing it 'through foreign eyes'. Then 'you' would quickly forget this experience, and become blinded by familiarity (Brandt 1936: 3). Unlike the English traveller, Bill Brandt saw England afresh, because though he was 'British by birth…he has spent most of his life abroad, and has thus been able to pick out what makes this country different from others' (4). As a foreigner and a Britisher, Brandt occupied an unusual space between states, places and conditions. He was present in a way that Spender could never be, but he was also entirely absent, separated from his own social roots. By 1936, Brandt was no longer who he was (a total stranger), but neither had he changed into what he was to become (a great British art photographer). As a foreigner gazing with apparent dispassion on the great disparity between the rich, middling and poor classes of England, Brandt occupied a moral betwixt-and-between. He observed strangers from a position unoccupied by the English; he was neither truly inside nor outside, occupying instead a liminal place not identified with any English class position. As a foreigner, he was structurally invisible to the class-conscious English.

Mortimer did his utmost to bring Brandt into the field of vision. In order to centre Brandt in England, Mortimer made the reader complicit in the journeys of strangers. He shifted ground between several positions, presenting Brandt as a foreigner able to make England 'strange' for longer than a 'native', and as an artist who had 'the artist's faculty for being surprised and excited by things other people would not notice'. In case this notion was considered to be disturbingly modernist rather than fashionably up-to-date, Mortimer added yet another attribute to the photographer: Brandt was an 'anthropologist [who] seems to have wandered about

England with the detached curiosity of a man investigating the customs of some remote and unfamiliar tribe' (Brandt 1936: 4). Of course, this argument from anthropology was familiar, and would have anchored Brandt in the English tradition of self-examination and critical scrutiny of the social scene if he had been writing rather than taking photographs, an activity which had long remained peripheral to social reform but which became increasingly popular in the late 1930s in magazines such as *Picture Post* (Hall 1972; Keating 1976).

For the purposes of exposition, Mortimer himself adopted the position of an outsider. He insisted on finding the English entertaining and infuriating, giving as an example their peculiar beliefs about clothes. Dress codes, he argued, were so bound by tradition, the state, and social class that they were readily understood by insiders, but so arcane that it would have been impossible 'to explain these customs to an intelligent cannibal from Equatorial Africa!' (Brandt 1936: 5). By inverting the process of reading, so that it was not from the centre to the periphery, but from the edge of civilisation to its heart, Mortimer prepared the ground for Brandt's view of England. He used the different perspectives of the foreigner, the artist and the anthropologist to cover up the apparent disjuncture in the book, the distance between seeing the English as comfortable and seeing them as condemned to live in 'hovels'. He claimed the tension between art and anthropology was the book's strength, amusing English readers with their own foibles, and also 'shocking' them with the stark contrasts between rich and poor. According to Mortimer, the urgency of Brandt's project rested in its depiction of 'humiliating squalor', which must 'modify' 'one's pleasure at being English'. Mortimer made no apology for sounding 'Bolshy', as it was 'not *talking* about these facts which makes people Communists' but the 'facts themselves'. If freedom in England was in danger, he argued, this stemmed not from communism but from the failures of capitalism so clearly seen in the photographs: 'children are less well nourished than our dogs and worse housed than our pigs' (Brandt 1936: 8).

In his attempt to site Brandt in England, Mortimer revealed his conception of readers' preoccupations. He engaged in a reasonable, reformist debate, which depended on showing that the true subject-matter of anthropology remained the working class. The middle classes, though dangerously complacent, were also the guardians of liberty and should awaken to their responsibilities.

Mortimer claimed the real divide between rich and poor was evident in the photographs, which were 'not of actors in realistic stage-sets, but of people as they are, in their real and unescapable surroundings' (Brandt 1936: 7). He claimed the book was mixing two other levels of signification – realism, which was reserved for the anthropological study of the working class, and theatre, which provided the stage-sets for many of the scenes of the upper- or middle-class life used to contrast with the squalor of the slums. But as David Mellor makes clear in his important essay 'Brandt's Phantasms', 'a very great number – perhaps the majority – of the photographs are posed by his English family…staging and restaging residual memories and childhood phantasies under his direction of their family dramatics' (Haworth-Booth and Mellor 1985: 83). In addition, Brandt used friends and members of his family as 'social actors' to stage scenes in rooms or in the night-time streets of the East End of London. Mortimer may never have known the extent of Brandt's staging. In any case, he could never have openly explored it in the climate of the period, when such store was set by the documentary truth-value of photography. Realism was a privileged discourse in documentary, along with surreality in art; but the myth of 'truth' in photography depended on realism or eyewitnessing rather than interior states or fiction. Mortimer claimed *The English at Home* was realistic because this enhanced its status as anthropology.

Shortly before he died in 1983, Brandt undertook another kind of journey, preparing a final resolution to his liminality, an incorporation and reception by curators and galleries then promoting art photography. He revealed details of production methods, sources of inspiration, and just how he built his personal version of England, to the art- and photographic historians, David Mellor and Mark Haworth-Booth (Haworth-Booth and Mellor 1985). To these writers goes the distinction of performing an archaeology of Brandt. With his co-operation, they retraced the documentary and surreal connections that Brandt had sped over in his few writings, establishing in more detail the biographical, intellectual and historical context for the body of work. In hearing his confession and writing it out in public in their own words, they ended Brandt's liminal state. *The English at Home* was given a new life – though one in which the class collisions of the 1930s are somewhat taken for granted and played down in comparison to the new paths opened to the biographical and psychological roots of the work.

In one of the finest essays of its kind, David Mellor abandons the traditional way of seeing Brandt in terms of genre, and reworks the complete *oeuvre*, mining much deeper into the personal sources of the work. He shows convincingly how

Obscurely and uncannily, all across his photographs, all across their formats and functions, Bill Brandt wrote a fragmentary and fantastic text. It is composed of emptiness, statues, secret chambers, and children's books. The phantasms from that text are to be found far beyond most received accounts of him; beyond the compartments of genre and style, in another place, where the imperatives of desire, dream, and phantasy disclose far grander, if darker schemes.

(Haworth-Booth and Mellor 1985: 71)

In his confession, Brandt 'admitted' to Mellor that 'It was my childhood book(s) that inspired me to be a photographer' (Haworth-Booth and Mellor 1985: 81). Brandt reshaped his family in line with his nursery text, the picture book *Cherry Stones*, and worked them into his photograph album too. As Mellor says, 'it was there, in [his wife] Eva's album, that the elements for *The English at Home* took shape as part of the album's continued memorializing of their new life in Britain from 1933 on: The Brandts at Home...Those scenes that he could not stage within his family circle he sought out in London and in Britain in general, [divining] them by Surrealist sensibility, by chance encounters' (Haworth-Booth and Mellor 1985: 83).

Having been taken by Brandt on the privileged journey into his motives, unravelling the 'concealed phantasmic project' of personal dreams, Mellor makes it clear that to bolster this discourse Brandt used the 'rhetoric of social differences that had some currency in the 30's genre of documentary' in *The English at Home* (and in *A Night In London* of 1938) (Haworth-Booth and Mellor 1985: 81). He relied on 'long-coined textual and figural stereotypes from the archives of British culture', such as the prostitutes, theatre-goers, night-workers, and policemen which 'were well sedimented in the British imagination as stock figures', a vast discourse of 'London types' stretching back into Victorian and Edwardian storytelling. According to Mellor,

A kind of lexicon of representations of British society begins to emerge, in profile, within this discursive field. In the 1930s the propagandist for the British Empire, Sir Stephen Tallents, called for 'national projection' in the media, which would stress during the period of the Depression 'the standing raw material of England's esteem in the world'. In his tract, *The Projection of England* (1932), Tallents outlined what might compose the iconography for such British propaganda. The Derby, Piccadilly, the Metropolitan Police, and London buses were cited, all of which Brandt employed in *The English at Home*. These were the received, manageable, and spectacular elements for representing England. But against them, while celebrating these institutions of the 'old time', Brandt and Brian

LATE SUPPER
SOUPER APRÈS LE THÉÂTRE

BEHIND THE RESTAURANT WHERE THE WAITERS COME OUT FOR FRESH AIR
À LA PORTE DE SERVICE D'UN RESTAURANT OÙ LES GARÇONS VIENNENT PRENDRE UN PEU D'AIR

65. Bill Brandt, 'Late supper' and 'Behind the restaurant where waiters come out for air', from *The English at Home*, 1936.

Cook, his publisher, pitted counter-images: pictures of a Dickensian squalor and deprivation, pathetic and grim. Brandt's rhetoric of darkness traced black pits in the East End, a picturesque social underworld.
(Haworth-Booth and Mellor 1985: 82)

In *The English at Home* 'the two Englands gaze[d] at each other' in contrasts too tendentious for the reviewer in the *Times Literary Supplement* who complained that 'Mr Brandt has hammered his point till it is in danger of being blunted' (Haworth-Booth and Mellor 1985: 82). Brandt used the genre of the collection of types and stereotypes of the nation and subverted it by critical juxtapositions, as we see in the rich/poor contrast in the pairing of wealthy diners and a tramp searching through the restaurant's dustbins while a waiter looks on, or in the rich/rich pairing of golf and a garden party. The reviewer, nonetheless, read the book as a social polemic in which realism succeeded in obliterating metaphor.

Brandt's long journey from the margins and his readoption by the centre, which began in 1948 with *Camera in London* and was finished for him in 1985 by David Mellor, required the overturning of the earlier readings, with the greater weight they gave to notions of realism and anthropology. It required the admission and

66. Bill Brandt, 'Golf in the rain' and 'Harrow garden party', from *The English at Home*, 1936.

valorisation of what would have been unacceptable in 1936 – the combination of family photographs, mock-ups, theatrical sets involving 'social actors' from Brandt's milieu pretending to be working-class, and a surreal sensibility in search of 'human *objets trouvés*'.

The value placed on *The English at Home* varies according to the readers. The book failed to signify in 1936 because it did not suit a popular market which was accustomed to reading photographs as direct evidence of reality. This market was not prepared to read a book which in 1985 Mellor describes as on the verge of 'deconstructing' itself: 'The Documentarist paradigms in *The English at Home* [were] riven by varieties of counter-realism', creating tension 'between documentary and its ethical and social dimension on the one hand and Brandt's irrational phantasy projections, his phantasms, on the other' (Haworth-Booth and Mellor 1985: 94). The photographer exceeded 'Documentary Realism' with 'catalogues of phantasy'; his 'adherence to a Realist text was deeply fissured, disclosing the figures of the woman's body, childhood, the obvious fictiveness of his tableaux, and strands of Surrealist codes' (Haworth-Booth and Mellor 1985: 81, 94). According to Mellor, the deep fissuring had two main consequences: firstly, it explained Brandt's invisibility in 1936. Secondly, it meant *The English at Home* was a flawed work which Brandt sought to bypass in 1948 with his journey into the transcendental. There was a third consequence when the photographer's confession and the art-historian's elaboration of it removed the book from the moment of its production and reception in the 1930s into a history of the uses for photography current in the 1980s. Writing and seeing are invariably marked by the prevailing ideology. As Abigail Solomon-Godeau argues, 'The language, terms, modes of investigation in which any cultural object can be considered are tied to the larger web of historical circumstance in which object and commentator alike have been formed' (Solomon-Godeau 1991: xxii). Brandt emerged in the 1980s in a newly privileged setting of photo-aesthetics and photo-history which were part of the current 'interweave of the social, political, and economic with the cultural in the production and reception of aesthetic artifacts' (Solomon-Godeau 1991: xxii).

Writing in the 1930s, Mortimer did not regard Brandt as invisible or the work as flawed. His major concern was the gaps between the classes, recognised in the photographs, and the danger they presented to the social fabric of England. Mellor calls these gaps a 'hierarchized, ritualized society of class gulfs and legible differences' which were supposedly 'erased' after the Second World War. Though the exposition of class and class conflict was central to contemporary ways of thinking about England, and photography was often used as proof of the great divides, it was not enough to save Brandt's book, which scarcely sold at all, slid into obscurity, and after some years was remaindered (Haworth-Booth and Mellor 1985: 13).

Brandt's disappearing book was a hybrid of warring signification, mixing documentary fact and surreal juxtapositions to the point where the simple story-book format of oppositional layout slowed or defeated the unfolding of class difference and class power. There was no encouragement to read the photographic book like a film, carrying storylines across many pages, reading images as an epitome of (or selection from) a cycle or roll of continuous narrative. When this book re-emerged as important in the 1970s, it was seen in hindsight as an early work, almost an apprentice piece, which explained some of the lack of resolution. In this resurrection, the historic intervention by a privileged explorer into unknown living-rooms was of less consequence than the abandonment of this practice in favour of transcendent art photography.

The history of Brandt's book has a bearing on both Orwell's and Spender's work. Orwell's altered *The Road to Wigan Pier* was turned into a text at war with itself by the publisher's decision to write a foreword and introduce documentary photographs. Regarded as a fiction in its original form, carrying insufficient political weight, the inadequate effort of the lone explorer was made good by the editorial team. Only when their concerns were consigned to history was the book resurrected as the author wrote it, and simultaneously misread as a true account. By putting Orwell back into the centre as its author, publishers of modern paperback editions emptied the book of its place in the historic debates over truth, reliable witnessing and their effects on political action. Once again, the fragile moment of documentary was swept aside in the pursuit of a totally different kind of authenticity.

Spender's case is not much different. His hidden photographs were neglected in a system which was unable to read them, gathering verbal testimony to the point of exhaustion. Yet in bringing Spender into the light, recent researchers and exhibition organisers have an agenda quite unlike that of the earlier social explorers. They do not share Mass-Observation's methods, nor their programme, and read the archive differently. Spender's photographs are documents of a slippage in the archive, a visual record to which there is no verbal equivalent. He signifies chiefly as a 'find' in the continuing excavation of the 1930s. His work is now seen in ways altogether different from those envisaged by Harrisson, owing something to the status of documentary photography as art, and also to the charm and nostalgia which attaches to pictures from a lost world. The repositioning of Spender has continued to obscure the photographs by locating them within the system of Mass-Observation. While we know that his pictures meant very little at the time, we also know very little about what it meant to fail to read them.

The cases of the disappearing and altered books, and the case of the hidden photographs, reveal the fragility of documentary in the late 1930s. The Second World War changed the nature of forays in the hinterland of class differences. The trope of exploration flourished in another guise, with muffled dissent replaced by a problematic unity.

6

History under fire

LOOKING FOR THE PUBLIC

WHEN FRANCE fell in 1940, *Picture Post* asserted that 'the war moves into every British family's back garden', but its photographs showed idyllic villages in four *English* counties (Anon. 1940b: 28). This slippage between England and Britain attracted no comment at the time. It was commonplace to think of England as a garden inhabited by a family (even if the wrong family members were in control – see Orwell 1982: 81). In this chapter I shall look at how writers and photographers took part in the search for an untroubled, public voice that spoke for the patriotism of all England – the touchstone for the whole nation, despite its divisions.

On a greater scale than any other war, the story of the Second World War was told through pictures, in the press and in official publications (Taylor 1991: 52–7). Photographs, films, the BBC and press reports were censored for reasons of security by the main source of news management, the Ministry of Information. The Ministry released official news and was responsible for the maintenance of morale, conducting publicity campaigns for government departments. It used photographs, posters, and pamphlets to develop a psychological and emotional culture of war which represented the British united against defeatism and the threat of invasion (Yass 1983). Since keeping up morale on the 'home front' was crucial for government, the campaign to advertise the war 'accentuated the positive'. Thus, in the way that England came to stand in for Britain, a similar slippage turned 'England as a reliable make' into 'Britain

67. Cover of *Britain under Fire*, *c*.1941.

can take it' or 'Britain carrying on'. This became the benchmark, and was repeated in numerous forms – for instance in the *Country Life* book *Britain under Fire,* in which photographs of bomb damage were intended to prove civilian resolve to potential allies – especially the USA (see illustration). As J. B. Priestley wrote in the foreword, 'let the camera tell its twofold story, of a great crime, and of a still greater people' (Priestley *c*.1941).

This positive, 'thumbs up' version of the war has been attacked by Paul Fussell in his book on understanding and behaviour in the war. He believes that 'the morale culture in wartime' was so successful that it has contributed to the power of the post-war media 'to determine what shall be embraced as reality'. Fussell writes, 'For the past fifty years the Allied war has been sanitized and romanticized almost beyond recognition by the sentimental, the loony patriotic, the ignorant, and the bloodthirsty' (Fussell 1989: preface). In order to 'balance the scales', he has looked for literary and eyewitness accounts to reveal the untarnished 'truth', privileging certain investigators who found otherwise silent people and gave them 'voice' in their books (in the manner of 1930s confessions which took on 'documentary' status through the authorship of writers). Fussell found that some of those who believed the uplifting, war publicity were disillusioned afterwards. They recognised that the dream world of songs such as 'There'll Be Bluebirds over the White Cliffs of Dover' was 'bullshit'

(Fussell 1989: 163). The optimistic songs and cheerful advertising campaigns projected through the media created an 'unreal war', a 'whole fictive world'. According to Fussell, this was the intended result of morale publicity, whereas the contrasting reality of military 'blunders' or the scientific work on atomic fission and cryptography was kept secret. These 'fascinating actualities' could not be mentioned until long after the end of the war. In their place, the official publicity machine offered the contemporary audience 'an image of pseudo-war and pseudo-human-behaviour not too distant from the familiar world of magazine advertising and improving popular fiction' (Fussell 1989: 164).

Fussell's work of clearing away the fictions of morale publicity, and allowing people to condemn it for misleading them is useful. It is limited, however, by overstatement and a ready acceptance of the power of 'media effects', or the idea that people allow what they see in the media to 'determine' their actions and understanding of reality. By separating the false but virulent media from the real but passive people, Fussell disallows the public realm. He avoids the fact that the advertising campaigns, the publications of the Ministry of Information and the press industry all produced material objects which constituted part of (and remain in) the public arena. As John Hartley argues in his book *The Politics of Pictures* on the creation of the public in popular media, it is newspapers, magazines and photography which constitute the public domain. The popular media is the place where and the means by which the public is created. Rather than dismiss this material as 'false', we have 'to look for the public in publicity' (Hartley 1992: 1).

During the war, the Ministry of Information and the press were constantly trying to frame their stories in ways which would seem true to broadly educated audiences which, though engaged, were highly differentiated and sceptical. As far as Government propaganda was concerned, the message was not necessarily accepted. For example, the poster headlined 'Mightier Yet!' showed warships and aircraft, but was so bombastic that it must have 'raised many a hollow laugh from shelterers in the tube stations during the blitz' (McLaine 1979: ill. 7, n.p.).

Historians gathering evidence of scepticism and placing it in the public domain have had to await the publication of books as different in method and widely spaced in time as Peter Fleming's *Invasion 1940*, Peter Grafton's *You, You, and You!*, and Angus Calder's *The Myth of the Blitz* (Fleming 1957; Grafton 1981; Calder 1991). Ian McLaine, in his book *Ministry of Morale*, demonstrates that the British often mistrusted official channels, especially when they were patronising or raised suspicions that the working classes were fighting for the upper classes. An infamous case was the poster which proclaimed '*Your* courage, *your* cheerfulness, *your* resolution will bring us victory', and thus separated 'you' (the many) from 'us' (the few) (McLaine 1979: 31). Errors of judgement such as this made Government look ridiculous, and in response it adjusted its campaigns to encourage harmony. It aimed its advertisements at widely different but particular groups, including mothers or single women, gardeners and factory workers. In place of the masculine heroics which characterised so much publicity in the Great War, the accent now was on different types and classes of people all pulling in the same direction. In the advertising campaigns, England was a nation which was tremendously varied but presented a united front.

The Government was concerned at the public's ability to withstand aerial bombardment. By the end of 1942, bombs had killed 43,000 civilians, and more women and children than soldiers (this rate did not continue – over the next three years the total of dead civilians rose by another 17,000) (Titmuss 1950: 335, 558–60). In order to find out whether or not people were 'taking it', in December 1939 the Ministry of Information's Home Intelligence Division gathered reports on morale after bombing raids. These were at their heaviest between 1940 and 1942, and the intelligence reports suggested that morale remained high, though possibly that was because the Division decided to measure how the public behaved rather than what it thought. Since people continued to perform their allotted tasks, the Government were not overly concerned by the sorts of evidence of open 'hysteria, terror and neurosis' gathered by Mass-Observation after the bombing of Coventry in 1940 (McLaine 1979: 119). Nevertheless, the Home Security reports were used by the Ministry to monitor the success of its campaigns, and alter them if necessary. In 1940 it found that people were both resolute and demoralised (McLaine 1979: 52–4, 62), and that some of their anger was directed at the Ministry. The reports showed that while the public appreciated the Government's recognition of their resolute qualities, they 'resented too great an emphasis on the stereotyped image of the Britisher in adversity as a wise-cracking Cockney', or propaganda which represented their grim experience as no worse than a 'torrid' game of rugby. In response, the Ministry officially abandoned the slogan 'Britain Can Take It', though the phrase continued to have currency 'in spheres outside the Ministry's control' (McLaine 1979: 125).

Though Government exerted huge financial and legal controls over the press, its

This is the village and down the road is the schoolhouse. Here the children will learn to know and love the things that are permanent and enduring ; of planting and growth, the ritual of seasons, the care of animals ; of the fecund quality of soil. For these things let us be glad. To this degree the war has lifted the reproach that we had forgotten the land—and the children.

62

68. Village scene from *Meet ...'the Common People...'*, *c.*1943.

stories were not written by censors (Gerald 1956). Nevertheless, those which appeared in magazines and newspapers during the war either suited Government or matched the tone of official pamphlets, because their aims and values were so often the same. The press depended on Government for access to information, and both shared a publicly stated belief in the patriotism of the people. The greatest difference between them was that Government was less sure of its audience than the press. The public discourse of government had to appeal to the whole nation, whereas the different titles which made up the newspaper industry wrote confidently in what they imagined to be the language of their readers (A. C. H. Smith 1975).

Both Government and the press based patriotism in 'home values' and simple history. At the level of popular, shared beliefs about history which children learned at school, it was common knowledge that 'we' had not been invaded for a thousand years. In this version of English (and consequently British) history, the British understood themselves to be diverse and yet a single nation. It was this communality that, in their different ways, the Government and press repeated. A nation which was comprised of individuals who had found common cause was best able to defend itself.

The problem for those bodies using public voices was to strike the correct tone, the one which would incorporate people rather than alienate them. They regarded Winston Churchill's speeches as suitably rousing, and the GPO, Realist and Crown Film Units borrowed his speeches to proclaim that the war was 'the common people' marching towards 'their just and true inheritance' (Carrick and Bradley c.1943; see Colls and Dodd 1985). Striking the correct note was complex, and often the safest way seemed to be to use stereotypes. For instance, this photograph taken from *Meet 'the Common People'* shows the village church, the river, and the washing hanging in the garden, while the accompanying text (which speaks of 'planting and growth' in relation to both the land and children) anchors the scene to the forces of permanence, fecundity and domesticity. Film-makers and book publishers were evidently not afraid of such sentiment, though how well it was received is less certain.

The danger inherent in public rhetoric was that it might be met with ridicule and disbelief. The 'common people' of the official imagination were resistant to the discredited promises left over from the Great War. After intelligence reports and social surveys had discovered this, the heroic imagery of soldiering and marching towards an indeterminate better future was replaced in publicity or propaganda by a lower-key, more 'feminised' sense of civilian determination among ordinary people on the 'home front'. When the defeated British army managed to escape capture at Dunkirk, this was widely reported in the press and illustrated weeklies to have been a victory for small people in small boats, civilians leading a rescue which was brave and spontaneous. This version of events has never been seriously challenged, and in popular perception Dunkirk remains a victory for the British way of life, for amateurs, for muddling through (Bond 1982). In public at least, the storytellers in press and Government imagined a range of civilian virtues and pleasures that extended from the picture of ' "the little man", the suburban husband pottering in his herbaceous borders, to that of Britain itself as a sporting little country batting away against the

Great Dictators' (Light 1991: 8–9). For example, the photograph of children at a residential nursery is in keeping with this degree of feeling (and different from the sentiment of *Meet 'the Common People'*) (see colour plate 9) – the picture by P. H. Hennell was published in J. B. Priestley's *British Women go to War* in 1943). Here the vibrancy of the scene, which we see recorded in brilliant colours, suggests feelings for the fate of children and the role of women without the false tone of so much public rhetoric. Stock types are in evidence, but not puffed up to become caricatures which invite ridicule. Instead, the picture (and the book) is very much in the mould of inter-war conservatism.

Just as England was transformed between the wars from the masculine, heroic nation of the late Victorian and Edwardian periods into a 'feminised' country, so the idea of history itself underwent a parallel transformation. Two of the most popular historians of the period, Arthur Bryant and G. M. Trevelyan, in trying to explain the present condition of England, looked backwards to the spiritual and political achievements which preceded the Industrial Revolution when English history rested on 'the world of manor houses, country pursuits, the rule of liberal and tolerant gentlemen' (J. H. Plumb cited in Wiener 1981: 87). The appeal of this view of England increased at the same time as popular writers of fiction such as P. G. Wodehouse and Evelyn Waugh turned a sense of loss and nostalgia for an older England into gentle humour or outright farce. Heroic history of all kinds began to dissolve. One of the most famous expressions of ridicule is Sellar and Yeatman's 1930 satire on public-school history, *1066 and All That*. Sellar and Yeatman noted ironically that the Great War (a 'peaceful and inevitable struggle') deposed England as 'top Nation' in favour of America, a shift in the balance of power which put an end to 'History' altogether (Sellar and Yeatman 1989: 111–13). They wrote 'History is not what you thought. *It is what you can remember*', and what people remembered were muddled bits of schoolroom patriotism left over from outmoded jingo days (Sellar and Yeatman 1989: v). At the same time as people rejected jingoism, they drew a less brittle kind of strength from the reformed sense of the nation as self-deprecating, understated, gentle, and at ease with itself. The difficulty for those addressing 'the common people' was to find the appropriate voice for patriotism. This was not straightforward, given that (in Orwell's words) their patriotism was 'not vocal or even conscious' (Orwell 1982: 42). Finding the public meant engaging its nascent, 'sleepwalking' patriotism and waking it up, to make the people consciously accept that their role in the war was purposeful.

PATRIOTISM

Orwell tried to describe English patriotism in *The Lion and the Unicorn*, which he wrote in London during the 'Blitz' of 1940. He called the book after the real and imagined beasts on the royal coat of arms and, like this crest, the book combined different histories and mythologies, subsuming them in England as the root of the nation. In a list which moved from the name of an actual country to the most abstract sensing of it, Orwell wrote 'we call our islands by no less than six different names, England, Britain, Great Britain, the British Isles, the United Kingdom and, in very exalted moments, Albion'. He declared 'the so-called races of Britain *feel* themselves to be very different from one another', but at the same time 'the vast majority of the people feel themselves to be a single nation and are conscious of resembling one another more than they resemble foreigners' (Orwell 1982: 47–8). This feeling of resemblance was surprising, given that England was 'the most class-ridden country under the sun' (52). Orwell believed that 'class-hatred' was strong, but not strong enough to destroy patriotism, which took different forms in different classes and enabled a diverse people to find common ground (48, 103; see Harrisson 1942).

Patriotism continued to bind the country together even when class distinctions loosened. Whereas in 1910 everyone could be 'placed' in an instant by their clothes, manners and accent, between the wars this was no longer the case. Orwell thought class was dissolving, or at least becoming less clear in outline in that 'indeterminate stratum' of people living a 'restless, cultureless life' centring around tinned food, magazines, radio and cheap cars (Orwell 1982: 68–9; see Summerfield 1986). He placed these glimpses of modernity among other more enduring fragments of 'the English scene', the basis of 'English civilisation' and community. The English had a culture which was distinctive and individual, and had 'a flavour of its own' which was difficult to describe precisely: 'somehow it was bound up with solid breakfasts and gloomy Sundays, smoky towns and winding roads, green fields and red pillar-boxes'. Most important of all, there was 'something in it that persists, as in a living creature' (Orwell 1982: 37).

England, to Orwell, was a mixture of contradictory forces. It was insular and xenophobic; it was riddled with class distinctions; it was more fragmented than ever, despite the development of communications; it was 'continuous', stretching 'into the future and the past'; it was patriotic without being nationalistic. The English enjoyed 'their old-fashioned outlook, their graded snobberies, their mixture of bawdiness and hypocrisy, their extreme gentleness, their deeply moral attitude to life'. They enjoyed being ordinary, private, and stubborn (37–41).

Declaring his connection with the stubborn nation, Orwell showed how determined and unbending he could be in the act of writing *The Lion and the Unicorn*. He opened the book with a description of himself choosing to sit at his desk during an air-raid rather than take shelter: 'As I write, highly civilized human beings are flying overhead, trying to kill me' (35). The German bombers' service to their country had 'the power to absolve [them] from evil', but Orwell resisted their force with his own 'national loyalty' (35). For Orwell, the act of resistance lay in beginning to record the threatened 'diversity', 'chaos' and 'muddle' of English civilisation in order to save it. Whether he actually wrote 'the English scene' during a raid, or only chose to open the book with the claim that he did so, this was an act of defiance against the perverse nationalism of the Nazis. Their system of regimentation would always be resisted by the English, who had proved themselves skilled in leading lives 'beneath the surface', unofficial lives away from 'Nosey Parkers', living 'to some extent *against* the existing order' (40–1). Orwell wrote himself into that tradition of bloody-minded opposition to threats from authority, whether coming from British officials or enemy invaders, by performing a stubborn act which he felt was *defiant*, and which was actually held up as a proud *characteristic* of the English temperament.

SURVEY

Orwell's literary, imprecise and polemical survey was part of a general scramble (begun in 1939–40 when invasion seemed likely) to record various aspects of England in order to preserve it. In its simplest form, the threat of mass destruction from the air or invasion led the English to replicate themselves on photographic paper for the purpose of insurance (Mortimer 1941: 124). This meant borrowing wholesale the recording mania of the nineteenth-century survey movement and attempt to record England in photographs. At that time, the 'whole duty of the photographer' (advanced by Cosmo Burton in 1889 – see page 54) had been to make an inventory of everything in the country. Now the idea resurfaced as something amateur photographers could do in the home without risking prosecution for taking photographs of installations of military significance (which covered almost every kind of outdoor subject). Inventories would be useful to them as individuals, since proof of house contents would help with claims for compensation. In a similar vein, private companies such as banks, legal businesses, stockbrokers, and accountants began to use photography to copy all books and documents of value.

However, from 1941 this private use of photography was restricted by limitations on the supply of photographic materials to amateurs. Inventories had to have national relevance – such as those undertaken by museums and by the Society of Genealogists which obtained supplies for amateurs to copy parish registers. Amateurs worked for the 'Central Council for the Care of Churches' on a complete photographic record of every church in the country, and the Royal Institute of British Architects oversaw the photographic work of the National Buildings Record (Mortimer 1941: 126–9). This project (begun in the survey movement) found support in the highest places, with funding from the Treasury, the Master of the Rolls as its president, and Lord Reith chairing the committee of what was then known as the Ministry of Works and Buildings (Mortimer 1942: 89–90). This survey involved other groups, such as the Royal Photographic Society, local preservation committees, architectural societies and county councils. The Ministry of Information, which was interested in recording every aspect of the war at home and overseas, envisaged even larger, open-ended records. Other official bodies were equally determined to make extensive use of photography: these included the Air Ministry, Admiralty, War Office, the Ministries of Supply, Aircraft Production, Health and Home Security, the General Post Office, the Board of Trade and the British Council (Mortimer 1941: 141; 1942: 88).

The vast scope of the work undertaken by these groups threatened to engulf them. Records piled on records, leading to stocks of pictorial information which had to be housed, catalogued and made useful by efficient systems of retrieval. The effort proved worthwhile: depositories of aerial reconnaissance, for instance, made sense as latent military knowledge (Powyss-Lybbe 1983), while other archives were used to advertise morale on the 'home front' (Moss and Box 1948).

Gathering information about England in these great archives and releasing it in the form of publicity helped to reinforce the sense of national strength within a diverse culture. Just as Orwell noticed, patriotism overrode class hatred, and the purpose of publicity was always to emphasise the place of national over local interest. It involved the pretence that antagonisms, rivalries and differences did not exist, or at least, did

69. Cecil Beaton, 'Bomb damage – St Paul's', 1940. Courtesy of Sotheby's London.

not exist 'for the duration' of the war (Harrisson 1940). The English found it difficult to pretend 'we' were one nation – it was an entirely novel requirement. This illusory harmony was especially difficult to sustain given the unusual upheaval which overtook civilians. Whereas in peacetime people could avoid each other, wartime evacuation, mobilisation, and new arrangements in industrial and office work ensured that class was thrown against class in ways which had never occurred before. Angus Calder has written that rural Britain, especially, 'was electrified by every sort of tragi-comic

Plate 13. John Kippin, 'Heritage, Markham Main , S. Yorkshire', 1993.

Plate 14. John Kippin, 'ENGLISH_IS_TORY, Alnwick, Northumberland', 1988.

Plate 15. Martin Parr, 'Stonehenge', 1989.

confrontation. Elderly gentlemen found their retirement invaded by half a dozen urchins from the slums of London or Liverpool. Neat spinsters who had agreed to take a schoolchild might be gifted instead with a sluttish mother who arrived smoking a cigarette over her baby's head and disappeared with her offspring as soon as the pubs opened' (Calder 1982: 47).

The language of morale publicity ignored local problems in order to save the idea of one nation united despite the social barriers of class. In contrast, authors working within some genres, notably the topographic book, never attempted to pretend the English were united as a whole. They aimed only at readers with 'taste' and a concern for the sort of history which is bound up in buildings. They adopted the methods of discovery rhetoric which we have already seen used in talking about scenery and factories in the late nineteenth century. A notable case is *History Under Fire*, written by the art-historian James Pope-Hennessy and published by Batsford in May 1941. The author described the recent air-raid damage to London buildings from the aesthete's point of view, lamenting lost architecture and ignoring considerations of human beings.

History Under Fire in many ways resembled other books in Batsford's topographic series, with plenty of historical fact and colour. This time, however, the author was forced to describe a world turned upside down, and readers were shown the damage in photographs. Apart from reproductions of old engravings and press-agency photographs of a few of the churches before the war, the fifty-two pictures by Cecil Beaton showed nothing but wrecked or burned-out buildings, as in the famous frontispiece of bomb damage near St Paul's (see illustration opposite).

At this stage of the war Beaton worked for the Ministry of Information and took photographs of bomb damage in London throughout 1940–41 (Danziger 1980: 40–1). He collaborated with Pope-Hennessy on *History Under Fire*, and the two men used to visit the ruins together. Modern writers on Beaton are caught between the familiar poles of claiming on the one hand that Beaton was engaged in documentary record but that, on the other hand, he enlivened this mundane task with his artistic 'vision'.

At the same time, recent writers are ready to subordinate Beaton's pictures to the art-historian's writing. For instance, Gail Buckland writes 'Pope-Hennessy and Beaton would go to the site of a once noble edifice, one to reflect and the other to photograph' (Buckland 1981: 17). This division between mental and manual labour, between thought and photography, or between historical and aesthetic sense and documentary record, was clearly important to Pope-Hennessy at the time.

In contrast to the positions of those who separate Beaton from his senior partner in the enterprise of *History Under Fire*, my own interest is not in Beaton's photographs as signs of his enhancement of documentary mode through his 'vision'. I am interested in Pope-Hennessy's determination to rise above the documentary evidence of the pictures, and the evidence of his eyes, in *his* attempt to restore London through writing and remembering. In this case, the photographs were visual texts which were literally contradicted by what the author wrote.

To countermand the evidence of the photographs, Pope-Hennessy adopted the methods used by early travel writers. He made the scene aesthetically pleasing, made it materially dense so that his readers would believe the truth of what he remembered, and finally ensured that art came to the rescue. He was determined to rebuild London, if only in his text, so the photographs were not allowed to contradict his belief in the curative powers of art. He thought the photographs might prove to be 'documentarily important' for 'posterity'. Though he refused to accept them purely as records, he granted them no more than an unspecified 'quality'. On balance, he decided the photographs invoked feelings that had artistic provenance. As records they were able 'to convey the early *horror* of the ruins, and also their *melancholy* appearance' (my italics). As art the photographs showed that London bombed was the city turned sublime in 'composition, grandeur, tragedy, the strange vitality of wreckage' (Pope-Hennessy 1941: vi).

Seeing Beaton's photographs as more artistic than factual helped Pope-Hennessy to ignore their status as evidence of destruction. To the contrary, they enabled him to begin the art of reconstruction, using his scholarship as an instrument of restoration. His commentary saved London by reversing bomb damage, turning it the right (aesthetic) side up. Ten Wren churches were burned in one night in December 1940, but in his text Pope-Hennessy was eloquent enough to conjure up 'these dear interiors' as they once had been, 'panelled, symmetrical, murky, personal, redolent of the eighteenth century, filled with monuments and busts, urns, tablets, organ cases, carved swags, pulpits and galleries, pews, hassocks, and hymn-books' (45).

When Pope-Hennessy asked himself how could they have been turned into 'heaps of ash', he decided the fault lay with modernity itself which had discarded refinement in favour of the ordinary 'banalities of contemporary destruction: the smell of burning, the nude columns, the vacant window frames'. Worse still, these 'banalities' forced him into a remarkable, personal loss of status: 'I became an amateur in Wren ruins as I had never been an amateur in Wren' (45). Pope-Hennessy saw modernity and high culture as mutually exclusive, and the clash endangered both national and personal histories. Writing the book was one way for him to restore his authority as an expert in refinement at the same time that he restored the buildings. He recovered his personal sense of place even as he saved London from banality.

The measure of success was objective: after the raid, Pope-Hennessy could count more of Wren's churches still standing than had been burned. There was a subjective yardstick too, measured by the art-historian's determination to exalt the aesthetic over all else, and to locate the continuing history of London (and so England) in its survival. The banal bombs had fallen on 'houses and streets that are not, from the historical angle, of great significance. It is a narrow, perhaps even an inhuman, viewpoint – but seen from it the bombers' attack upon our London past has failed' (Pope-Hennessy 1941: 113).

In his patrician view of the 'prospect', Pope-Hennessy never attempted to imagine the nation or even London as a whole. Moreover, he never tried to imagine that civilisation existed anywhere else but in buildings of the past. He contrasted these signatures of an old civilisation with '*Blitzkrieg*', the use of the German word signifying a German act, as if there were no equivalent in English. 'Blitz' was the word for the actions of a modernised and uncivilised race (113).

This point of view was not confined to topographic books aimed at specialist audiences. It was also expressed in *Picture Post*'s story of the 'Baedeker' raid on Bath (which is reproduced on page 197). It was one of the five (largely tourist) cities (the others being Exeter, Norwich, York and Canterbury) which were bombed between April and June 1942 in retaliation for Bomber Command's destruction of Lübeck in March that year, itself an exercise in the terror bombing of civilians under the guise of precision bombing of military targets.

Instead of turning the bombing of Lübeck to their advantage, the Germans made a propaganda error when their press and information spokesman at the Foreign Office said that in response they intended to bomb 'every building which is marked with three stars in *Baedeker*'. The British used this to claim that the Luftwaffe (on Hitler's orders) were using the guidebooks for the deliberate destruction of ancient and historic sites rather than aiming at military targets (Rothnie 1992: 131).

Picture Post, July 4, 1942

THE HOUSE THAT DESERVED A LONG LIFE
Bath's climate is kind to old age. But in one night Nazi bombs destroy work that has lasted for centuries.

THE STREET THAT IS MORE FAMOUS THAN EVER
A strange disorder comes to the boldly sweeping Royal Crescent which Wood the younger started in 1767.

ALL THAT REMAINS OF A REGENCY VILLA
A great rent from roof to basement. Walls blackened by fire. A garden filled with masonry. But next door the walls stand.

IN THE ASSEMBLY ROOMS THE CHAIR SURVIVES
John Wood the younger built the historic Rooms in 1769-71. Just before the war they were restored. Now they are gutted.

BATH—WHAT THE NAZIS MEAN BY A 'BAEDEKER RAID'

20

WALKING round Bath after the Nazi raid was like looking into an elegant drawing-room after a grimy, spiteful urchin out of the gutter has tried to do his worst in it. His spite does the guttersnipe no good : it is beyond his power to destroy the walls and furniture of the room he has invaded. All he can achieve is trouble for his betters. But while the mess remains, people of taste shudder a little, less at the amount of damage done than at the evidence that there are still people in

70. 'Bath: What the Germans mean by a "Baedeker Raid" ', *Picture Post*, 4 July 1942.

The *Picture Post* story on Bath, published in July, used eight photographs by Bill Brandt to illustrate the bomb damage to eighteenth-century buildings (Anon. 1942: 20–1; Haworth-Booth and Mellor 1985: 91). The captions' only references to human beings were to famous artists, architects and socialites of that period. Apart from the damage, the single note of regret was that 'people of taste' woke up to what 'we' were losing only when the bombing had begun (there was no mention of the 400 deaths in the raid on Bath – see Rothnie 1992: 141).

Censorship alone would have prevented *Picture Post* from publishing any details of what happened. Even so, the concentration on these historic buildings (which were relatively easy to restore) showed that the magazine chose to blame the Germans for deliberate damage to 'our heritage' while ignoring altogether the haphazard bombing which wrecked houses and shelters in working-class parts of the city.

Moreover, the article turned fascism from a political creed with appeal across classes into the image of a bad child of the lowest social class: the text claimed the fascist was like the 'guttersnipe' who wrecked the 'elegant drawing-room' of his 'betters'. Walking round Bath was 'like looking into' such a room 'after a grimy, spiteful urchin out of the gutter has tried to do his worst in it'. In this image, the Germans are not the threat at all: what the anonymous author of the caption fears is the invasion of wealthy houses by the ragged children of the poor. The author has conflated Nazi bomb damage with the destructive desires of the unpoliced and envious English. This caption withstood the editorial process, and shows that it was permissible even in a popular magazine to link guttersnipes (who might be children from industrial cities) with Nazis. After all, as the article makes clear, 'heritage' and 'taste' did not belong to everyone in the country, and those with a stake in neither were dangerous.

These stray remarks were unusual in *Picture Post*: they indicate a moment when the mask of unity slipped to allow a glimpse of prejudice against an unregenerate class. The journalists and editors must have felt the language of lower-class spoiling was appropriate when talking about art, heritage, and the special history of England which belongs to upper-class houses. These remarks demonstrate the complexity of patriotism and class even in a popular magazine such as *Picture Post*, since the editors were comfortable with this mode of address to their readers, considering them sympathetic to wealth and history rather than to poverty and envy.

LANDSCAPE FOR EVERYONE

In *The Lion and the Unicorn* Orwell showed how patriotism ran deep, and ran away from reality towards emotion. Its strength came in part from a mystical sense of the past. England was a country where the voices of ancestors or mythic leaders were heard (often through the poetry of Chaucer and Shakespeare), and where the unconquered nature of historic sites overtook their peacetime significance as holiday resorts (see, for instance, Massingham 1942; Scherman and Wilcox 1944). Landscape was a route to levels of emotion which were acceptably patriotic without being too nationalistic (in contrast to the warmongering fascists).

It had long been conventional to look at the English landscape and see through it, as it were, to the past. In 1926, C. F. G. Masterman's subsumed other nations to English history in his introduction to E. O. Hoppé's book *England*, (first published in Germany and retitled *Great Britain* when issued in London in 1929) (Hoppé 1926 and 1929). Closing his review of the isles, Masterman imagined 'looking down on England at intervals during the centuries'. He wrote of turning the wheel to move time along, pretending that he could see the history of England unfold (as in a funfair or seaside 'Mutoscope', which provided the illusion of movement when the viewer rapidly turned stills from a cine film). Masterman turned the wheel and allowed his readers to watch the country grow, pausing at key historical moments. England emerged from a prehistoric 'jungle', and was then guided by mercantilism and monasteries through the Renaissance towards the 'black blots on the landscape' that were the legacy of the Industrial Revolution (Hoppé 1926: 28; 1929: 27). Fears that the countryside would be destroyed by industry date from the early nineteenth century at least, and Masterman's comments are in a long tradition that retained its force in describing the contemporary scene.

In 1940 these fears for a blackened or suburban England were overtaken by the fear of invasion from abroad. Then Masterman's perspective on a long, unbroken English history was more relevant than anxieties about creeping industrialism. Suddenly the mythic history of the country 'unconquered for a thousand years' was central to patriotic propaganda which imagined England to be magical, and centred on the village, the squire and the sense of a community close to the past and to nature. This variegated but close-knit aspect of the English landscape meant that it would 'triumph' even if the enemy invaded. In 1941 the journalist C. Henry Warren wrote a book called *England is a Village*, in which he insisted that 'England's might is still in her fields and villages, and though the whole weight of mechanized armies roll over them to crush them, in the end they will triumph' (Warren 1941: ix). As long as people kept the 'dream' of old-fashioned villages before their 'waking eyes', England would defeat Nazi Germany, which was being portrayed by J. B. Priestley and H. J. Massingham, for example, as 'an industrial society run amok' (Priestley 1941: 21, 25; Massingham 1942: 127; Wiener 1981: 77).

In practice the desire to save the miraculous fields and villages meant that the countryside was rendered illegible to strangers. From May 1940, directional and mileage signs were removed from the highways, and some local authorities forced hotels to blank out or take down signs erected on their private property, which mentioned town names and distances (Anon. 1940a: 200). Everything that had been easily read in England before the war was dismantled, hidden or otherwise obscured by blackout and camouflage. Fields and open spaces were obstructed by concrete blocks, stones, and wire to prevent enemy planes from landing: 'Tradesmen painted addresses off their vans. Church bells were silenced, to be rung only as an invasion warning. The big garage on the main road was shut. Petrol had to be fetched from a garage right off the map' (Anon. *c*.1945: 132).

Travel for its own sake ceased, to be replaced by the obligatory, ceaseless journeying of evacuees, refugees and the military. Since most of the armed forces remained in Britain until 1944, it was they who moved around the most, 'shuttling to and fro on leave in their cumbrous equipment in cold, ill lit, overcrowded trains' on manoeuvres, or shunted to another end of the country for no apparent reason (Bond 1975: 223). Enforced train journeys and night-trekking out of the cities to avoid the 'Blitz' were two of the most familiar and unwelcome reasons for travelling into or through the countryside. It was no longer a place for pleasure, but had become a bleak refuge or blacked-out interval between destinations.

Because the countryside was no longer a simple, rural scene, or because military restrictions and petrol rationing meant it could not easily be visited for leisure, its pastoral beauty had to be remembered. As an aid, in 1941–42 Batsford reissued topographic books that had been published in the mid-1930s in their *Pilgrim's Library*. These books extolled the freedoms of travel before the war when the English had revelled in the diversity of the English landscape. The country was so different from one end to the other that the poet Edmund Blunden said no-one could agree on 'the typical English scene' (Anon. 1941–42: 3). Mocking the idea that England could be identified with a single place, he helped give weight to the idea that England's strength was unity in difference.

Before the war, the way of viewing the country that Blunden exemplified had become ordinary. From the summer of 1939 the question for writers and photographers was how to reconcile the pre-war combination of variety and familiarity with the new cut-off view and diminished experience of the landscape. They joined the convention of comforting diversity with the convention of recording current events in the established documentary mode. Bombing threatened the taken-for-granted transport systems, so these now became the object of attention in their own right. Referring to Vera Brittain's *England's Hour*, the historian Graham Dawson writes 'delays, diversion, closed railway stations and bombs on the line became a key mode' for registering the war and marking a modification of 1930s documentary (Dawson 1984: 4). Documentary, however, was not disruptive of social norms; on the contrary, it confirmed them. England was seen in two different lights at the same time – England was first made strange by war and then made familiar again because the war was fought, as the public were constantly reminded, to preserve the historical nature of English freedoms in an English landscape. The strange and the familiar were not in any direct contrast or contradiction. The tension between them was an effect of war and, in a conservative resolution to the problem of conflict, the familiar gained the upper hand in the end. This was in essence the promise and reward of victory.

Wartime viewers and readers were offered numerous small victories in the ways England was pictured and written up in books and magazines. Here the country could be seen in its variety, seen whole, and seen to be worth fighting for. The solution worked by appealing to the viewer's sense of history in three dimensions: a generalised feeling of continuity with the past – deriving in part from layered historic periods evident in the English landscape; the Romantic's love of English scenery which had become common coin by the twentieth century; and the moves made in the nineteenth century for social reform. By the 1940s, these old ideas confirmed what people already assumed to be the case. History in the form of feeling – ancestral, aesthetic and moral – was a conventional form. It resolved the puzzle of instability by turning it into the bedrock of certainty.

This conventional, stock-in-trade history appeared in the simplest and most direct speech and picture-making. We see this in advice offered to press photographers in 1939. Picture editors had begun to turn down the 'pretty-pretty' landscape views which had been best-sellers before the war, so photographers had to give them 'a war angle'. For instance, it was much easier to sell photographs of the Lake District if children evacuated from coal-mining areas were included in the foreground, with a caption saying the 'war has given [them] their first glimpse of the beauty of England' (Sansom 1939: 648). The discovery of 'beautiful England' may have been a strange experience for the children, but for magazine readers it was a recollection of what they already knew, a reminder of what the war was supposed to save. For these viewers, seeing working-class children in the pretty landscape was novel, but also showed them how wartime social change could be accommodated. If viewers had any sense of England gone wrong, the appeal and the picture showed England put to rights.

Picture editors turned down pretty views because it was no longer enough to remember the country as it had been before the war. The landscape had changed, and prepared for an impending invasion, which required it to be turned upside down, blanked out, or forbidden. Locking it up in this way protected it, and removed it from immediate experience and scrutiny. Before the war, visiting the countryside was linked to the healthy, outdoor life. Hiking and rambling was one of the most popular weekend pursuits or holiday activities, and was widely represented in the subjects printed in the photographic press (see illustrations on pages 121, 125). Class movement had caused conflict in Norfolk in the 1880s and 1890s, and the increased movement of working-class people into the countryside led to trouble with landowners in the 1930s. A well known case is the mass trespass of ramblers from the industrial city of Manchester at Kinder Scout in the Derbyshire dales in 1932 (Lowerson 1980: 276; Stephenson 1989). This led to piecemeal reforms and some increased rights of access to mountains and moors. But the war ended the idea of England as an internal battlefield. The 1930s battles between ramblers, conservationists and landowners for the land as a holiday haunt, social amenity or exclusive reserve were replaced by a search for a common purpose, and in this endeavour the landscape symbolised the English way of life even more than before. The Ministry of Information and the press promoted the idea that the diverse but beautiful landscape of England belonged to the whole people, encouraging them to see it as their own and so worth defending.

Looking through the English countryside to its past, and seeing it as the source of spiritual and patriotic renewal was a common feature of stories in *Picture Post*. Before the war it had also used picture layouts to highlight social inequalities, always

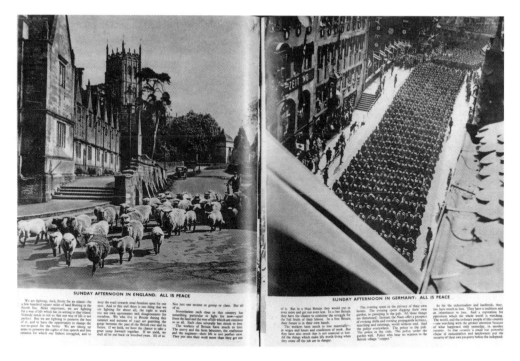

SUNDAY AFTERNOON IN ENGLAND: ALL IS PEACE

SUNDAY AFTERNOON IN GERMANY: ALL IS PEACE

71. Comparing Sunday afternoons in England and Germany, from 'What we are fighting for', *Picture Post*, 13 July 1940.

referring in positive terms to the pursuits of the decent working class. Now it used these methods of comparison and contrast to reveal the differences between Britain and fascist Germany. *Picture Post* published an especially graphic version in July 1940, when invasion fears were at their height. 'What we are fighting for' was the topic, and the front cover depicted 'The British way of life' in the shape of a boy with a cricket bat next to 'the German way of life', represented by a 'Hitler youth' (13 July). The layout contrasted fair play and boyish freedom with the narcissism of an elaborate uniform and militarism. Everything German was stiff, while everything English was genial. A photograph of Hitler saluting was placed opposite a picture of Churchill smiling and puffing on a huge cigar: the captions read, respectively, 'Totalitarianism' and 'Democracy'.

Picture Post guessed that its readers would be impatient with politicians, who had had their say, and whose aims sounded 'unreal and far-away'. To reach its audience, the magazine set out to show 'in the simplest possible terms' the things the British people – 'you and I and the man next door' – were fighting for:

72. Views of England, from 'What we are fighting for', *Picture Post*, 13 July 1940.

This is a war for everything that we can see from our own window. For the cottage at the end of the lane, and the old bridge by the mill. We are fighting for the very soil and stuff of Britain. Intact for a thousand years, it is not to be tampered with now. Lambeth Walk is not to be a stamping ground for the storm-troopers. Stratford-on-Avon is to be no site for Goering to build a castle.

It was important to forget differences at home, because each class had much to lose. The workers would lose the benefits of union and the freedom to dig their own garden or gossip in the pub. The industrialists and landowners would lose their inheritance. The 'great mass of the middle classes' (which included lawyers, journalists and tradesmen) would lose 'the pleasant margin of choice in their lives', and be dictated what was legal, what they could write, or they might be 'squeezed out of business'.

As we see here, these warnings were accompanied by photographs which showed the difference between a peaceful afternoon in the two countries. In England a shepherd walked with his flock in a village High Street, but in Germany the street was filled with marching soldiers. Other photographs showed German workers in a bar listening to Hitler's never-ending speeches on the radio, while in England workers played darts, a pleasant 'game that never ends'. The theme of the text and the pictures was that in Germany all individual freedom was lost to the mass preparing for war, while the English way of life was individual and leisurely, allowing for play on the rivers, on the greens and in the parks. 'English girls' relaxed in deck-chairs on the promenade, whereas 'German girls' sat in lecture halls and were given a 'good talking to' by Nazi leaders. In Britain, families sat down to tea together, whereas in Germany children were encouraged to denounce parents to the police for criticising 'the Nazi regime'. The caption to a picture (reproduced above) of a man by a half-timbered house read, 'England: where a man's home is still his castle'. A photograph of a country cottage stood for 'England: where each one can work out his own life'. People in a park were said to enjoy 'England: where it is still no crime to lie on the grass, to speak one's mind, to wear clothes instead of uniform'. In contrast, the Germans had set 'race against race, religion against religion, class against class', and the picture spreads showed the victims of persecution paraded in the streets, interrogated, or marshalled into concentration camps (for German propaganda against England, see Knop 1939).

According to the publicity, though England appeared peaceful and relaxed, the country was no longer simply full of genial, accommodating people, whose genius was compromise. Instead, they combined two popular forms of self-image: a proud history of battle against would-be invaders from mainland Europe, and the stubborn streak in the British character. Thus armed, they mobilised to withstand the threat from Germany. In 1940 readers of *Illustrated* saw imposing photographs of Dover Castle, 'the key of England' which had been 'in the front line of Britain's history for centuries' (24 August). The old castle was still a rampart with thick, upstanding and unbreached walls, linked to the natural barriers of the famous white cliffs. At the same time, and inevitably so, the coast was no longer a resort, but had been turned inside out. The beach at Dover, like other points on the south and south-east coast vulnerable to invasion, were transformed into a 'Defence Area' and so closed to holidaymakers. Another picture story in *Illustrated* in 1940 showed the cliffs of the 'Channel front' photographed through the barbed wire which lay along the shoreline. The caption spoke of the topsy-turvy effect of defence which closed the beaches and promenades:

'Gone are the bathing belles, the motor caravans, the ice-cream stands and the pleasure craft that were so integral a part of our English seaside in summer. Now the grim, majestic panoply of war has succeeded such pleasant amenities, and wire entanglements, trenches and gun positions tell their own tale of an England at war and on guard' (7 September).

The cliffs at Dover came to stand for a complete ring of natural bulwarks. Moreover, the white cliffs remained unsullied. The barrier of the cliffs also stood in for a message of farewell and recognition as airmen, and troops later, left them behind and returned to them as a marker of what was supposed to be the absolute and inviolate boundary of the country.

THE BATTLE OF BRITAIN

Though the beachhead never fell to invading armies, the symbolic, protective coastline was breached in daylight almost every day in the summer and autumn of 1940 by the Luftwaffe. From August to October 1940 the Germans bombed Britain for eighty-four days and nights. According to the Ministry of Information pamphlet on the battle, the enemy lost 2,375 aircraft in daylight, a figure which excluded those lost at night and those severely damaged but escaping to France. In contrast, the Royal Air Force lost 375 pilots killed and 358 wounded: 'such was the Battle of Britain in 1940' (MOI 1941: 31–2).

During these air raids, the picture press remained optimistic, and after the British won the victory the Ministry of Information's pamphlet demonstrated how alive it was to the variegated nature of the reading public, drawing on ways of looking and speaking to its audience which were already established in the popular press.

In the early days of the battle, the illustrated press showed civilians looking upwards for signs of threat and salvation as home defences engaged the enemy. This line of sight, which is the civilian equivalent of military targetting in which eyeshot precedes gunshot, was already a popular viewpoint in the weekly magazines (Virilio 1989: 2–3). Pictures of civilians looking up had two effects. They showed that the topsy-turvy world could be set right by the eyeline artillerymen used to shoot down the enemy, and that by looking up civilians were as vigilant as gunners or Home Guard spotters. Equally important, civilians with uplifted gaze suggested they were optimistic, looking to the future.

73. Cover of *Frontline 1940–1941*, 1942.

The new eyeline was used by *Illustrated* to cover the progress of the battle. The magazine linked civilians to soldiers by showing both looking skyward: anti-aircraft batteries were seen in action (20 July); journalists 'watched a tremendous air battle over the Dover area'; a warden 'gaze[d] into the sun through his parted fingers [and] carefully watch[ed] the dog-fight overhead' (24 August); people in the 'front-line village' of 'Kentville, Kent' were all looking up as 'a "Hurricane" squadron blazed into a throbbing crowd of enemy fresh from France' (21 September).

Looking up was suddenly normal, and the gaze appeared frequently in government publications, especially those which reported the work of home defence, seen here in the pamphlets *Front Line 1940–1941* (MOI 1942) and *Roof Over Britain* (MOI 1943). Whatever apprehension was associated with looking up at bombers disappeared from the public record, where the look always signified vigilance and hope. Its symbolic meaning was made explicit in *Britain Can Take It – The Book of the Film*. A photograph of a woman looking out of a window (which was also used in

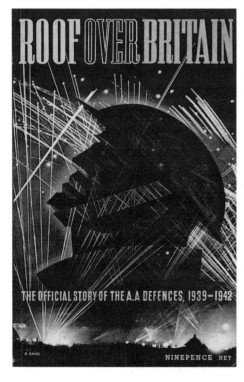

Britain doesn't look down upon the ruins of its houses, upon those made homeless during the night, upon the remains of churches, hospitals, workers' flats. Britain looks upwards towards the dawn and faces the new day with calmness and confidence.

74. Cover of *Roof over Britain*, 1943.
75. Page from *Britain Can Take It*, 1941.

the illustrated version of *The Battle of Britain*) was captioned 'Britain doesn't look down upon the ruins of its houses, upon those made homeless during the night, upon the remains of churches, hospitals, workers' flats. Britain looks upwards towards the dawn and faces the new day with calmness and confidence' (Williams and Reynolds 1941: n.p.). Of course, individuals did look on ruins, but in the official record 'Britain' had its eyes steadfastly trained on the brighter, peaceful future. The eyes of the nation were trained upwards anticipating a victorious end to the war.

In the end, the new line of sight was a measure of confidence. It was an example of how the grim likelihood of attack was 'mingled with the normal', how anxiety was acclimatised, and bombing defined as an interruption which would pass (Calder 1982: 197–9). For instance *Illustrated* showed the incongruity of the times and the strength of people's resolve by contrasting a 'lovely pastoral picture' of sheep with a brief description of the unseen 'dog-fights'. It epitomised the necessity of war in a clash of 'voices' in which country sounds were drowned by the roar of aircraft. The feeble bleating of sheep was replaced by the 'growl' of guns, and this difference was expressed in children's words that resemble sounds: the complaint of 'Baa! Baa!' was unequal to the times, whereas the guns' 'Drrrr! Drrrr!' brought the enemy down to earth (21 September: 16–21). New sounds in the pastoral scene were acceptable, just as the wreckage of enemy aircraft was acceptable as proof of victory. Throughout the Battle of Britain *Illustrated* celebrated the way enemy aircraft were spotted and 'Spitfired', which meant they were brought down – 'down on the beaches', 'down in the streets', 'down in the cornfields', 'down in the woods, on the roofs, in the back gardens' (24 August). This was the victory of the airborne fighters over 'felled' bombers, 'our' aviators forcing the enemy down into English soil, where they were reduced to nothing, the 'wrecked carcases of aircraft' as twisted as 'the crooked symbol of Nazi power' (MOI 1941: 16).

While the British wrecked the latest German aircraft with one hand, they refurbished old-fashioned forts with the other. Ancient castles, in particular, suddenly enjoyed a new lease of life. They were either fitted with dummy artillery weapons which looked real from a distance, or they were used by civil defence spotters as look-outs. Castles were also linked to the past, and so were useful reminders of heroic England and memories of days out in the country before the war. One revitalised fort was Pevensey Castle in Sussex, which figured in a *Daily Sketch* story as a picturesque reminder of peace. Referring to a photograph of the castle, the *Sketch* told its readers to 'enjoy this picture' as 'a moment's respite from the war' (9 September 1940).

While castles were familiar holiday haunts the newspapers sometimes used them to accompany and contrast with headlines referring to the 'Blitz'. Censorship forbade them to picture bomb damage immediately after a raid, if at all. Making do, they used pictures of castles as reminders of both peace and the need to make a stand against the enemy. Castles were the props of history, holding up against all-comers.

The Ministry of Information made this explicit in its account of the Battle of Britain, one of its numerous pamphlets covering all phases of the war (Moss and Box 1948). Enemies might escape from their 'downed' aircraft, and 'watchers, like those upon the keep of Hever Castle [in Kent], would see the blue field of the sky blossom suddenly with the white flowers of parachutes' (MOI 1941: 16). Spilling enemies' blood in England, or turning them into surrendering white flowers, made sense of old and not-so-old castles (the ruined Tudor house at Hever had been extensively restored by a wealthy American, William Astor, in the early part of this century). The Ministry

Plate 16. John Kippin, 'Muslims at Lake Windermere', 1991.

Plate 17. Karen Knorr, 'Pleasures of the imagination', 1991.

imagined a line of sight connecting roof-spotters on ramparts to aerial fighters, a line of sight which not only joined the watchers to the battle, but joined the new sky-fields of England and the Channel to more familiar battlegrounds. Describing spotters on Hever Castle implied that England was alert now as in the days of masted warships when men aloft in crow's nests spotted enemy ships on the horizon. Spotters became the eyes of the nation, what Churchill called his 'Jim Crows', the first defence against invasion (21).

Churchill was already talking of how a few airmen were 'turning the tide of world war' on 20 August when he made his famous 'Never in the field of human conflict' speech to the House of Commons (3). But as the Ministry of Information said, the battle was 'still at its height', with 'the last throw' coming against London in the autumn, and it was not until the end of October that the enemy air force 'virtually abandoned its attacks by daylight and began to rely entirely on a policy of night raiding – its tacit admission of defeat' (3).

Unlike any other battle, this was fought and won in the English Channel and over southern England, over London and the counties of the south coast from Kent to Dorset. The battlefields of England, like the field of human conflict, stretched to include not only the sea but the sky too. It was a new type of war fought at speed by aviators in the 'fields of air' (4), with none of 'the majestic and terrible smoke of a land bombardment'. Most people in the country had no idea what was taking place above them, and those who looked would have seen 'only a pattern of white vapour trails, leisurely changing form and shape, traced by a number of tiny specks scintillating like diamonds in the splendid sunlight' (4).

For those who missed the battle, or never guessed its significance, the Ministry recreated it, using several 'voices' in its attempt to reach a wide audience and to suggest its historic significance. As I have shown, it repeated the high-flown rhetoric of the Prime Minister and used the descriptive language of novels to paint a picture of the scene. It also gave many facts about the design and armaments of aircraft and the formation of battles. It was vague about geography in the manner of official communiqués. It used the style of newspaper headlines to introduce new sections, such as 'First Great Air Battle in History' and 'The German Command Plans a Knockout'. It included 'laconic' snatches from pilots' reports, such as 'I gave him everything I had' (28). The combination of different types of writing, and the points of view of politicians, strategists, fighters and people watching from the ground, demonstrated

76. Cover of *The Battle of Britain, August–October 1940, c.*1942.

that the battle was for everyone, and that it was to be remembered in everyday speech as well as in a literary style of language which strained after effect. The multiple voices were ordinary and familiar, or deliberately distant, mandarin, 'historical' in tone. Shifting between 'low' and 'high' tones, the voices took the experiences of ordinary civilians and incorporated them in the common struggle on the 'home-front'. These shifting voices took death in its banality and raised it to the level of 'sacrifice'. Ultimately, they placed the battle alongside the heroic victories of 'Marathon, Trafalgar and the Marne' (32). Thus the peculiar, and modern, battle was endowed with historical significance, and the fields of air were joined to the land by British fighters rising and German aircraft falling.

Similar combinations of voices and collusions between anonymous authors and readers took place in the way the battle was seen in photographs. On its cover, a later edition of *The Battle of Britain* (reproduced above) pictured the white vapour trails above the city skyline. The pamphlet also reproduced maps of the battles and gave an artist's impression of a dogfight. It showed planes in formation. It illustrated 'I gave him everything I had' with a photograph of a plane exploding, and ended with photographs of wrecked enemy aircraft described as 'the melancholy remnants of a shattered and disordered armada' (MOI *c.*1942: 33–5). Occasionally the line of sight was the pilots'; sometimes it was a 'bird's eye' view, as in the maps and diagrams; most often it was the view from the ground, looking at downed planes or looking upwards because 'Hurricanes and Spitfires Stay in the Air' (MOI 1941: 14).

The Ministry presented metaphor and history mixed together. With the authority of Churchill, it turned ships' crows into sky-watchers, ruins into defences, holiday haunts into fortresses, and any would-be invader (since the sixteenth century) into Germans. Plain talk and cold facts sat easily beside different types of exalted 'prose'. Helped by photographs and other graphic devices, the Ministry fixed the progress and meaning of the battle for audiences which, it promised, could win the war and have the peace.

7

At home with Fox Talbot

MODERN AND POSTMODERN STORIES

THE RHETORIC of the Second World War has not been forgotten in reproducing 'England' in contemporary times, but it has been subtly altered. 'Heritage' is a form of history which is supposed to be all-inclusive and accessible. It is also a type of history that is not so evidently tied to politics or the state, to statutes and treaties. Instead, heritage is an entertainment.

In the next two chapters I intend to discuss how photographers have engaged with this version of the English past. In this chapter I shall examine contemporary hopes for settled times or the end of historical upheaval. The example I have chosen to discuss is 'A Celebration of Photography', an event which took place at Henry Fox Talbot's family home at Lacock Abbey in 1989 (see illustrations). The 'celebration' was intended to mark the one hundred and fifty years since Fox Talbot's discovery in 1839 of the negative/positive process and the 'invention of modern photography'. In the next chapter I shall look at how contemporary photographers have engaged with the tourism of heritage attractions, and the English landscape as a forbidding, exclusive place. These photographers often give expression to a widespread disenchantment, rejecting the idea of happy settlements, and revelling instead in dislocation and disharmony. I shall continue this theme in the third and final chapter in this section, which examines photography of the landscape as a metaphor for even greater disruptions and destruction.

77. Amateur snapshot of banner at 'A Celebration of Photography', Lacock Abbey, Wiltshire, July 1989.

Before discussing the ways in which 'A Celebration of Photography' was a dream of English coherence, I intend to comment briefly on the changes in beliefs about history that occurred in the period following the end of the Second World War. By the 1980s and 1990s the sense that the United Kingdom was a country at one with itself became almost insupportable, and the term 'Great Britain', referring ambiguously to geographical extensiveness, military power and moral authority, became 'more and more problematic in the course of the decade' (Corner and Harvey 1991: 12; see Nairn 1977). It is generally accepted among academics that traditional assumptions about national identity and unity, based on the 'assumed superiority' of England over Ireland, Scotland and Wales, men over women, and the metropolis over the regions, along with the centrality of the values of white, Western Christendom, have become 'less and less tenable'. Education and the media have created a social space for 'the recognition of differences' in language, culture, class experience, family and domestic life. The construction of differences in public space 'has sketched in the limits of the older, imperially based and pre-democratic concept of "Great Britain", offering a modest challenge to its sway' (Corner and Harvey 1991: 13). For the purposes of this chapter, whose main subject is the longevity of conservative beliefs about England and Englishness, the key word in this passage is the recognition that the challenge has been 'modest'. The great changes in Britain which Corner and Harvey outline were simply denied at the Lacock 'celebration'.

This conservatism, in which the past is recreated and then held up to be in some ways preferable or superior to the present, should not be dismissed as archaic or outmoded. On the contrary, the wish to save England in one of its past forms is a powerful, motivating force in the country. In line with tourists' expectations, the imaginative return to the past is the search for reassurance and confirmation. It runs in direct contradiction to the everyday experience that in elusive ways life is dislocated, rootless and unsatisfying.

In leaping forward more than forty years from the widely publicised optimism and patriotism of the war years, from the certainty afforded by the repetition of familiar narratives, we move into an age of uncertainty, where such narratives seem no longer to account for change or present circumstances. Some cultural historians believe there is a profound difference between earlier periods and contemporary times (Jameson 1984; Lyotard 1984). As David Harvey writes, in the last thirty years the 'modern' epoch has been overlaid by that of the 'postmodern'. Whereas the former period 'transformed itself over five centuries', the latter emerged 'as a full-blown though still incoherent movement' in the late 1960s or early 1970s (Harvey 1989: 38). In the modern era it was still possible to imagine a world of rational connections and differentiations, and to imagine that it was possible to control the representation of a quintessential English scene and limit its meaning. Though these beliefs led to tensions and struggles between groups over which should determine the meaning of these treasured sites, each group believed there was a meaning to impose. In the postmodern environment there is no hope of regaining the control which was the project or ambition of modernity. Instead, postmodernists abandon the illusion of control and engage with what David Harvey calls 'the immediacy of events, the sensationalism of the spectacle'.

One aspect of postmodern experience is its lack of a sense of historical time, or of sequential, deep history into a remote but connected past. Harvey argues that the breakdown of 'the temporal order of things gives rise to a peculiar treatment of the past' in which postmodernists lose all sense of historical continuity and memory, while plundering history and absorbing it into some aspect of the present (Harvey 1989: 54–7). Whereas the experience of modernity was the fragmentary and ephemeral nature of everyday life – a fundamentally alienating experience – at least the resulting alienation was set against the beauty and truth of an ordered world. In contrast, the postmodern experience of fragmentation and ephemerality never seeks comparison with essential or stable meanings. In postmodernity all experience remains without roots, without history, without overarching narratives that oppose the dream of coherence to the experience of alienation. Harvey refers to Robert Hewison's book *The Heritage Industry, Britain in a Climate of Decline* (1987): 'Post-modernism and the heritage industry are linked' since 'both conspire to create a shallow screen that intervenes between our present lives and our history'. History becomes a 'contemporary creation, more costume drama and re-enactment than critical discourse' (Harvey 1989: 62–3, citing Hewison 1987: 135).

There is a problem with this last point of view, since it suggests postmodernism and the heritage industry have lost contact with an underlying, 'real' past. In its place, Harvey seems to suggest postmodernism and heritage each promote only a substitute form of historical consciousness, which is shallow and false. The division implied here between real history and contemporary false history is problematic since a sense of what constitutes history is always a contemporary creation, and one in which re-enactment of myth and costume drama is at least as significant in the creation of tradition as critical discourse (Hobsbawm 1983; Porter 1992). Indeed, a satisfactory popular understanding of historical events depends upon recasting 'the past' in forms which are still continuous with the present, and not as a disconcerting world known only at the surface. Despite the onset of postmodern times and the end of 'deep' history, the everyday experience of time is one of continuity and depth.

Another writer on the heritage industry, Adrian Mellor, places continuity at the root of 'everyday consciousness'. He argues that 'ordinary people, going about ordinary lives, do not feel themselves to be part of "the postmodern condition" ' (Mellor 1991: 94). Mellor states that the end of explanatory narrative may be a constant feature of postmodernity, but it does not impinge on everyday life. He writes 'You can't walk through a shopping mall, watch late-night TV, attend a seminar, buy a sweater, or spend the day out at Wigan Pier, without...meta-narratives dying at your feet'. Nevertheless he argues that people do not see everyday cultural practices as evidence of 'fragmentation' or 'depthlessness'. Nor do people frame contemporary products in terms of pastiche or nostalgia: 'when they go shopping, they stubbornly insist that they are buying something to wear, rather than constituting their subjectivity' (93–4). This determination on the part of people to save the everyday, narratable reality of the world suggests that postmodernity has not become part of common sense. Instead, easily understood and reassuring narratives still establish meaning and continuity among large sections of the population who believe they have a stake in society, which they establish and sustain through consumer 'spending power' (Featherstone 1991; Lee 1993).

WINNING THE WAR AGAIN

We see the authority of readily understood narratives in everyday consciousness in the relation of contemporary Britain to the Second World War. In leaping forward into the 1980s, we enter the period of reminiscence and anniversaries. In a sense, the war has never ended in Britain. Remembering the battles and heroes of the war has been a perpetual activity since 1945, a national pastime with greater resonance in daily life than the annual Remembrance Day would suggest. The British have continuously made use of their victory to make sense of the present – either to escape to or draw strength from a time when the people of the nation were supposed to have worked together for the common good. Some references continue in the heroic mould of wartime patriotism: the genre of feature films such as *In Which We Serve* (1942) carried over into celebratory post-war films such as *The Dambusters* (1954). Other references sought to clarify and fix the history of the war by narrating it in long-running and repeated television documentaries using 'archival' film, such as the twenty-six part series *The World at War* (1973–74). Similar 'historical', well-researched and 'authentic' versions of the war have been staged as imaginative reconstructions by museums and art galleries, as in *The Blitz Experience* at the Imperial War Museum and exhibitions in local museums and galleries (see Ballard 1985).

Not all references to the war have attempted to stage or repeat historical events accurately, have used film and photography as documentary proof, or have been pedagogic or sombre in their appraisal of the British at war. On the contrary, we see the continuation of the war in the form of a popular entertainment in television programming. The long-running series *Dad's Army* (1968–93 including repeats), and *Allo Allo* (1985–91) emphasised the comedy of social manners sharpened by the humorous collision of a military style and civilian lives. In short, the war registers in a mix of comic and 'historical' representations at the popular level.

These national–popular memories are continuously joined by official remembrances. At the time of writing (June 1993), the fiftieth anniversary of the Battle of the Atlantic is being commemorated on Merseyside with a week of events, and visits from the Queen, Prince Charles and Princess Diana. This is one of a series of fortieth or fiftieth anniversaries of wartime events – all of which keep the war alive through spectacular displays. Despite protests about wartime horrors, blunders or atrocities, commemorations neither apologise for the war nor glorify in it. They are nationalist propaganda, but through their use of pageantry, slow movement and dignified silence, commemorations are meant to be a time for honouring and remembering the 'sacrifice' of lost comrades. The ceremonies are carefully constructed to be times when the nation is symbolically united in sorrow and nostalgia, represented by marching veterans, tearful reminiscence by survivors, the presence of royalty, the eulogies of religious, military and political leaders. The supposedly unified response to a threat in the past renews a sense of community in recent troubled times. The everyday use of the Second World War is a 'cool' form of historical reference, so ordinary that it causes no special excitement.

Accompanying this is the 'cool' use of state pageantry and the figure of the Queen, which are also part of the normal round of everyday, continuous enactment of what it means to be English (Cannadine 1983). The place of the Queen in commemorations of war is crucial, because she signifies a deep, familial link with 'our' history. The Queen, and by extension, the Royal family in its ideal, aristocratic and mystical form, contrast with the British political scene, in which history is altogether less stable. In the 1980s the Government of Margaret Thatcher displaced the ideal stability of the monarchy and the continuous 'cool' re-enactment of the war. Thatcher tried to capture the mystic ground held by the Queen, and she created a 'hot' version of the Second World War to reinstate Britain as 'Great'.

The 'philosophy' of Thatcherism required that the past be divided in two. In its more despised form, the 'past' was cut off from the present. This past was largely the source of ancient and useless beliefs about society based on class conflict, with different class interests being represented in class-based organisations such as trade unions. In contrast, the idea of the superior nation depended heavily on the affirmation of one factor of the 'past' that made sense within Thatcherism. This was the rediscovery, in 1982, of a new, 'hot' use for the Second World War, which was redeclared on two fronts. The first front was discovered when the 'fascist' Argentines invaded the Falkland Islands (Barnett 1982). At the same time, Thatcher opened a

217

second front against the 'enemy within', who were trade unionists, strikers and socialists. Churchill's 'bulldog' spirit and the imaginary unity of purpose among civilians in wartime became the model for organising social and industrial relations on the home front. Thatcher turned the professionalism of the military Task Force into a model for the civil state, a place where everyone obeyed orders and played their part, 'sterling qualities which shine through our history' (Thatcher 1982). She folded the sacrifice of the 1940s on to the 1980s, and used it to dismantle the internal enemy, the workers who clung to outmoded practices, and who (in the words of conservative historian Corelli Barnett) had become a 'subliterate, unskilled, unhealthy and institutionalised proletariat hanging on the nipple of state maternalism' (Barnett 1986: 304).

Thatcherism transformed complex history into simple heritage, a disconnected series of complete and comforting tales about beneficent patriotism, selected 'Victorian values' of invention and enterprise, and the supposed unity of civilians during the Second World War. Thatcherism provided a climate for enterprise policies and the end of 'entitlement society'. Under Thatcherism, the only right the individual possessed was the right to participate in a deregulated market – including the market for heritage. The entertainments of heritage were not crudely determined by the policies of Thatcherism, but heritage as history for sale was a characteristic product of the 1980s.

Since the end of Thatcher's premiership in 1990 there have been two complementary moves in the systematic promotion of a popular national history. Firstly, the Second World War has returned in its 'cool' form (and became a constant point of reference during the Gulf War of 1991). Secondly, the Government has moved away from Thatcherism's contempt for the 'past' as a dump, and has selected moments from the past other than Victorian values to be shining examples for the present. Current Tory philosophy sees the past as customs and castles, but considers it to be most palatable when mixed with modern entertainments and diversions. The Government has disbanded English Heritage, a quango – or quasi-autonomous non-governmental body – established by the National Heritage Act of 1983 to care for and market historic buildings and ancient monuments. It has lumped its properties, together with sport, broadcasting, and plans for a national lottery, into a new Ministry for Heritage. In this version, the past exists in line with the present; it can be said to have delivered the present, and can be honoured as 'tradition'.

Perhaps the links with a traditional past were always too sinuous to break.

Looking at the case of the celebration at Lacock, it is clear that neither Thatcherism nor postmodernism disturbed an orthodox version of Englishness, though, as I intend to argue, this Englishness was not without its own internal tensions and contradictions.

THE CELEBRATION OF PHOTOGRAPHY AT LACOCK ABBEY

In June 1989 Kodak and the National Trust, founded in 1894 to preserve 'places of historic interest and natural beauty' (Gaze 1988), staged 'A Celebration of Photography' at Fox Talbot's home at Lacock (see illustration of Souvenir Programme on page 220). Kodak paid for the 'celebration' in the grounds of the Abbey, which has been held by the Trust since 1944. These two powerful vested interests had potentially quite different audiences. In this chapter, I shall look at how Kodak attached itself to and inflected the usual meaning of the place. This alliance was temporary, of course, but their different interests might easily have produced a clash of purpose between Kodak and the Trust. The two organisations proceeded to cover up the differences between them by agreeing on a general effusion of English heritage.

Though some previously unseen photographs by Fox Talbot were on show at the museum in Lacock dedicated to his memory and work, Kodak's 'celebration' was purposefully not dedicated to the art of photography. That came later in London at the Royal Academy of Arts' exhibition (which had nothing to do with Kodak) called 'The Art of Photography 1839–1989'. This show deliberately restated the orthodox 'grand master' history of the medium nurtured by American collectors and curators over most of this century (Weaver 1989b; Berger and Richon 1990). Unlike the Royal Academy exhibition, the 'celebration' at Lacock was remarkable for its lack of continuity with conventional histories of photography-as-art. The only point of contact between Kodak's 'celebration' and the Academy show was the emphasis on the life of Fox Talbot and the ideas of origins, progress, and continuity. As I shall argue more fully below, even this minimal link with photography-as-art was at odds with the Trust's own sense of the history of Lacock. For the Trust, Lacock's history is much deeper than mid-Victorian England, and is tied to changes in function and architectural styles rather than the 'invention' of what became commercial

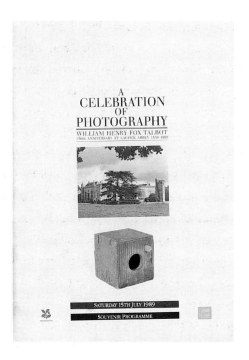

78. Kodak celebration souvenir programme of 'A Celebration of Photography', Lacock Abbey, Wiltshire, July 1989.

photography. If there was a gap between Kodak and the Trust over the place of photography at the Lacock Abbey 'celebration', it might have been widened by Kodak's decision to promote the popular hobby of photography. Its goals are seemingly irreconcilable with the Trust's advocacy of a superior national identity found in, or reconstructed through, the homes and artefacts of the landed gentry and aristocrats. However, Kodak self-consciously linked photography with other popular but 'heritage' pastimes. It used 'traditional' Morris dancers and staged a concert of popular 'classical' music to address a communal sense of Englishness. Thus the live elements of the 'celebration' corresponded with the Trust's general aim to preserve places of historic interest or natural beauty for the benefit of the nation. Kodak thus managed to raise the 'popular' to the level of the 'national'.

Given their differences, the convergence of Kodak's and the Trust's interests is not at all obvious. Kodak looks for mass audiences with unspecified interests, though advertising tends to concentrate on personalised family memories, while the Trust appeals to those interested in communal and public visits to sites of national significance. The public expression of convergence and the key to Kodak's sponsorship of 'A Celebration of Photography' lay in what Erroll Yates, the Chairman of Kodak, said were their common interests in 'hallmarks of quality and excellence' of service (Souvenir Programme 1989). Kodak had always catered for small groups with high rates of consumption. At the end of the nineteenth century it had nurtured the small market of serious amateurs who were interested in art photography; at the end of the twentieth it was seeking to align itself with the significant consumers of the heritage industry. Similarly, the Trust's own audience broadened in the 1980s as the travel industry sewed 'attractions' into 'heritage tourism' (Yale 1991; Prentice 1993).

What Erroll Yates did not need to say was that both his company and the Trust aimed to make specific types of memory easy to gather and preserve. For both, repetition is the key. Both were trying to instil in their public the desire to *repeat* the occasion of memories of (possibly family) day-trips to stately homes, castles or other ancient places. To encourage this desire they worked to make the experience easy, and this they achieved by meeting the expectations of their customers through the reliability and standardisation of their products. Customers coming back to repeat the experience form the bases for profit among companies, and repetition is the basis for the sense of belonging among communities. One hundred and fifty years of photography was the unique moment for a 'celebration' of *continuity* in the identities of business and nation.

This type of order through memory exists in the ways of looking and touring which Kodak and the Trust encourage. Kodak published a free leaflet of 'photo information', called 'Photography at National Trust Properties', which gives 'tips' to amateurs on how to 'concentrate' on the 'photography of buildings, follies and monuments'. The Trust often prescribes tourists' routes with signs that indicate which door to enter next, ensuring that people move in one direction through the building. The public presentation of touring and remembering underscores how dependable the experience is, so long as visitors abide by rules made to seem less like governance than helpful 'tips'. Though neither the Trust nor Kodak can determine the memories of visitors, both do try to guide their customers towards preferred readings. Every visitor to Trust properties is eased across the threshold, literally and metaphorically, into an experience of the past; everyone engaged in photography is eased into it by promises of 'good pictures' every time they use Kodak film (unfortunately, some of the public began to use photography to 'capture' security systems, leading to theft and then a ban on indoor photography – see Anon. 1992).

The sense of the past is experienced in the interrelation of time and place, which have objective existence and mythic dimensions. In the case of the 'celebration', the objective facts representing *time past* were the reality of Fox Talbot's photographs; the mythic dimension of these objects in time was how they signalled a critical moment in the history of seeing and recording. The objective fact representing *place* was the landscape, and the built environment of ancient buildings; the mythic significance of this place was (in the words of the souvenir programme) its status as a 'quintessentially English village'. Lacock as an English *place* was defined in *time* by 'its Medieval Abbey' and by the 'museum dedicated to the photographic achievements of Fox Talbot' (Souvenir Programme 1989). Tourists can only visit places, but they want to be assured that these places have links with the past. As Michael Bommes and Patrick Wright suggest, contemporary tourism depends upon the notion that ' "the past" is really there to be visited' (Bommes and Wright 1984: 294). At Lacock, the linkage of time to place created memories not only of the beginnings of photography but of an abbey next to a picturesque village. These discoveries of place and the memories attached to them delivered a celebration of something more than photography – nothing less than an enduring Englishness, and its preservation in the undisturbed countryside.

According to Kodak's leaflet for tourist photography, difficulties are designed away or deliberately avoided. The leaflet says entering the past is as simple as using modern photography, and requires no more than a small adjustment in the point of view: 'Avoid background clutter. Move your viewpoint to hide unsightly factory chimneys or pylons.' Adjustments in position or place result in the desired version of the landscape or view, with all its historical resonance; a shift in space produces a shift in time. Being an old place, Lacock gives a sense of continuity in time, and direct access to the past, contributing to the belief that England and heritage are synonymous.

THE PLACE OF LACOCK

Part of the problem in understanding heritage is that concentrating on the *past* might conceal the importance of the spatial dimension in producing a sense of history, so I shall show how the meaning of heritage derives much of its force from *place*. Though time and place are intermingled, so that it seems perverse to separate them, I shall

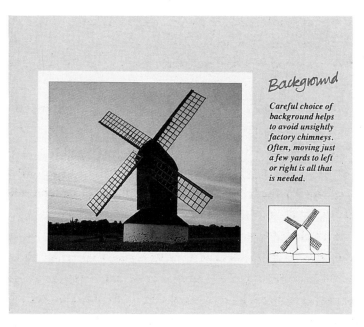

79. Example of advice to amateur photographers in Kodak's pamphlet *Photography at National Trust Properties*, 1989.

examine Lacock in both its spatial and temporal dimensions, looking briefly at Lacock's unusual force as a place, along with its use as a time-machine. If place and time are separated at all, it is usually to name the site and give its historical significance. We can see this in Kodak's press release announcing the 'celebration', which reminded readers that the family bequest to the Trust was *the whole village* of Lacock. As if to underline how place and time are inseparable, Kodak then overlaid the place with the weight of its history: 'With its four streets, Lacock still resembles a medieval town, with houses of every century from the 13th century to the 18th, but with very little building of the 19th or 20th centuries' (*News from Kodak* 1989). Places which are clearly defined (for example, museums or sporting arenas) provide the foundations for order in everyday life. Lacock is a place for what sociologist Kevin Hetherington (writing about Stonehenge) calls 'the collective expression and discovery of identity and culture' (Hetherington 1992: 90).

However, places do not have meaning in themselves but always in relation to others which are believed to be different. In thinking about geographical dualism, the opposition of high/low (which we encountered in the chapter on Emerson on the Norfolk Broads) can be turned into the opposition of centre/margin. In the same way that the 'high' tries to reject the 'low' for reasons of status but finds it cannot, so the centre depends on and includes the marginal (Stallybrass and White 1986: 5) (see next chapter).

Whereas groups at the centre and margins will always disagree about the meanings of a site, occasionally they clash over its actual occupation, which happened in the early 1980s at Stonehenge. Kevin Hetherington writes that the contest over the meaning of Stonehenge, culminating in the suppression of the summer festival and consequent 'battle' of 1985, existed between two broad groups: on the one hand counter-culture New Age travellers who transgress the conventional routines of everyday life and, on the other hand, groups which sustain the dominant culture, including landowners, local authorities and English Heritage. The contest between marginal and central groups stemmed from completely different ways of thinking about social life. Marginal groups wanted to break with dominant public life and hold a 'festival' to 'create new meaningful identities' out of a 'disordered existence'; centre groups wanted to concentrate on the continuity of time and what they perceived to be the certainties of the national story. According to Hetherington, whether Stonehenge is defined as a heritage space or a festival space, both meanings are the resolution to the feeling that communal and meaningful spaces are destroyed by the disruptive experience of time and the spatial instability of everyday life in capitalist societies (Hetherington 1992: 90; see Giddens 1990). Instead of remaining a heritage site, Stonehenge became 'a topos of insecurity' when it was fought over. Then, if only for a few days, it came to seem a place where the counter-culture might be installed as symbolically central.

Though Lacock never experienced or represented a clash of cultures as clear-cut as the 'battle' for Stonehenge, it was none the less a place which had a dominant meaning already established by the National Trust which was then challenged, if only for a weekend, by the intervention of Kodak. Binary oppositions are subject to minute discriminations so that the tension between Kodak and the Trust, though it did not exist on the scale of that over Stonehenge, was discernible even though it was easily resolved.

The Trust aims to move visitors through its properties with little interruption. Popular pastimes and hobbies which might break the flow of reverent traffic are not encouraged. This includes the hobby of photography, which even at the Abbey has been pushed to the margins. The Trust has never presented the Abbey as a shrine for photography, and has always shown it to be something much more than the home of Fox Talbot and birthplace of modern photography. Kodak accepted this state of affairs, and even though its 'celebration' set aside all photography other than Fox Talbot's, it did not use the Abbey to present original photographs as art, nor did it exalt Fox Talbot himself as an artist or scientist. This separation of Fox Talbot from the Abbey had been established for many years. Visitors who wished to see original pictures or know more of his life needed to pay a separate entrance fee to the Fox Talbot Museum, which was not founded until 1975 and is situated in a converted barn outside the Abbey gate.

At Lacock the National Trust has custody of a site whose meaning is rooted in a world in which everything is pre-modern. The visitor does not need to be a connoisseur of architecture to know that the Abbey is a mixture of styles, none of which belong to this century. The building is a mixture of medieval religious cloisters, Tudor extensions and late-eighteenth-century alterations and enlargements which form one great complex. In being ancient, and in presenting several faces from the deep past to the moment of photography in the nineteenth century, the site represents a full stop to history. It remains 'unspoilt' by subsequent progress, including the discovery and progress of photography itself, or the coming of mass tourism.

At the same time the Abbey is in another sense turned into 'spoil'. The Trust has saved a treasure house from the past, since the Abbey itself is treasure. The Trust has performed archaeology-above-ground – but at a price. The meaning of the site is established in distant and sanitised times, settling for heroic periods. Those visitors who are interested can quickly discover from the National Trust leaflet that the architecture of the Abbey stems from the thirteenth century when it was built as a nunnery; nothing happened until the sixteenth century when, following the dissolution of the monasteries in 1539, one of Henry VIII's courtiers turned it into a private house and (in the words of the Trust's leaflet) 'commissioned some of the best Renaissance architects for his alterations'; nothing happened again until the eighteenth century when some additions were made in the new styles; the architectural history of Lacock ended in the nineteenth century with the few changes then made, the most important being the three oriel windows in the South Gallery, one of which Fox Talbot used as the subject for the 'earliest existing negative'.

For the Trust, the significance of the building is the combination of fine architecture from medieval, Tudor and 'Gothick' periods. Fox Talbot's incumbency

80. Martin Parr, 'Club photographers at "A Celebration of Photography", Lacock Abbey, Wiltshire, July 1989'.

and the impact his discoveries had upon subsequent generations is noted in passing, but is certainly not at the heart of the Trust's use of the bequest. To pass into the Abbey is to travel much further back in time than mid-Victorian England and its scientific discoveries which later became the subject of mass production and mass entertainments. To enter the Abbey is to seek alignment with times which are older, more aesthetic and more patrician – times ordered by religion and the sequestration of women, the notion of Renaissance man, the beginnings of Romanticism.

Given the Trust's inclination to speed its patrons into pre-modern times, the 'celebration of photography' within the grounds of the Abbey was a unique event. Had Kodak wished to turn the 'celebration' into a trade show, or attempted to hijack

81. Martin Parr, 'Club photographers and a Fox Talbot tableau at "A Celebration of Photography", Lacock Abbey, Wiltshire, July 1989'.

the Abbey and turn it into a permanent shrine to the origins of modern photography of which the company was the most illustrious representative, then there would have been a battle (though probably not in public). But Kodak had no interest in such a commitment, and never looked likely to embarrass the Trust by emphasising trade over-much. It certainly made no attempt in the 'celebration' to deal with the issue of modern, mass entertainments which Fox Talbot's work set in train.

For Kodak, the significance of the place was its original coupling of art and science. The press release implied this marriage of aesthetics to a system of record, stating that Lacock 'is still a photographer's paradise – 150 years after the science was invented'. Tying art and science together was one unusual link in Trust properties, but it was not the only tie. The 'invention' of photography had eventually grown into a massive commercial enterprise servicing huge numbers of snapshooters which, like so many other manifestations of tourism, might have threatened Trust sites. Yet photography proved no threat to the 'paradise' of Lacock. On the contrary, Kodak returned its profit in the form of *sponsorship* to save the heritage. Furthermore, the alliance of commerce and conservation was mutually beneficial, paying for an expansion in the Trust's photographic library, and giving Kodak exclusive rights to points of sale at Trust shops.

At Lacock the gap between the Trust at the centre and Kodak at the margin was not great but it was significant. Though Kodak mentioned its interests in art and science, and the commercial potential of their alliance, the company chose to base the 'celebration' on the ground of holiday pastimes and amusements which recapitulated Englishness. There was a church flower festival, a display of brewery dray-horses, hot-air balloons bearing Kodak advertisements, street entertainers including a man on stilts, Morris dancers, clog dancers, various early bicycles ridden by people in period costume, and old-style children's entertainments such as Punch and Judy. These events were national–popular heritage, and obviously had nothing to do with the 'Gothick', Renaissance or medieval worlds which were otherwise so much in evidence in Lacock's architecture. Their uncertain relation to the austere history of the place as a religious settlement, or its history as the private home of landed gentry, made these entertainments potentially disruptive. In contrast to the Trust's engagement with the long history of the place, the 'celebration' confined itself largely to the recent past. It continued to celebrate modernity by staging English traditions of a relatively low caste. Furthermore, it encouraged amateur photography, which had also been restricted to wealthy patrons before commerce turned it into one of the main pleasures of mass tourism.

The gap signified by the perpetual separation of the Fox Talbot Museum from the Abbey, and the lack of interest by the Trust in mass forms of entertainment, was made much narrower by the decision to include in the programme an equivalent form of higher but accessible culture and hold it in the grounds of the Abbey. An amphitheatre was erected for the Royal Philharmonic Pops, which played before an invited audience for one-and-a-half hours. The music was carefully chosen. It extended the 'paradise' of Lacock as an ancient village and Abbey towards the way Englishness is denoted in national–popular music which bears the definable quality of courtly patronage, along with the folkloric and mystic associations of the landscape. There were *English Dances* by Arnold, Vaughan Williams's arrangement of the anonymous Elizabethan song *Greensleeves*, the *Trumpet Voluntary*, the *Pomp and Circumstance March no. 1* by Elgar, and thirty minutes of his *Enigma Variations*. This was followed by a *son et lumière* 'celebration of photography' with narration and specially composed music. The evening ended with a great firework and laser display accompanied by eight minutes of excerpts from *Music from the Royal Fireworks* by Handel. Thus were photography and Kodak itself tied to English courtly music, patriotic tunes, folk-dances, and the musical invocation of the English countryside. This programme came close to the Trust's own perception of itself presiding over an essential Englishness dignified with middle-class taste, and no doubt it was important that the audience was special, and that music, fireworks and lasers at night were the part of the show only for insiders.

Kodak inserted itself early on into these more sedate and dignified signs of Englishness. The first item of music played by the Royal Philharmonic Pops was the National Anthem, arranged by Britten, lasting two minutes, but it was followed by the *Kodak Fanfare 'Energy'* (now called *Trailfinders*), and also lasting for two minutes. This juxtaposition suggests that it was important for Kodak's vision of the 'celebration' to stop short of merging with the Trust but to stand next to quintessential signs of Englishness. It managed this successfully, testing the central, dominant meaning of Lacock as an ancient Trust property by intruding some popular, uncontroversial 'traditions', and inserting its trade name and fanfare among the stable tunes of English glory.

The weekend was carefully named: it was not called a 'festival' because that word has been tainted by its association with marginal groups. Similarly, visitors to Lacock were not entering a carnival. Indeed, they moved in a direction which denied carnival: instead of crossing the threshold from the everyday world into a lifestyle of excess, intoxication, instability and waste, to enter this 'celebration' meant all pleasures were held within tighter limits. The entertainments were carefully staged and orchestrated. There was a definite timetable which had to be met, and a hierarchy of events, ending in the climactic firework and lasar display (for the hierarchy of invited guests). The series of daytime popular entertainments was similarly carefully staged, so the whole event proceeded like clockwork. This orderly presentation of amusements and diversions was a repetition of middle-class social protocol *and* the ideal form of workplace management. Together, the Trust and Kodak presented to their audience a place in the world where events might unfold and still be regular and predictable, firmly fixed in place. The event was most correctly named a 'celebration' because the term suggests entertainment adapted by a type of adulation, or softened by an air of satisfaction.

Comparing the 'celebration' to the use of Stonehenge in Hetherington's analysis, we can see how Lacock signified as a public space for the reinforcement of existing values, adapted by the sponsors to their own ends. If there was a noticeable gap between Kodak and the Trust over the *place* of Lacock, there was an even smaller gap (though for similar reasons) in their conceptions of Lacock's *time*.

THE TIME OF LACOCK

As we already know, photography's history is short, but Lacock is ancient; the history of photography begins where the history of Lacock ends. Like Stonehenge, the place 'resonates with pastness', but this is a past that can only be recaptured in memory. Tourists visiting a site tend to invest it with mutually understood meanings – articulated for outsiders or newcomers by helpful captions and maps. These signposts point tourists to the past, and for their part, ready to be nostalgic, they are emotionally equipped to undertake the journey. Whereas nostalgia ordinarily might be a suspect, enervating feeling that hinders a realistic assessment of the present, tourists actively use nostalgia to remove them temporarily from the present. The day-dreaming effect of nostalgia leads tourists to invest the site with a sense of the past, or to what Hetherington calls 'the re-temporalizing of heritage spaces'. This activity of investing a site with time is supposedly completed by its guardians – hence the emphasis at Lacock on time before 1840. The tourist uses an institution like the National Trust to establish the time-scale of the place, to establish a link between the place and time which 'is to be preserved...gazed upon but not changed, used or touched' (Hetherington 1992: 89). Nevertheless, as Hetherington himself makes clear, places are continuously used and touched, and this helps determine who is able to 'gaze' and what type of site they will see.

In 1989 Kodak and the Trust collaborated in using Lacock for that one specific celebration. This moment was unusual because it overlaid the great age of Lacock, and its beginnings as a nunnery, with the relatively recent times of Victorian invention. Fox

Talbot had used the grounds of the Abbey for group portraits, and the exact sites and poses of his subjects were shown in enlarged copies of reproductions of his original photographs glued without ceremony to boards and nailed to stakes hammered into the ground (see Martin Parr's pictures). These forlorn, amateurish signposts simply stood before a wall, doorway or barn, showing what once had taken place there. Their chief purpose, however, was to foretell impending tableaux: young actors from the Bristol Old Vic theatre company toured the grounds in period costume and paused by the signs, striking the pose that Fox Talbot had favoured. When the actors were in place the signs helped photographers to adopt the line of sight which corresponded most precisely with Fox Talbot's. The tableaux compressed Fox Talbot's activities of many years into a few hours of rapid and repeated reconstructions. Despite the relentless pace the actors, with commendable professionalism, held their positions for minutes on end, until the last of the numerous amateur club photographers was satisfied that he (rarely she) had captured the simulation and therefore repeated the original.

Repetition of Fox Talbot's photographic scenes saturated the narrative space of Lacock. This repetition contained any potential contradictions, purified difference, and collapsed distant time into a resolved, homogeneous and complete narrative. The effect of this repetition was to block time-travel to the deep past of Lacock, limiting it to the Victorian moment of invention. It also helped observers to identify themselves with the past, offering a narrative which fulfilled a wish for the survival of bygone times. The pleasurable effect of this repetition was achieved by moments of recognition which had nothing at all to do with the domestic arrangements at Lacock *before* 1840, but related only to the first use of photography in a modern, bourgeois home. Fox Talbot showed that photography was capable of recording artefacts and architecture, but more than that he demonstrated the use of photography in suggesting order and hierarchy within families, among middle-class men at play, or between himself and his employees at work. By resurrecting these scenes and encouraging photographers to repeat them by using their own machines, Kodak and the Trust underlined the importance of exactly that familial, centred, and controlling existence which had been the first subject of photography and the yardstick of normality.

The club photographers were time-travellers in a medieval cloister, using later versions of a nineteenth-century machine. They repeated the celebration of domestic life imagined by a Victorian gentleman, setting the gender and social authority of the landed gentry at the heart of the English pastoral. The club photographers expected not to depart from the text already given. There was no interest in the *staging* as such, and it was only a few photographers who were interested in the event as a whole and looked at the audience (see photographs by Martin Parr, and one of the amateur snapshots). The club photographers concentrated on the tableaux, intent on simulating the first modern man to photograph the home itself, the domestic family, with men and women fixed in the normal hierarchy and with servants or estate 'hands' arranged as if labouring or displaying the magic fruits of labour.

Though the time-tunnel from 1989 back to the 1840s was shorter than the Trust preferred, commerce and conservation were used to celebrate a particular form of history. Kodak's ideas converged with the Trust's in suggesting that historical time might be regained by cutting straight from the present into the past. In addition, without any sense of irony or tension, the photographic tableaux suggested a continuity between a pre-industrial hierarchy and a highly differentiated sector of modern consumers. Exactly as Kodak suggested in its pamphlet, a small shift in the line of sight could alter the perspective altogether. Photographers chose to aim towards the representation of the past. They ignored the crowds of tourists which mirrored themselves in the present: looking at them would have spoiled the illusion of and pleasure in contemporary order.

Restaging and copying old photographs brought to the forefront a binary opposition which we may add to the interaction of high/low and centre/margin, namely the coupling of life and death: the resurrection of Victorian home life required the simulated resurrection of the dead. This enactment brought together the inescapable conclusion to life – its finale and its negation – and sought to reverse it. In the tableaux the dead were made to live again. They appeared not as macabre apparitions of decay but in their prime, fully alive, alert and utterly separate from the onlookers, moving through their routines as if they had no idea that onlookers were watching them. The separate spheres of actors and audience corresponded with the absolute division between the cozy Victorian scenes depicted and the fact that these were acted. The correspondence between the original photographs and the tableaux meant that the figures were dead and alive at the same time. The whole activity showed that certain of the dead (those in photographs) continue to have some presence in life. This mixture of life and death in photography – where people long dead appear as they were when alive – is uncanny. At Lacock the tableaux mixed the home-like, which arouses a sense of peaceful security, with the pretence that the dead had come to life and were repeating their movements, magically unaware of the presence of twentieth-century observers. The separation of actors from observers was crucial. The actors' obliging repeat performances with no interaction between themselves and the photographers enabled the time-travel to unfold without threat: the dead who came to life remained in their time-zone, stood in their historic spaces, and did not cross over into the present. Similarly, none of the photographers tried to join the tableaux. To have done so would have been to break faith with the illusion, and end the separation between the zones of the dead and those of the living. The recognition that life and death are separate but conjoined was one of the effects of the tableaux. Moreover, this recognition is a characteristic of space and time which is exploited in the heritage industry. In this case, the intrusion of the peripheral dead into the central, occupied space of the living met several needs. It resurrected Victorian values as well as Victorian bodies and gave them validity then and there. It demonstrated the power of photography to create a long-lasting simulation of life. It allowed photographers to place themselves close to the living–dead and fix the Victorians, the actors and themselves to that place by making photographs as permanent records.

Recognising the proximity of life and death is an ordinary experience when thinking about history, which both recedes into the past and extends into the future. This ties history into photography, since both are reminders of time measured in periods much longer than the lifespan of individuals. As I have argued throughout this book, photographs are 'clocks for seeing' or *memento mori*, yet the sting of death is drawn by selling history and photography as amusements, as the safe expression of nostalgia. The sense of morbidity in history and photographs is altered by nostalgia, which ensures that the simulacrum of death can be contained, unlike its actual experience.

Despite its ability to weaken harsh realities, nostalgia is not an innocent form of day-dreaming about the past. It is widely believed to be a symptom of personal crisis. As the sociologist Bryan Turner writes, 'Being content is somehow incompatible with knowing that we are [mortal]'. It is also a sign of social crisis, associated with what Turner calls 'the loss of rural simplicity, traditional stability and cultural integration' following the impact of industrialised capitalism (Turner 1987: 152–3). According to David Lowenthal, nostalgia is commonly attacked as a shallow and false feeling. If

82. Martin Parr, 'Tableau of "Three Estate Workers" at "A Celebration of Photography", Lacock, Wiltshire, July 1989'.

nostalgia is a yearning for the lost past then it seems like a failure of nerve, wilfully turning against the present and its problems. Contradicting this point of view, Lowenthal argues that nostalgia does not 'necessarily connote despairing rejection of the present [since few] admirers of the past would actually choose to return to it' (Lowenthal 1989: 28). He concludes that nostalgia has a widespread use: it 'mainly envisages a time when folk did not feel fragmented, when doubt was either absent or patent, when thought fused with action…in short, a past that was unified and comprehensible, unlike the incoherent, divided present' (29).

This cohesive, forgetful aspect of nostalgia enables individuals to think about their mortality without succumbing to despair. On the contrary, sharing past times in

83. Martin Parr, 'Tableau of "The Chess Players" at "A Celebration of Photography", Lacock , Wiltshire, July 1989'.

ancient places enhances group recognition. Thus the 'celebration' of photography at Lacock provided the grounds for communal belief in the reality and longevity of English history and nationhood. The place of Lacock was the site for what the sociologist Rob Shields calls 'the crowd-practices and emotional community of affective groups, of institutional policies and political-economic arrangements [which take effect] right up the scale to the "imaginary community" of the territorial nation-state' (Shields 1991: 7).

The power of place in the 'imaginary geography' of the nation is matched by the power of time in creating a sense of belonging to what Patrick Wright calls an 'old country' (Wright 1985). Place and time are joined by the power of photography,

84. Amateur snapshot of tourists looking at 'The Chess Players' at 'A Celebration of Photography', Lacock, Wiltshire, July 1989.

which *limits* time to particular, observable acts in space. At Lacock time flowed in two directions. Most obviously (since the dead were resurrected) past time flowed forwards into the here and now. But present time also flowed backwards, since the place itself and the tableaux invited the club photographers to ignore their immediate surroundings, enter the imaginary past and imitate Fox Talbot. The double movement of time in a place distinguished by its age and identified with past characters and events is crucial to the experience of history, especially in its popular commodity form as 'heritage'. It must provoke a sense of survival, of preferred moments from the past surviving into the present. It also reminds tourists that they have survived, and are able to take advantage of current time-travel facilities.

It is possible to criticise historical re-enactments (whether in unique events at Lacock or in their widespread use in theme parks and heritage centres) for inaccuracy and for presenting a sanitised or comfortable version of the past. Yet these criticisms fail to recognise that many heritage attractions never set out to attain historical accuracy, which is anyway chimerical, but are popular entertainments. What makes

85. Amateur snapshot of a photographer in Lacock, Wiltshire, July 1989.

them distinctive is their difference from elitist and impenetrable 'knowledge' displayed in some museums: they aim to replace 'learning' with the pleasure of the spectacle. Re-enactments are loosely based on what their organisers take to be historical 'facts', but they do not attempt 'true histories' of events. Instead, they seek to entertain, divert or amuse through more or less elaborate spectacles. In this guise, historical re-enactments take on the authority of stories, abandoning dry-as-dust 'history' for tales of mythic significance.

Patrick Wright points out that history in its mythical form (taken away from facts, though not absolutely divorced from them) 'appears to flow *backwards* rather than forward in time'. This element of myth in staging heritage means that the force of time flowing backwards ties the event to those points which, altogether, make up the preferred, collective memory. In turn, this draws from and reinforces a dominant, national consciousness. 'Mythical History', Wright argues, is not oriented towards the future. Its purpose is to tie the present into a national essence which is then put forward as an unchanging though not always ancient past. The function of restaging the past is identity, rather than difference.

Identity as a historical theme has the ideological effect of producing a sense of continuity between past and present. Citing the philosopher Agnes Heller, Wright continues 'what is ancient serves as a model for repetition; thus the ancient and the present are not distinct. Anyone who repeats the ancient *is* ancient.' For the outcome to be reassurance, the ceremonies of re-enactment must be 'carried out and respected' (Wright 1985: 176–8). According to Wright, the nation exists through ceremonies and anniversary celebrations, and those who organise the repetitions, or take part in them, sustain the national past as something immutable and conservative.

Mythic history is one way of recreating a living sense of the national past and, as Wright observes, this explanation is not only fundamental to everyday life, but 'should also be seen more pointedly as its *project* – as the connection in which the prevailing symbolism of this old imperial nation works to establish its own over-arching constituency of support' (Wright 1985: 5–6). Everyday life is not merely what stands in contrast to the unusual or to 'History' (6). On the contrary, it is easy to transfer the experience of the everyday into those places which charge an entrance fee or which offer membership, and yet on admission prove to be not at all intimidating. All that tourists leave at the gate is any expectation of individual ownership, which is replaced by a *feeling of belonging* to the amorphous 'national heritage'. This was the purpose of the 'celebration' at Lacock, and it did not concern the Trust or Kodak that heritage and its audience was narrowly defined.

According to Robert Hewison, heritage is an anodyne entertainment which demonstrates that the British state of mind and the nation-state is in a terminal condition. He illustrates this on the cover of *The Heritage Industry* with a drawing which shows the island itself (rather than its inhabitants) to be dead, looking like an extinct bird, the pathetic 'Dodo Britannicus', stuffed and mounted in a museum case. Writing in this vein of mockery about what he considers to be the moribund National Trust, Hewison criticises it for being the repository of old, undemocratic forms of society, 'the fiefdom of "the amenity earls", or those who would like to live like them' (Hewison 1987: 55). Within this analysis, the Trust is seen to be a system of relief for the old upper classes, using public funds to maintain their stately homes, with its support coming largely from conservative or retrogressive groups of white, middle-class, middle-aged southerners.

Patrick Wright also makes links between what he considers to be reprehensible changes in the institutional 'body politic'. He argues that the way the Trust represents the past as a relic has serious 'political implications'. He writes that 'a society which understands itself through a preservationist perspective is in a morbid state', accusing the Trust of being sepulchral, 'an ethereal kind of holding company for the dead spirit of the nation' (Wright 1985: 56; 1986: 32–4).

Against this, I would suggest that the heritage industry, rather than being a sign of decline or morbidity of society, functions to allay anxieties about mortality. It is a secular assurance of continuity. Heritage – like photography – demonstrates that memories do not remain clustered around the sadness of lost time but shows how the past lives on, suggesting a possible after-life. One way of dealing with death is to pretend that it is not absolute, and to *bring the past to life* (with the important proviso that it lives in appearance rather than dangerous actuality). Morbidity in heritage and photography alike is contained by means of the promise of time-travel without the obligation to stay in the past. Displays and photographs offer a way to deal with lost youth or times before any of those presently living were born, a way simultaneously to have and to suppress the knowledge of the country as a boneyard of lost generations.

8

Pleasures of the imagination

OPPOSITIONAL PHOTOGRAPHY

IN THIS CHAPTER, I intend to discuss the techniques of a relatively small number of photographers who stand in opposition to the comfortable and contained world of the 'celebration' at Lacock. These critics claim greater seriousness as photographers than club amateurs. They do not seek for themselves the tourists' goals of reassurance, and they do not recognise the characteristic tourist anxiety of missing the essential experience of a treasured landscape or site. They do not share the contempt for tourists and trippers that I have drawn attention to in the work of P. H. Emerson on the Norfolk Broads in the late 1880s, but they do distance themselves from groups of unreflecting, uncritical holiday-makers. Unlike Emerson, they deliberately adopt a parodic or quizzical stance in relation to the kinds of photographs which tourists produce or which are produced for them in guidebooks. They refer to snapshots, postcards and advertising, but they do not reproduce the confirming nature of such mainstream imagery. Whereas to conform to the rules of standard, clichéd imagery defeats the imagination, or renders its work unnecessary, oppositional photographers often break the rules of composition, subject matter and captioning. Their disruption of normal tourist imagery is evidence of what they take to be the problematics of touring, which tourists are discouraged from noticing at all. For oppositional photographers, the pleasures of the imagination are precisely those which enable them to sharpen the historic complexities of race, class and gender where they have been

86. David A. Bailey, 'From the Sheffield residency on the centenary of the Mappin Art Gallery', 1987.

softened and weakened by conservative attitudes often found in tourist entertainments. Despite their difference from Emerson, they mark their difference from tourists and from popular, formulaic landscape imagery in a movement that he would have recognised – by producing monographs and exhibitions for the narrower audiences who visit bookshops, libraries and galleries of contemporary art.

Though oppositional photographers separate themselves from standard tourist fare, they do not segregate themselves from the reassuring imagery of 'normal' tourism. Opposition depends on harnessing the dominant modality of tourism, especially the identification of core English values which are constantly repeated. Oppositional photographers rework the language of tourism, and play with its appearance and concerns. They take part in a constant dialogue with the everyday practices of tourism and with its standard imagery. Their success depends upon their ability to embrace the cliché and alter it, making it appear new in ways which are surprising and not necessarily subtle.

Rather than re-create the tourist photograph, which is an analogue of a beautiful, numinous world, oppositional photographers are more likely to suggest the impossibility of its being coherent, defined or positive. Some of them, such as Martin Parr, utilise sardonic humour. Others, including Paul Reas, Peter Kennard and Ingrid Pollard, try to unsettle the viewer, and aim for irony and confrontation. Their subjects include the comic gap between expectation and experience which opens up when tourist attractions claim to speak to individuals who then find themselves in crowds and unable to pause for long in any one place, or are discouraged from leaving the prescribed route. Another of their targets is tourism's use of difference as 'exotic local colour'. This orthodoxy promises that the differences between tourists and their hosts will not only be entertaining, but will strengthen identity rather than weaken it. In contrast, oppositional photographers use difference to highlight social inequalities and exclusions. In dealing with tourism, they are critical of the political nature of so-called 'heritage', and they express doubts about the 'imagined community' of England fashioned in the image of the dominant white middle-class.

None the less, this stance remains within the hierarchy of tourism outlined in the introduction, in which trippers scarcely see at all, tourists only glance in order to find reassurance, and travellers practise a long, reflective gaze across the too tranquil interval of English landscape tradition. Like Emerson, oppositional photographers might be regarded as travellers. They would no doubt reject the hierarchies that were so important to Emerson, but at the same time they sustain the gap between themselves and the object of enquiry. To express their disquiet, they rely on the existence of standard behaviour among tourists, who accept and demand the assurances of clichéd imagery. Whereas tourists prepare to collapse into the experience of holiday-making, the photographic practices of its critics are designed to prevent their incorporation. They deliberately alter many of the signs which tourists expect. They do so not from fear of being mistaken for tourists, but because they are engaged in a very different activity. Their aims are different from tourists'; they are not even looking in the manner of tourists towards treasured landscapes. Quite unlike tourists, they are engaged in critiques of tourism, of heritage, and of certain failings or disasters of nationalism. They are concerned with the inequalities that stem from political choices, often feeding on xenophobia, racism and class anatagonisms; or, as I argue in the final chapter, they are concerned with violence, often based on gender difference, and generally meted out in the name of culture by men to women and nature.

REPEATS

Before I discuss the practices of oppositional photography, I must describe one of the chief characteristics of 'normal' tourist imagery which it alters or subverts – namely repetition. At both practical and ideological levels, repetition is the basis of successful tourism. The tour is designed to deliver large numbers of people to a site at any one time, and the logistics of the operation demand control and routine. Operators know the routes, the hotels, the sites, and to ensure the smoothness of the enterprise they are prepared to 'guide' customers, even reduce them to dependency.

Tour operators offer a high level of reassurance and predictability to lessen the effects on their customers of unsettling new experiences. Even more importantly, operators endeavour to allay fears that tourists might be denied the pleasures they have paid for. Operators hope to provide the appropriate experience and prevent disappointment.

The foremost hope of tourists is that pleasure will outweigh anxiety. In order to achieve this, they seek reassurance through familiarity: repetition is crucial, since it returns to tourists whatever they are looking for. Repetition not only smothers the unexpected but also reliably re-presents the already known. It guarantees a high level of group solidarity and satisfaction.

Critics of tourism tend to see its repetitive nature as the source of unintentional comedy. Martin Parr photographs tourists using stepping-stones to cross a stream in the Peak District of Derbyshire from his book *The Cost of Living* (see colour plate 11). The image shows the site crowded with people, with someone standing on every stone (Parr 1989). The photographer reveals that tourists in a mass are fixed in several ways: they are literally fixed to the spot; limited by their inability to choose another visiting-time; fixed by Parr in a picture which reveals their plight.

It is characteristic of this photographer to ignore the beauty spot and concentrate on the party of tourists. In images from the Peak District and Lacock, Parr remains outside the group in the privileged position of the observer. This position establishes him as a traveller, looking with greater authority than trippers can. Parr travels in search of trippers, who become objects of wonder. In his photographs it seems that trippers see only entertainments which have been carefully prepared for them, distilled, and often narrowly defined, such as beauty spots in Derbyshire or actors restaging Fox Talbot's photographs at Lacock. If Parr was the traveller who turned trippers into objects of ridicule or comedy, then he would be in a position similar to that of nineteenth-century writers laughing at the embarrassments of class which derived from the sieve-like nature of inland waterways as holiday resorts. But Parr is working in a completely different historical situation – one in which it is the political and social consequences of tourism and the 'heritage industry' which are the actual objects of enquiry and fascination. In other words, Parr and the other photographers discussed in this chapter are not aiming simply to set themselves up as travellers distinct from trippers or tourists as objects of fascination. Instead, they are placing themselves in a wider debate about the foremost industry of tourism. They set out to demonstrate that the practices and presumptions of tourism actually reveal the opposite of what the industry intends: instead of making clear that the nation coheres in a deep horizontal comradeship through its historical sites and treasured landscapes, tourism reveals that contemporary England is deeply fractured.

QUOTATIONS

Nevertheless, the attempt to save the coherence of the world is central to tourist practices, as well as to its cultural politics, so that it remains one object of fascination among oppositional photographers. Repetition and reliability, as I argued in chapter 4, are mainstays of the photographic industry, and correspond to the tourist industry's goal of encouraging tourists to indentify with each other and recognise that they have achieved their purpose as sightseers.

I now intend to discuss in more detail how oppositional photographers use repetition against itself, so that it ceases to provide reassurance and, in their work, becomes the source of comedy or anxiety. Successful repetition and group identity depends on correct quotation, so that, as I argued in the previous chapter, the participants at Lacock identified themselves as serious amateurs by copying Fox Talbot's photography. Repeating the scene in the manner of the originator required that all signs of contemporary life be omitted. Only correct 'nineteenth-century' information must fall between the quotation marks, or be held within the frame. This was relatively easy, since the desired images were known and already framed: photographers had only to copy or quote the originals.

In repeating the scenes and searching for accurate quotations, photographers were underlining their ambition to identify their work with originality, or a certain notion of authenticity. Yet even as they tried, they also unintentionally underlined how their versions differed from Fox Talbot's. Instead of permitting the identification of copies with originals, the act of repetition emphasised that the quotations were not originals. Even so, the amateurs' overwhelming desire was to ignore the articulation of difference for an easy transition into a perfect, miniature world. By placing the restaged scenes within the frame, they established themselves as distanced viewers, and entered into the fantasy of over-seeing orderly domestic life in Victorian times.

The use of 'Fox Talbot' as an emblem of value is a rare case of how photographic 'authors' contribute towards a special type of cultural map in England – one which directs tourists to places which have inspired original creation. It is much more common for heritage guardians to draw on poets and novelists than to use artists or photographers to show how genius, entertainment and nostalgia for the past flourishes in England. This canon of writers creates its own geography. Besides 'Shakespeare Country' there is 'Brontë Country' in Yorkshire, 'Hardy Country' in Wiltshire and Dorset, 'Catherine Cookson Country' in Tyneside and 'Beatrix Potter' tourism in the Lake District (Squire 1993).

One painter who has a 'Country' is Constable, whose work stands for the reassurance of pre-industrial England. As we see in Paul Reas's photograph, visitors enter this art-historical world at Flatford Mill in Suffolk in search of the original rural scene (Reas 1993; Yale 1991: 241). As I intend to show, this photograph suggests that 'Constable Country' is held together by a mixture of desire and anxiety, identification and difference (see colour plate 12).

In the photograph, the tour guide carries a miniature reproduction of the original painting of the mill and indicates the area which Constable painted. This confirms that the party has arrived at the site, and overcomes the tourists' fear of failing to see the desired spot. Using the copy as a frame for the view enables tourists to repeat and enjoy the 'correct' quotation; the copy is an equivalent of the painting and a safeguard against missing the point. The gesture and the copy together mean 'here is the view that Constable saw', or 'this is the spot where Constable stood'. To confirm themselves as serious tourists, the visitors expect to measure what they see against the print. This practice establishes similarities and differences between the present site and the copy of the painting, which, if not too great, might be used to measure Constable's artistry, or otherwise be blamed on the passage of time. The guide intends both the copy and his authoritative gesture to provide sufficient evidence for the authenticity of the view, to delimit wayward readings, and to deter people from looking in the 'wrong' direction.

Still, the guide's use of these signs in the presence of tourists also indicates that the excursion risks disaster. The guide and the tourists might be forced to acknowledge the absence of the artist in 'Constable Country'. Instead of supplying a measure of reassurance that the site had been found and the quotation correctly repeated, the miniature might set off a whole chain of disappointments. The guide's print of 'Flatford Mill' is a copy, a second-order image alluding to the absent first-order painting. In turn, the original work of art alludes to a scene which is no longer available, or never was available except as it is represented by painting. Hence, if the aim is to discover Constable, staring at the view is futile. Indeed, coming across the site and looking at it marks the beginning of disillusionment. Tourists cannot hope to restore the original scene, reconstitute the act of painting, repeat the original act, or put an equivalent in the frame. In the search for origins they discover only a series of absences – the missing site, the missing artist, the missing painting, and the gap between desire and achievement.

Nevertheless, despite the disappointment of recognising nothing but the absence of original material, it is the miniature copy itself that saves the tourists' experience before the landscape. The print measures neither the artistry of Constable nor the authenticity of the view, but the authenticity of the visit. Tourists accept it as a souvenir of the artist, the painting, the scene, and themselves. They accept the souvenir as authentic, material evidence of either location or the original object, and this acceptance becomes the authentic experience of tourists. In addition to looking at the print, they might take photographs or purchase them, collecting miniatures to mark their own experience.

Their replicas, postcards and prints are none the less signs of dispossession, because souvenirs merely substitute for originals. Despite this, the distance between the self and the original signified in the miniature copy is not experienced as loss, silence, or the absence of 'correct' quotation. Above all, the copy is a way of placing something authentic between the quotation marks or in the frame. The print or postcard puts an end to the anxiety of failing; it becomes the tourists' report, their narrative of exploration and proof of arrival. In Paul Reas's photograph, the guide holds the talisman which saves the tourists.

These signs exist within the world depicted in the photograph, but Reas's image has its own context in his book and exhibition, entitled *Flogging a Dead Horse*. Reas's photograph of tourists in 'Constable Country' must be seen not only as their display of tourism, but the photographer's criticism of the 'heritage industry'.

Reas's work stands in the tradition of cultural commentators and historians who oppose the 'heritage industry' because they believe it promotes nostalgia and the ideology of conservation (Wiener 1981; Horne 1984; Wright 1985; Hewison 1987; Walsh 1992; for a critique see Davies 1988). They argue that heritage is not real, has no authenticity, no aura, and no foundation in history, and that it represents a break with a politicised and complex historical appreciation of contemporary English life. It is a substitute for the problems of history, a panacea for audiences who receive simple narratives designed to allay anxiety and anchor them in a profoundly stable present. As such, heritage is merely another example of what Benjamin called 'the phony spell of a commodity' (Benjamin 1973: 233) cast over a deluded or self-deluding public by a manipulative 'culture industry', the purveyor of conformity, boredom and 'flight from reality' (see Swingewood 1977: 12–18). The regular shape of heritage experiences leads its critics to characterise it as history up for sale, or history reduced to its commodity form. The heritage industry is in the business of inserting clichés in the frame, without inflection or uncertainty.

Though the various critics of the heritage industry highlight its morbidity or its misreading of history, they are not claiming that an underlying 'true' history has been neglected. Focusing on the popular use of spectacle by powerful groups such as English Heritage and the National Trust, they argue that heritage entertainments displace a sense of continuity and replace it with its opposite – a past which is complete in itself and has no bearing on present conditions. The periods represented by designated 'heritage centres' in England, such as Wigan Pier Heritage Centre or Ironbridge Gorge Museum Trust (Yale 1991: 102), for all their apparent difference, appear to be self-contained, autonomous moments of history. Uncoupling the representation of the past from its context encourages heritage audiences to perceive the present in selected ways. They teach audiences by omission to fail to see the contradictions which existed in the past; or they suggest that conflicts are quickly resolved and isolated. What visitors learn at heritage centres is 'unreal' because it is uncomplicated and sanitised to such an extent that it can neither be grasped nor truly believed in.

In his book *The Representation of the Past* Kevin Walsh criticises the numerous 'living-history' events organised by English Heritage, including its re-creation of the best-known ancient battle and date in English history. In 1990 almost 20,000 people saw mock Normans defeat a stand-in King Harold again in '1066 Country' in Sussex (Walsh 1992: 133). Though such re-creations of English history are presented and presumably accepted by their large audiences as national–popular entertainments, Walsh regards them as 'mere titillation, meaningless amateur dramatics promoting the postmodern simulacrum, a hazy image of a manipulated and trivialized past [in which] history is decontextualized and mixed with non-history in a promotion of pastiche' (103). Walsh sees nothing innocent about these enactments, since they always carry a political message which need never be openly declared. This has important consequences for the way people think about the past, how they think it relates to the present, and whether or not they consider the historical, dynamic nature of experience. He writes that the 'living-history' past is 'promoted as that which [is] no longer important to and contingent upon people's daily experiences', intensifying to the point where the past emerges as 'a reservoir of shallow surfaces which can be exploited in the heritage centre or on the biscuit tin' (3). Walsh argues convincingly that heritage becomes a distinct ideological tool for sustaining class and regional divisions, promoting and reinforcing the values and tastes of higher-status groups as well as privileging the south of England (123–40).

When English working-class experience becomes heritage, it remains a trope of the midlands or the north. It is celebrated in places such as the Black Country Museum in the midlands, Wigan Pier in the north-west and the North of England Open Air Museum at Beamish in the north-east. At these centres, working-class life is a thing of the past; it is recognisably situated in the modern, industrialised world, and its harshness is softened only by the sense of local community. Throughout the experience, visitors find a past which was primitive in comparison to their own times, yet was homely, straightforward and decent. These centres suggest that working-class life, though thankfully over, was not so bad after all. This effect is achieved in two ways: either the past is brought into sharp focus, and its materials laid out with a startling clarity but empty of harmful effects; or the past is seen in soft focus, tinged with the glow of nostalgia rather than discoloured by smog (see illustration opposite).

Paul Reas works against the idea that working-class life is over, and against nostalgia for the past. His photographs need to be seen within the larger context of criticism provided by authors such as Walsh and Hewison. The title of his book makes

87. Publicity leaflet for Black Country Museum, *c*.1990. Original in colour.

clear what he considers to be the status of a country where real work has been replaced by false make-work, and a whole politicised history has been erased by turning it into 'industrial heritage'. *Flogging a Dead Horse* is scathing of heritage, particularly when it subsumes the history of former industrial areas. The political decisions made under Thatcherism to run down or close much 'traditional' manufacturing industry such as coal-mining, steel and shipbuilding, were matched by the boom in the heritage 'industry' on the same sites. In *Flogging a Dead Horse*, Paul Reas pictures the few redundant miners who are employed as 'interpreters' providing 'authentic' personal reminiscence. They are surrounded by tourists who wait to have their picture taken as mementos of holidays in places in Wales and the north-east of England which until recently were sites of work, relative wealth, and community.

Whereas Reas maintains the realism of photography and preserves its associated ambiguity, others prefer to underscore their views by writing texts over their pictures. John Kippin's photograph 'Heritage – Markham Main, South Yorkshire' clarifies this photographer's belief that the de-industrialisation of Britain and the destruction of the coal-mining industry is a political choice with profound consequences (see colour plate

13). The photograph declares that the traditional work of that pit is lost, and the community destroyed; moreover, Conservative Party policies have ended a way of life and yet turned the destruction into another site for the national–popular celebration of 'heritage' – which empties the place of both its life and bitter ending. When factories are knocked down, sometimes fragments of machines are placed in museums and exist as illegible signs of both industrial processes and social, working life; in contrast to this practice, Kippin seeks to write the history into the picture.

As well as commenting on social change openly designed by Conservative policies, Kippin argues that heritage entertainments are covertly political. His postcard called 'ENGLISHISTORY' (from the exhibition 'Futureland') suggests that the past has been annexed by the Conservative Party (see colour plate 14). Under the Tories, the past is at the mercy of anti-intellectualism and contempt for the historic experiences and struggles of whole sectors of the population. As Neal Ascherson wrote in the *Observer* in 1987, 'the Tory historical message simply tells the public that "your heritage is the story of how we came to rule you" ' (cited in Lowenthal 1989: 25).

Both Ascherson's remark and Kippin's photograph are overstatements, since the purpose of heritage displays is not to tell the story of ruling, nor is 'English history' owned by Tories. There is some truth, however, in their claim that heritage is exclusive. Kippin's work, Martin Parr in *The Cost of Living* and Karen Knorr in *Marks of Distinction* (1991) draw attention to exclusivity and the way it centres on treasured landscapes and rare objects (see colour plate 17 and illustration on page 253). They show that heritage does not exist primarily in the artefacts of working lives drawn from disparate places and amalgamated into a 'centre'. It exists, rather, in the ancient landscape gardens, great houses and precious objects of the gentry and aristocracy.

Yet in these forms heritage might not be recognised as national–popular at all. On the contrary, it might provoke the question 'whose heritage is it?' – and the response that it does not belong to the pasts of most visitors. Despite the blandishments of trustees, visitors might recognise the wealth on display as evidence of exploitation.

Though such readings cannot be prevented, they do not form the appeal of heritage. It speaks to the deep comradeship of being English, attempting to silence protest. Heritage, as an adjunct of nationality, is exclusive. Recognising this might encourage the reactionary bent of much nostalgia for the past, yearning for a return to those more certain times when people knew their place. Heritage celebration might then become a form of continuous deference in a nation still nostalgic about class distinctions and hierarchy – reaching its extreme, conspiratorial form in what David Lowenthal describes as a 'perspective designed by the wealthy and powerful to justify their control of the present' (Lowenthal 1989: 25).

This deep suspicion of heritage as a plot by the wealthy or politicians to establish on their terms what it means to be English and patriotic is joined by an equally strong suspicion of heritage as a commodity. Other oppositional photographers such as Alison Marchant, Ingrid Pollard, Victor Sloan and Peter Turley, are concerned that history in England has been hijacked and distorted by market forces which encourage tourists to seek out and reinforce the orthodox view of England as 'pretty as a picture'. In contrast, these photographers decide to place the 'incorrect' information within the frame (see Wombell and Deslanders 1990). Unlike the photographic experiences designated as appropriate or correct in 'normal' tourism, the emphasis in their photographs is not on identification and comforting reassurance but on dislocation and disturbance.

Rather than accept the authenticating function of the souvenir, oppositional photographers use it as a familiar reference which they can disrupt. Consider Peter Kennard's well-known image 'The Haywain, Constable (1821), Cruise Missiles USA (1983)' reproduced on page 252. In this work Kennard collaged photographs of missiles into a reproduction of one of Constable's best-known paintings – a picture which now has wide popular appeal as a memory of 'old England' and the riches of the countryside. The photographer adopts the cliché that *The Haywain* stands for an idyllic, pastoral England, an age of innocence before the advent of industry. He uses Constable to establish the tranquillity of the English countryside so that he can underscore the hostility of foreign bodies. Kennard's subversion of Constable gives sudden and graphic warning of greater erosions taking place on English soil, the erosions of national sovereignty and safety that began when England became the land-carrier of the machines of American 'defense'. By misquoting or misrepresenting the painting by Constable, he demonstrates jarring discontinuity in the idea of England. Furthermore, by placing the missiles in the cart rather than in the landscape, he suggests the complicity of the English in their own putative destruction.

The success of Kennard's intervention depends on the widespread acceptance of the painting as emblematic of 'England'. *The Haywain* carries more weight than any

88. Peter Kennard, 'The Haywain, Constable (1821), Cruise Missiles USA (1983)', 1983.

single photograph of the countryside. Kennard takes advantage of the painting's double authenticity: it is a sign of 'Constable' (which means English genius) and a sign of 'England' (which means unspoilt and unconquered). This double authenticity of genius and purity is the strength of the country, and it is that which is endangered by foreign armaments. By juxtaposing the powerful signifiers 'Constable' and 'missiles', the collage shows that the Government and its supporters break faith with the past. It is Government, Kennard implies, which 'misquotes' England.

Peter Kennard uses Constable as a signifier of English value in order to show how by contrast England is in danger from current policies. In a different fashion, Paul Reas's sardonic photograph of 'Constable Country' reveals tourists engaging in the repetitions which are central to keeping alive an idea of England. Both photographers refer to a reassuring source, though they force it to tell different, contrary tales.

89. Karen Knorr, 'The employment of a housewife in the country', 1991.

Kennard's image suggests the reality of a fundamental 'England'. For this photographer, 'Constable' stands for an underlying, stable idea of the country holding out against a Government held in thrall by a dominant foreign ally. This idea of a stable England was endangered by the political imbalance in the so-called 'special relationship' between Britain and the USA, as he and anti-nuclear protestors saw it, in 1983. The photograph was a demonstration of and a protest against an imbalance which might ensure that nuclear war between the USA and the USSR would start in England.

For Reas, working with the signifier 'Constable' ten years later, the political situation is quite different. The end of the Cold War and the break-up of the Soviet Union meant that nuclear weapons and American bases in England were no longer such bones of contention. For Reas, the signifier 'Constable' does not stand for an underlying sense of the 'old country' so much as the ludicrous promise of authenticity made by the tourist industry. Reas believes that neither 'Constable' nor 'England' can be reclaimed on tours around treasured landscapes. 'Constable Country' is a spurious entity, an invention of the guidebooks, and the artist's genius is not to be found in Suffolk in 1993. Though 'Constable' continues to stand for England, this is clearly neither unitary nor precise (see Daniels 1993: 200–42).

DIFFERENCE AND EXCLUSION

Identity and difference, the one creating the conditions for the other, are crucial to tourism. The ability to recognise and repeat signs is basic to belonging to any 'imagined community', including that of the nation. At tourist sites, the signs of Englishness are meant to be easily read: this is achieved partly by connecting once distant, treasured sites with ordinary social life and reinforcing a sense of identity through familiarity. Many historical sites become inviting because they have shops and tearooms. In addition, especially at English Heritage sites, tourists see history restaged as family entertainment in the form of colourful re-enactments. History exists in pageants or living histories which make identification with the past easier than wandering around mute buildings. Thus these sites and events create a sense of belonging for participants: they are signs of England's heritage even for those who remain outsiders. In other words, the loss of aura has a positive effect in defining the land and suffusing it with English national history, defining Englishness and leaving it to visitors to feel whether or not it belongs to them. Some tourists will be seeking confirmation of their belonging to the imagined community; others might feel resentment that their histories are excluded from the core of values; others yet might feel relieved that Englishness remains quite other and foreign to them. The mix of tourists from different ethnic backgrounds at heritage sites, seen in Martin Parr's photograph of Stonehenge, is itself a signal of belonging and difference (see colour plate 15). The nationality of both figures in the picture is unknown, and they might both be English, but because they look as if they originate from different continents, the photograph makes the point that visitors to heritage sites might be engaging in different activities: they might be identifying with their own national past or recognising its otherness.

   In both cases, they will measure the tourist experience of English heritage

... a lot of what
MADE ENGLAND GREAT
is founded on the blood of slavery,
the sweat of working people...an industrial
REVOLUTION without the
Atlantic Triangle ...

90. Ingrid Pollard, from the Pastoral Interlude Series, 1987–88. Original in colour.

against their sense of themselves as belonging to specific communities. In the first place, individuals see themselves as distinct and separate, and then recognise others who share the same sense of integration, thus creating a sense of being inside the group. To these insiders it seems real and natural that there should be outsiders. Indeed, English tourists together at English sites make a formidable body of insiders. The heritage sites encourage them to share a sense of integration in opposition to foreign tourists, who can gain a sense of the English national heritage as observers, though it remains foreign to them, and they remain foreign to it. Outsiders are by definition excluded from entering the local group; they fail to recognise or to repeat signs in the appropriate manner, and so fail to integrate. This is not merely a passive effect of being an outsider: it invites those who share and practice the core values to take positive steps of exclusion or to acquiesce in them (Wright 1985: 8).

Nevertheless, if foreigners are left outside, many English people feel that they too have no central place even in the national–popular, let alone the core values of traditional England. Those who belong to marginal groups may be integrated in themselves, but that does not mean they have access to the national; indeed often the contrary. Marginal or subordinated groups have to defend their particular identities against the social mainstream, which appears to be irresistible, unyielding and unforgiving. As a result, individuals who are English can find themselves excluded from the core heritage of 'England' because of their colour.

In recent times a number of independent photographers have attacked the narrow definition of national identity. A significant collection of these works was drawn together in *Heritage, Image + History,* an exhibition and catalogue organised by Cornerhouse in Manchester and Impressions Gallery of York (Wombell and Deslanders 1990). In their introductory essay Paul Wombell and Gerald Deslanders suggest that 'previously neglected areas of the past are now being brought into view' and that the issue of diversity of historical experience is now at the forefront. Questions of race, gender, class and regionalism are being raised among photographers who attend to the special unease of Blacks or Muslims when faced with the established meanings of countryside or museums (Tawadros 1988). For example, in order to demonstrate her inability to insert herself into the hegemonic culture, Ingrid Pollard uses quotation and its simultaneous destruction to attack the assimilationist idea that Black people can take on English pastimes unproblematically. She demonstrates her exclusion from the dominant sense of national identity in two registers in the photograph reproduced on page 255 and in the colour plate 23. Firstly, she alters the usual subject matter of the pastoral scene. She sets up a version of the popular English sport of fishing, but the fisherman is Black, so that observers would recognise him as an individual conventionally excluded from enjoying countryside pastimes or rural sports. Furthermore, he is fishing with a net rather than angling with a rod, and the photograph is hand-tinted rather than naturalistic in colour – alterations to the idyll which suggest greater differences between white and Black experience of country pursuits. The second alteration is to the caption. Instead of a description of place or time, she writes '…a lot of what MADE ENGLAND GREAT is

Plate 18. Jem Southam, 'Cook's kitchen' from *The Red River*, 1989.

Plate 19. Keith Arnatt, from *Miss Grace's Lane*, 1987.

Plate 20. Ron O' Donnell, 'Waterfall', 1992.

founded on the blood of slavery...'. This statement wrecks what remains of the cohesion of the picture.

Opposition in this manner might appear too polemical and insufficiently sensitive to the relative ease with which minorities in England now cross barriers, compared even to recent times. However, such social mobility threatens those who perceive traditional (white) English culture to be weakened by multi-culturalism. To take an everyday example, the English 'national cuisine' of roast beef and Yorkshire pudding, or fish and chips, is in decline, complemented or supplanted in every High Street by food of other nations. This might be regarded as the armchair colonisation of exotic lands via their cuisine. It might also be regarded by some traditionalists and purists as a loss to the guarded core of Englishness, bringing on a dangerous 'weakening of the attachment of cultural heritage to specific places' (Prentice 1993: 31–2). This weakening of attachment has been described with some regret as a sign of cultural 'slackening': 'one listens to reggae, watches a western, eats McDonald's food for lunch and local cuisine for dinner... "anything goes", and the epoch is one of slackening' (Lyotard 1984: 76).

If slackening is characteristic of postmodern times, it has plenty of opponents among the traditionalists. When the specific cultural meanings of heritage sites are weakened, a discernible tension ensues. The right-wing politician Lord Tebbit favours the insularity of 'the island race' as a protection against 'waves of immigration' and foreigners who refuse to identify with (or submit to) the dominant English culture. Tebbit and other campaigners against what they believe to be the 'slackening' of a multi-racial society support the continuing attachment of orthodox meanings to heritage sites and to the English countryside. They prefer to see 'old England' occupied by white Anglo-Saxons. Otherwise, whole sets of 'new residents', even in the second generation, might simply disregard traditional meanings and habitual behaviour.

In 1991 Tebbit invented his 'cricket test' for national loyalty: the Pakistani touring side defeated England in a Test Match, and the victory was rapturously received by 'new residents'. In response, Tebbit questioned their loyalty to England, suggesting that many non-white Britons would support the visiting cricket team from their country of origin when it played in England rather than the home team whose nationality they held. Tebbit's 'cricket test' demonstrates the pertinence of the question 'Whose heritage do you want to claim?' That sense of the bourgeois-imperial so crucial to Anglo-Saxons can no longer be promoted as universal, nor is it necessarily dominant – though it is obviously so in certain well-defined activities such as visiting treasured landscapes and country houses, or taking part in countryside sports.

Ingrid Pollard finds no slackening of white hegemony in the countryside. Indeed, she finds it insular and more racist than ever. As I argued above, she demonstrates this by inserting the 'wrong' person into the picture, and giving it the 'incorrect' title. In another well-known image, she testifies to the success of the pressure which she feels excludes her. As we see, she captions this photograph of the Lake District with the words 'A visit to the countryside is always accompanied by a feeling of unease, dread…'. This is a surprising, shocking caption to what at first sight is an image of someone who seems to be enjoying herself in the countryside, appearing to be 'at home'. Yet, as we learn from the caption, despite the commodification of the countryside as a haunt for well-equipped ramblers following in the footsteps of the Romantics, for Pollard the landscape is disenchanting: the spell it casts as a commodity seeks to discount her as a customer. In emphasising her exclusion, she also indicts what she takes to be the oppressive homogeneity of visitors to the Lakes.

The testimonies of both Lord Tebbit and Ingrid Pollard suggest that the meaning of the countryside is in transition. This makes for uncertain readings. Looking at John Kippin's photograph of 'Muslims at Lake Windermere', we discover that the tendency to 'read' the view in terms of traditional English activities is hard to resist: the men are praying, while the women and children wait (see colour plate 16). Describing this scene in *Creative Camera*, Paul Wombell writes that the party are 'picnicking'. Wombell surmises 'They're probably from Lancashire and came to work in the mills, and now they are tourists in this heritage England. It turns the idea of British landscape upside down; who goes there, what meanings can people get' (Wombell 1992: 22). Of course, Wombell arrives at the progressive point – suggesting that the meaning of heritage is altered by participants and audiences, though he incorrectly assumes the group are engaged in a 'traditional' picnic. The picnic has specific meanings. Though, as John Hartley writes, it has long ceased to be restricted to 'a pleasure party' drawn from 'the fashionable social classes', and now signifies 'the widest reaches of global-American family ideology' (Hartley 1992: 52), still the traditional picnic is not linked with prayers. Although there is a spiritual tradition to English landscape, prayers in this fashion are quite unconnected to the pantheism or Romanticism which is usually associated with it.

The question 'Whose heritage do you want to claim?' is answered by David A. Bailey in a decidedly ambiguous way. Bailey, a Black photographer, poses with a white, marble bust in the Mappin Gallery in Sheffield where he was artist-in-residence (see illustration on page 241). In his casual embrace of this precious object, as if the thing were alive and a friend, Bailey displays a certain insouciance or 'lack of respect'. He refuses to accept the museum object as a normalising sign of ruling culture. At the same time, his nonchalance cannot simply destroy the authority of the white bust, which remains there still. He was able to approach this symbol of the ruling culture, which has historically excluded him, only by adopting for a time the special guise of a bona fide artist. In other words, the rarity of the Black man throwing his arm around the white bust signifies his general exclusion, not his sudden incorporation. Writing about the relations among such objects, cultural institutions and 'the people', Tony Bennett points out that museums intentionally exclude everything which is defined as 'other and subordinate'. He writes 'If we know that we are out of place, we also know that this effect is not accidental, that we are in the midst of an object lesson in things which, in some measure, instructs us through its capacity to intimidate' (Bennett 1988: 73). Though evidently not intimidated, Bailey remains an outsider, along with many other sectors of 'the people'.

This projection of Englishness as white and middle-class and used (historically) to governing other nations is the central, immovable fact of national belonging. Consequently, heritage can be formidably exclusive – witness the preponderence of white, middle-class, middle-aged members of the National Trust, which has most of its properties in the rural south of England (Hewison 1987: 87; Walsh 1992: 123–35). As Patrick Wright stresses, 'the bourgeois-imperial sense of national identity and belonging is often projected as the absolute essence of a social life which it also places conveniently beyond question' (Wright 1985: 17). This sense of national identity deriving its authority from the middle classes means that individuals who are English can find themselves excluded from the core heritage of 'England' because of their social class.

Kevin Walsh, in *The Representation of the Past*, uses statistics to demonstrate the class basis of the dominant culture. This is significant because of the relative neglect of class as something which can be measured. According to contemporary myths, social class is unimportant. Class struggle has ceased, and class identity has been ironed flat by the spectacle of the malls. As part of this process of denying the existence of class, the Tory Party has developed an ambitious rhetoric to proclaim the 'classless' society. Though they overstate the case, there have been important changes in the perception of class difference. It does appear that class-consciousness as a discursive formation has disappeared, just as the agencies and structures which were once such clear expositions of class differences, and especially of working-class identity, have been dismantled or become redundant. Class-conscience apparently has no language to speak itself, no structures to form itself except inadequately among the fag-ends of the jealous and the dispossessed. But, as Walsh demonstrates, certain preferred 'pasts' which have been turned into commodities and established as standing for the whole 'imagined community' of England, are often centred on definite class-formations. These, however, are now supposed to be 'historic' and therefore without currency in contemporary life. None the less, as Walsh shows, 'Englishness' continues to incorporate and exclude on grounds of social class. These activities are evident in the audiences for 'traditional heritage, country-house visiting, and the wider consumption of images of rurality', which remain the holiday haunts of the white middle-classes (Walsh 1992: 123–35). The sites most favoured by the middle classes are the great houses and gardens which they do not own, but to which they aspire.

The intimidating and socially exclusive character of upper-middle-class aspirations for high culture has been the subject of Karen Knorr's photography. In her book *Marks of Distinction,* Knorr moves to and fro between high culture's guardian institutions such as public, 'national' galleries and private country estates which outsiders may sometimes visit (Knorr 1991). In the photograph 'Pleasures of the Imagination' an anonymous man stands with his back towards us, while we see the landscape painting he is studying (see colour plate 17). The photograph reveals the signs of exclusion not only in the ropes that bar entry into the space reserved for the paintings but also in the way the narrow space occupied by those chairs and pictures, with their vistas into landscapes puncturing the grey walls, is symbolically richer and more spacious than that occupied by the viewer caught on the wrong side of the barrier. It is as if the space on offer for viewers is a space of allowance, permission or sufferance – a very limited and class-bound type of freedom *outside* the pale the aristocracy draws around itself. In the gallery space, the pleasures of the imagination are predominantly aesthetic. They are not supposed to be soured by feelings of exclusion for whatever reasons. At the same time, the shape of the gallery expresses the knowledge of exclusion from ownership, and so the pleasures of the imagination *include* the recognition of not belonging, of a heritage which is exclusive rather than common.

According to Knorr, it is a normal and not perverse activity of tourism to take pleasure in hierarchy, exclusion and the partiality of heritage. There is something that rings true in her assessments of a heritage drawn from a few successful dynasties, which is allowed to stand in for the past of all those millions whose ancestors did not write themselves into the landscape, build houses, amass fortunes or patronise the arts. To write history and sell heritage remains the spoil of victors or their apologists. In her series of photographs on 'Country Life' (which refers to an upper-class journal of the same name), Knorr refers ironically to 'The Employment of a Housewife in the Country' in the caption for a photograph of a classical statue that signifies 'plenty' placed in a carefully-designed vista (see illustration on page 253). Since neither work nor housewifery is in evidence, which are the business of servants, Knorr indicates that they are absent and irrelevant among the landed gentry. Among the features of this world is the erasure of real work, and all signs of causality and effect. What remains important is the idea of 'plenty' and the unbroken, unspoiled view across a landscape. The pleasures in looking at the photograph are mixed. We are invited to look at something which has the romance of contraband, a sight stolen from the owners, since few onlookers dare presume this world belongs to them. On the contrary, the image represents a blockage, forcing the majority to recognise their personal exclusion, except on sufferance. Moreover, the photograph might force viewers to contemplate the permanent exclusion and invisibility of generations labouring to produce 'plenty', but for whom?

In the following chapter, I shall continue to discuss various ways in which exclusion operates by exploring landscape as the scene of everyday violence. I shall also examine the significance of boundaries, where many of these assaults take place. In some ways, this common violence is similar to the deferential and safe mock battles of English Heritage of which the outcomes are already known. Everyday violence in the landscape, though not always tolerated, is continuously exercised. The exercise of present power by routine means of exclusion, such as low-key fortifications and the landed gentry's habitual use of stone, iron, wood or earthwork to deter 'trespassers' is part of the historical nature of the landscape. Nevertheless, current barriers, which have historic roots and political bite, are not yet turned into commodities and celebrated as heritage.

9

Wastes and boundaries

GAZING AT WASTE

LEAFING THROUGH tourist brochures, or looking at advertisements which use treasured landscapes, one notices that their most striking characteristic is an apparent newness. Everything appears to be fresh, shiny and smooth. This is most obvious in photographs of exhibits at heritage centres and museums, where even if the place itself is ancient, in the publicity photographs it appears to be unblemished. The way things appear to be so bright and youthful in these promotional photographs recalls an ideal world of beauty, in which everything remains young, whole and symmetrical.

The main subject of this final chapter is photography devoted to despoliation, enclosure, or the reduction of landscape to a species of wasteland. Whatever the characteristics of tourist brochures, there are some portions of land which are so neglected or spoiled that they appear to be the opposite of treasured landscapes. These are no-nonsense wastelands, places which are decomposing fast (represented here in John Kippin's photograph of a rubbish tip). Other wastes are urban. We build dumps (landfill or slum housing); we also deliberately spoil landscape when we dig, burn, spill and blast.

Landscape and wasteland express a form of the binary pair utopia/dystopia, both of which hold different fascinations. In one interpretation, the idealised view of treasured landscapes or 'beauty spots' requires the prolonged look of the gaze. The

91. John Kippin, 'Rubbish tip', 1987. Original in colour.

prevailing feeling is satisfaction that change has ceased, leaving aesthetically pleasing forms of landscape or tranquil intervals. These spaces, the preferred destinations of tourists, have national significance. Another, contrary interpretation of 'beauty spots' is that they produce anxiety. Tourists are supposed to feel uplifted when confronting beauty spots, but they might feel nothing of the sort. They might fail to perceive the scene and fail as tourists.

At first sight, wastelands are not so ambiguous, since they do not pretend to offer peace and cannot threaten to replace it with disappointment or failure. Wastelands appear to be negative in relation to beauty spots. Educated not to notice wastelands, tourists routinely avoid them, or look at them quickly and neutrally – searching beyond them for 'real' landscape.

In this duality of utopia/dystopia it appears that countryside in its imagined and ideal state of landscape can be spoiled by development and agri-business. Then landscape is no longer 'green and pleasant' because the countryside is so patently 'rationalised' for profit, and much of its picturesque detail erased or corralled in parks. But the purpose of this chapter is not simply to compare the (mis)representation of England as a blessed, sceptred isle with the (mis)represention of the country as septic or spoiled.

I am not concerned with examining these erasures or alterations to the landscape in their objective form, for instance as part of the political struggle between conservationists and landowners, since to do this would move the discussion into the framework of planning, which can appear benign. I am concerned with wasteland in its symbolic form, and the significance of liminal, border ground. Both are where struggle and resistance take place over using the countryside as the plot or space in which landscape is established as female, and where 'she' is wrecked. My chief concern is the violence performed on two terms, which become effectively interchangeable – 'nature' and 'woman'. Before examining the rhetoric of violence which shrouds these terms, I intend to draw together some threads from the previous two chapters, and look at them in a slightly different light.

Throughout this book I have been concerned with sight, with landscape as an effect of looking. I have discussed the steady gaze required to 'read' landscape; the use of discovery rhetoric, in which the observer (metaphorically) stands on a promontory and relays everything from that masterful point of view; the observer as one who sees within prescribed sets of rules, codes, regulations and practices. It seems at first that it should be straightforward to ascribe a way of looking at wasteland, drawing on one of three ways of looking which attach to three types of tourist: travellers use the gaze, which is contemplative and assured; tourists glance, which is a much more superficial and anxious look, deliberately avoiding what does not belong to the idea of scenery; trippers scarcely see at all, except in blinks, glimpses, or blurs (see page 14). Taking the first two, gaze/glance, it seems there might be some correspondence between landscape/wasteland. The assured gaze is the appropriate way of looking at the calming landscape, whereas the glance is suitable for land that stands in a kind of negative relation to landscape – in the way that tourists will pass by wasteland as accidental and peripheral to the main pursuit – which remains the exercise of the prolonged look across a tranquil interval.

However, the gaze is also used to contemplate wasteland. Indeed, the gaze remains one of the most favoured ways of looking at wasteland precisely because it is so prolonged and serious. Attaching the gaze to wastelands has a long history, beginning with the definition of the picturesque, which always incorporated strange sights, and signs of ageing and decay. Before the advent of photography, lists of picturesque subjects included not only old mills and gnarled oaks but well-worn paths through fields, sluices covered with moss, backyards filled with junk, and ramshackle cabins (Kemp 1990: 105).

During the nineteenth century and into the early days of photography, this list for tourists became settled around abbeys, birches, brooks, canals, oaks, tombs, water-mills and windmills (see chapter 2, page 69). Age and decay were attributes of these subjects, and suited the startling ability of photographs to pick up details of dust and dirt, or signs of ageing such as cracks in plaster, withered leaves, or broken panes in windows of distant buildings. As Wolfgang Kemp argues, since any photograph could capture these details, to suggest that every photograph of decay is 'a cultural critique or a melancholy reflection on the mutability of earthly things is to over-interpret them' (Kemp 1990: 118). Though photographs are always reminders of death, this link is conventional even if it is rarely promoted. What has always received much greater publicity is the equally conventional link of photography to picturesque haunts.

But for those who considered themselves to be rather more like travellers than tourists, the picturesque was not confined to conventional subjects and their links with ageing. As I suggested in chapter 3, artists and others educated in making aesthetic judgements sought out the wetlands of East Anglia. Lowlands, though they were signs of economic underdevelopment and moral concern, were not signs of decay. 'Dreary landscapes' were a popular background among painters in Britain from around 1870 for scenes of rural poverty (Rodee 1977). These images demonstrated the superior ability of artists and serious photographers to take 'disinterested pleasure' in the object of their look 'by consciously disregarding the object's utilitarian value' (Kemp 1990: 107). Of course, disinterested pleasure was also open to tourists who took in ivy-clad walls, but these were satisfied with more conventional picturesque subjects which were easier to reach than marshes, bogs and tidal estuaries at dawn or sunset on gloomy autumn afternoons. The way late-nineteenth-century artists and photographers concentrated on low wetlands, rather than on leafy lanes in Devon or Surrey, suggests that the category of the picturesque was elastic. It also showed that it was always possible for artists or travellers to distance themselves from ordinary tourists by identifying subjects which, while within the genre of the picturesque, were not as conventional as rustic bridges and so forth. This choice of subject was reserved (so they thought) for finer sensibilities and richer pockets than those with which mundane tourists had to settle.

Photographers' interest in 'dreary landscapes' continues into contemporary times, though now it is concerned with the degradation of the environment by pollution. For instance, Jem Southam's book *The Red River* on the valley in Cornwall of the same name concerns 'the continued ravaging and despoliation of the Earth' (Southam 1989: 3). The image of 'Cook's Kitchen' (see colour plate 18) appears in the section on Dolcoath in which Southam turns his back on what the 'eager tourist' usually looks for – 'the granite cliffs and rocky coves, the sandy beaches and fishing harbours, frequently represented on postcards and in paintings and films of Cornwall'. Instead, Southam goes in search of evidence of mining activities which lies scattered across farms and smallholdings – 'Tracks, heaps of waste, piles of rubble, arsenic chimneys, collapsed walls, dry addits, dank pools' (3).

Southam's book is a complex of different types of voices – his own descriptions, his photographs, poetry by D. M. Thomas, quotations from (among others) the works of Milton, Bunyan and T. S. Eliot, and an essay on the valley by local historians. *The Red River* narrates the tale of the valley, and is not content with the binaries of landscape/wasteland or insiders/outsiders. Instead, the book encourages its readers to take part in a complicated journey across time and space, though the points of reference remain artistic and historic. This journey is evocative and learned – not the easily-digested fare of tourism.

In a different vein, Keith Arnatt has long been interested in ironically employing the designation 'Area of Outstanding Natural Beauty', which normally attaches to conservation areas and beauty spots of national significance. He photographs patches of unsightly, desolate ground, and titles them with the acronym 'AONB'. In the picture from his series 'Pictures from Miss Graces's Lane', Arnatt depicts the dreary landscape (see colour plate 19). Yet he inflects the meaning of the picture in a way foreign to nineteenth-century artists by focusing on the grey tyre in the foreground.

Photographs such as this demonstrate that it would be wrong to tie the artist's interests in marginal picturesque landscapes to the aesthetic and educated sensibilities of self-styled travellers which was usual in the nineteenth century. Though determined to distance himself from tourists, Arnatt's frame of reference, like Jem Southam's, is the collision of nature and culture, despoliation and ecology.

Arnatt is interested in decay itself: he often photographs material rotting on rubbish dumps. The fascination for decay resulting in beautiful works of art and photographs now makes specific reference to the dangers of polluting the environment (Mellor 1988). This is clear, for example, in Ron O'Donnell's installation 'Waterfall' (see colour plate 20). In his artwork O'Donnell demonstrates the modern experience of distance from nature by replacing fresh water with its commodity form – the promise of pure, spring water in plastic bottles. The installation contains other detritus which stands in for nature packaged, tinned, skinned and 'dressed' for supermarket shelves. Decay is present in natural ecological systems, but O'Donnell's piece suggests that in modern life this decay can be progressively poisonous, ultimately clogging or eliminating the natural systems with waste which never degrades.

His installation invokes other considerations about the relation of nature and culture, such as the modern experience of water and food as utterly distinct and consciously *preserved* from any sense of origin in nature. Now that nature is so much associated with decay and disease, especially at the invisible level of microbes and viral infections, products originating in nature must be purified through heat, irradiated or subjected to other processes that halt their dangerous propensity for further, quickening degradation.

THE GENDER OF LANDSCAPE LOOKING

Though artists, serious photographers or travellers gaze at wastelands, tourists either do not notice them, or try to avoid seeing them, only glancing at them furtively. Norman Bryson draws attention to the way that in English, gazing and glancing are separate activities. He writes that in contrast to the steady look of the gaze, the *glance* is 'a furtive or sideways look whose attention is always elsewhere, which shifts to conceal its own existence, and which is capable of carrying unofficial, *sub rosa* messages of hostility, collusion, rebellion, and lust' (Bryson 1983: 94). This list implies that the *sub rosa* messages of the gaze are altogether pure, standing in contrast to the pejorative attributes of the glance. However, this attempt to separate the gaze and the glance cannot succeed for long. Attributes of the glance are attached to the gaze, despite attempts to empty it of bad associations. The inherent instability of verbal and visual signs is that the characteristics which are preferably attached to one side of a dichotomy can cross over to the other side. Attempts to sustain dualities and separations are always likely to fall apart, just as tourists might experience either pleasure or anxiety when confronted with a landscape. The gaze, in short, is not a disengaged, objective look. Like the glance, it has characteristics of hostility, collusion and lust in everyday usage. Though the gaze (in one of its guises) is a 'prolonged, contemplative [look] regarding the field of vision with a certain aloofness and disengagement, across a tranquil interval' (Bryson 1983: 94), this practice alone is insufficient to rule out hostile messages. Lovers gaze into one another's eyes in admiration and lust, but the observer might gaze without permission or reciprocation. The contemplative gaze might be the prelude to or begin the process of furtive, interrogative and destructive effects. The motivation to separate the 'pure' gaze from the 'impure' glance is similar to that which drives other hierarchies, such as the differences between travellers, tourists and trippers, or the differences between having 'taste' and not – namely, the motivation is one of separation of knowing groups from those others who by definition are excluded. This motivation to separate derives from the desire to differentiate on the basis of class or race, for instance, and also on the basis of gender. The gaze and the glance, variously disinterested and investigative, are commonplace ways of 'taking in' landscape. Landscape thus viewed is commonly conceived to be the body of a woman.

In response, Susan Trangmar has literally turned her back in the attempt to defeat or resist the colonising gaze, as we see in photographs from her series 'Untitled Landscapes' (see page 10). The woman in several pictures sometimes appears like the small figure in a postcard landscape, a marker of scale (see colour plate 21). More importantly, she turns her back on the camera (see colour plate 22). At other times the woman fills the frame, obscuring the view. In her account of Trangmar's work, Susan Butler argues that this is a way to deny 'the "landscape" image as an open accessible view'. This strategy is 'a telling instance of woman as the "ruin of representation" ': the position of the woman is the agency which both foregrounds and denies conventional ways of appearing in photographs and calls into question the expectations of viewers. According to Butler, this strategy subtly positions both the viewer and viewed 'within traditional patterns of looking that reproduce unequal relations within culture' (Butler 1989: 11). As Butler demonstrates, Trangmar works *against* the convention of the gaze. Trangmar succeeds in 'confusing categories', but none the less her work remains a point of resistance. It could not be otherwise, since the dominance of the (male) gaze continues to reproduce unequal relations within culture.

Let us now consider the symbolic and actual experience of the English countryside as a gendered space, returning to do so to the 'celebration of photography' at Lacock Abbey. Besides an enthusiasm for photography, what *gender* relations were expressed in this reconstruction of historical events? In brief, it was a supreme (though not rare) moment of male/culture dominating female/nature. It enabled the amateur photographers who copied the tableaux of Fox Talbot's original compositions to replicate his position as an originator in science and as the head of a household. Fox Talbot enjoyed both domesticity and the world of men's work. As a family man he enjoyed Lacock as home, and as a scientist he turned it into his laboratory. This circumstance gave him a peculiar authority, though not an unusual one: in line with the widespread tendency to describe male inventors and artists as 'fathers' and to appropriate birthing imagery in descriptions of their work, Fox Talbot became both the 'father of photography' and its mother. At Lacock, Fox Talbot created his technological infant in the laboratory, and nurtured it in the home by establishing its application in family photographs.

When amateur photographers 'took' these scenes in 1989, they were not simply replicating photographs, nor were they simply taking part in English amusements and national–popular entertainments. Whether they knew it or not, they were engaged in a symbolic repetition of the moment which reaffirmed the role of men in technological 'breakthroughs' and 'birthing'. The 'celebration' allowed men to appropriate 'generation', taking this away from the metaphor female/nature and granting it to themselves. The return to the origins of photography at Lacock was a return to narratives in which the male hero completes his task. Through the tableaux the amateur photographers discovered the origin and repeated the task of the original father, and so awarded themselves a moment of self-birthing.

In addition, by mimicking Fox Talbot these photographers achieved a kind of immortality that was denied them in their first mortal, maternal birth. In these acts of representing themselves through the 'original Fox Talbot', the photographers symbolically mastered the passage of time, and sidestepped the problem of mortality given in their original, maternal birthing. The ground which Kodak and the Trust prepared at Lacock was suitable for nostalgia, but this was only achieved by writing the masculine narrative of scientific domination of nature over the other histories which are inscribed in the Abbey.

As I shall demonstrate, organising the view and overwriting the landscape are part of the same process of control and conquest of female/nature by male/culture. The object of male violence is the concept of landscape itself in which the terms 'nature' and 'woman' are interchangeable (and expendable) (see MacCormack 1980; Merchant 1980; Kappeler 1986; Caputi 1988; Shiva 1989; Hekman 1990; Plumwood 1993; Rose 1993). The association of women with nature and men with culture has been understood as a hierarchical dichotomy for centuries, with men, as usual, occupying the privileged side of the dichotomy (Hekman 1990: 111–12). As Carolyn Merchant shows in *The Death of Nature* (1980), the coupling of female/nature was central to the origins of Western capitalism, linking a masculine imaginary to the discourses of science and technology, so that the virile adventurer unveiled the earth for profit, legitimating even deeper penetration. 'Nature' is the all-encompassing environment, fertile and fecund, like a mother or lover; or it is wild, untamed, unbridled, like a lover or mistress. Whether compliant or tempestuous, nature is frequently feminised. The equation works just as well the other way round, with the idea of women becoming synonymous with nature.

One affect attributed to both nature and women in the earliest years of photography was domesticated 'bliss'. Another was rage (see Green 1990: 147–52). Bliss and rage as two attributes of female/nature have been established for centuries in

European thought, and in certain circumstances the attributes cross the divide and belong to masculine/culture. The hierarchical relation of masculine/culture and feminine/nature – with all that implies for domination and violence – has a long history. According to the political scientist Susan Hekman, it can be found in Plato, who defined knowledge as the masculine thrust out of the 'cave' of mother nature (Hekman 1990: 111). Yet the movement of philosophers, scientists and mercantile adventurers towards determined control of female/nature gathered pace in comparatively recent historic times. The language of domination is found in the Renaissance 'New Philosophy' of Francis Bacon who advocated that men must 'lay hold and capture [Nature]'. For eco-feminists such as Vandana Shiva, modern science (dating from the end of the sixteenth century) is a consciously gendered, patriarchal actvity: 'For Bacon, nature was no longer Mother Nature, but a female nature, conquered by an aggressive masculine mind' (Shiva 1989: 17). Other contemporary authors such as Susan Hekman, Carolyn Merchant and Susan Kappeler, referring to the history of ideas and the growth of science in England during the sixteenth and seventeenth centuries, demonstrate that the idea of female/nature as a benevolent, innocent principle (or as merely unruly and subject to containment) was overtaken by its representation as so dangerous that it required interrogation and forceful subjugation. Susan Hekman argues that 'the dominating attitude toward both nature and women...is a product not of the inherent nature of men, but, rather, of Enlightenment thought and the rise of modern science' which replaced an organic model of the world with 'a mechanistically conceived universe that could and should be manipulated and dominated by the scientist' (Hekman 1990: 113–4).

The key role of 'woman' in nature was overtaken by the mechanical conception in which 'she' was completely passive. This mechanistic model of the world served capitalist and patriarchal interests because it opened up the territories of the earth and women's bodies to discoverers and prospectors. The nurturing and mysterious qualities of women and nature were lost in a world that extractive sciences laid bare for economic advance (Merchant 1980: 165). The representation of women as malevolent in nature paralleled the sense of nature as an extreme and mysterious force, with both becoming the objects of probes to 'extract her deeply guarded secrets' (Caputi 1988: 196; Kappeler 1986: 63–81). From the sixteenth century, the scientists' conflation of women with nature, and the consequent hardening of the definition of masculinity as extracting secrets from female/nature entailed 'her' perpetual interrogation. The scientist-adventurer engaged in the programme of domination over nature used violent metaphors of rape and torture to describe 'her' conquest (Shiva 1989: 17, 29). Scientists and explorers always put the 'question' to nature, and their endeavour was always to prize 'her' open. 'She' was torn apart in the process, resulting in the continuous depletion of species, habitats and resources, and the increasing and unending pollution of water, land and atmosphere.

This penetration imagined and practised by an expanding Europe at the 'birth' of modern science and capitalism had several consequences. There was no question until the recent rise of ecology movements and eco-feminism that the explorer/scientist/lover had to be 'masculine' in 'his' relations to nature and to the objects of knowledge and raw materials 'he' generated from 'her'. Nature was conceived to be raw and innocent partly because 'she' was imagined to be without technology. Correspondingly, as we saw in Jonathan Smith's 'common reverie', the explorer/discoverer was not *in* nature partly because he was not seen. He was not himself the spectacle – being instead the eye and the author (see pages 9–12). According to masculinist accounts (which form the bulk of Western literature), 'his' place in culture is achieved by *disconnecting* 'himself' from the category of 'nature'. Still, disconnection does not mean that 'nature' is left to 'herself'. On the contrary, when 'she' is developed, entered or penetrated by explorers, whether mining engineers or tourists, 'she' is subject to what Teresa de Lauretis calls 'a rhetoric of violence' (de Lauretis 1987 and 1989).

THE RHETORIC OF VIOLENCE

De Lauretis argues that the *meaning* of a certain representation of violence depends on the depiction of the gender of the violated object. Surveying such representations, she finds two kinds with respect to its object: male and female. These definitions of gender are relational rather than biological, and their perception establishes the meaning of the represented act. The perpetrators of violence are understood to be masculine while, in turn, victims are perceived to be feminine (de Lauretis 1987: 42; 1989: 249). The subject or agent of violence 'is always, by definition, masculine; "man" is by definition the subject of culture and of any social act' (43; 250). Rape is violence done to whatever is female in a social sense, the feminine other 'whether its physical object be a woman, a man, or an inanimate object' (42; 249). Violence against nature is

Plate 21. Susan Trangmar, from 'Untitled landscapes', 1986.

Plate 22. Susan Trangmar, from 'Untitled landscapes', 1986.

... it's as if the Black experience is only lived
within an urban environment. I thought I
liked the LAKE DISTRICT, where I
wandered lonely as a BLACK face in a sea of
white. A visit to the countryside is always
accompanied by a feeling of unease, dread ...

Plate 23. Ingrid Pollard, from the Pastoral Interlude Series, 1987–88.

ordinarily described as 'rape' which, as de Lauretis argues, at once defines nature as feminine.

In sum, there are two main oppositions which interrelate: in mythic plots the active male hero defines himself against passive female objects, and there exists a historic divide between male/culture and female/nature. When the 'male hero' enters the space of the 'female', 'his' action and language is always interrogative. 'He' puts the land in the position of the 'social female', and often alters it forcibly.

Of course, the representations of female/nature and male/culture are the twinned poles of binary oppositions, and do not exist in either raw or absolute states. Nature in England, for instance, has been subject to cultivation for centuries, and there is scarcely any remaining old-growth forest, and no wilderness. When farmers, miners or builders uproot forests and fields in order to 'develop' the land for agri-business, industry, transport and housing, they write themselves into a land which has already been subject to earlier inscriptions, alterations, invasions. Such interrogations of the land are not diminished by being recent, and remain masculine in function against whatever they replace, which shifts into the feminine position of object on which or to which the violence is done.

To demonstrate to what degree violence is 'en-gendered' by discourses, de Lauretis discusses a theory of plots in mythical texts where there are only two characters, the mobile hero and the space through which he moves. De Lauretis links this theory to the structure of pleasure in narrative cinema, where the woman is fixed in the position of the image to be looked at and bears the mobile look of both the spectator and the male character(s): 'it is the latter who commands at once the action and the landscape, and who occupies the position of subject of vision, which he relays to the spectator' (de Lauretis 1987: 44; 1989: 251; Mulvey 1975). The mythological hero's movement through plot/space establishes differences and norms, and to be the originator of differences is to be the author – the defining position for the masculine gender. The other character is an obstacle or boundary, representing the limit of his action, and is structurally female: 'indeed, [she is] simply the womb, the earth, the space of his movement' (de Lauretis 1987: 44; 1989: 251).

Though women have been and remain identified with nature, in the mythic text nature remains an enclosed space which men enter for leisure, pleasure *and* to test themselves and their authority. Nature is what men are not. In other words, the mythic experience of nature is not primarily addressed to women, but establishes and reinforces a patriarchal version of masculinity. The plot/space of the hero is opposed to the obstacle or boundary which does not have its own meaning but rather produces *his* action and subjectivity. The female becomes his work and his product when he crosses the boundary and 'penetrates' the other space. For many traveller-adventurers, the rhetoric of discovery engages with the rhetoric of violence, as landscape/woman becomes the object of curiosity to be explored, conquered, domesticated and if necessary destroyed.

The catastrophes of gender and colour

The description of plot, heroes and their objects is useful in thinking about the movements of tourists in search of treasured landscapes. Though tourists move about the countryside and would seem at first sight to occupy the position of the active male in the mythic tale, appearances are deceptive. Tourists are feminised by their precarious position in relation to the established authority of ancient sites or beauty spots. Numerous properties and whole tracts of countryside in the hands of private or state owners are designed to keep out the less powerful, including would-be invaders such as tourists. The work of the estate manager is either to control the movements of tourists or to exclude them altogether. In both cases, the bounded site is an example of a kingdom within a kingdom, terrain which has been developed in contradistinction to whatever is outside it, just as landscaped gardens were differentiated from worked land.

There is a continuity of purpose between exploring and landowning, which are two stages of a continuous process. The male hero explores, conquers and extracts, but in another guise 'he' establishes boundaries. The boundary is the sign that the task of the hero has been accomplished in the stake-out, the conquest of land and the establishment of estate – but this is a conquest which is never complete. At one level, the boundaries of properties (understood in terms of the mythic narrative plot) are the signs that the active hero has in fact completed a task and defined himself by establishing his space against the matrix of the inactive, feminised space which he rejects. Borders represent the end of one heroic stage of his narrative. Moreover, they also suggest the inequality of power between centre and periphery, and are thus the point of resistance. The hero's further tasks are to repel all bodies who dare to challenge the boundary or try to cross the border. In other words, the task of adventurers and landowners is to keep the view from the centre to the edge to themselves, denying the privilege to others.

The promontory occupied by the explorer and the estate established by the conqueror remain out-of-bounds to tourists and women, except on sufferance. Even so, it is difficult for them to command the field of vision. According to Mary Louise Pratt, the few women explorers in the nineteenth century found it difficult to write in a genre in which 'Explorer-man paints/possesses newly unveiled landscape-woman'. Explorer-women, in their writings, did not spend a lot of time on promontories: nor were they entitled to, as 'the masculine heroic discourse of discovery is not readily available to women' (Pratt 1992: 213).

The exclusion or refusal of entry to vantage points and estates is often contested by pressure groups such as ramblers' associations, who attempt to assert their right to break a boundary. Often they simply dare to enter the forbidden space or attempt to use the law against the owners. Though it seems that the active ramblers, for instance, stand in the character of masculine hero against the feminine space of the owners, the opposite is the case. Local invasions or activity around the edge of property leaves the ramblers or other pressure groups in the feminine position, since their movements simply provoke the 'hero' into sustaining 'his' borders.

The catastrophe of gender is complicated further by the colour of nature. This was not an issue for Wordsworth in the Lake district. His use and development of the literary genre of the 'romantic sublime' enabled him to write the landscape in terms of an ecstatic, transcendent and powerful version of himself (Yaeger 1989). In contrast, when Ingrid Pollard visited the Lakes and walked in the path of Wordsworth, she scarcely saw the countryside at all (see colour plate 23). She found herself wandering not like the poet 'lonely as a cloud' but 'lonely as a BLACK face in a sea of white'. The whiteness may have been literal, in that she met no other Black ramblers, but it remains metaphoric. As a Black woman, Pollard was doubly denied the equivalent of the promontory, or the viewpoint of the 'explorer-man'. Within white landscape rhetoric it is difficult to code persons of colour as lonely heroes writing themselves over a white space. To the contrary, explorer-heroes in the binary story fields of mind/body usually investigate and conquer the dark spaces of unknown territories, whether of continents or their populations. The white explorer has the attribute of mind, and thus symbolic power, whereas his object of enquiry, the body of nature, is darker than himself, denser, and not as warm. In those fields, coloured women stand in for the dangerous, fecund, and animal. Since this hegemonic structure left no place for Pollard to command a view, nor any comfortable structure to be viewed within, she became afraid. As I mentioned above, she captioned one of her photographs with the words 'A visit to the countryside is always accompanied by a feeling of unease, dread…'. It is this sense of unease or dread that I wish to follow in the issue of assault upon the interchangeable bodies of women and landscape.

ASSAULT AND RESISTANCE

The binarism female/nature which is destroyed by male/culture is incomplete, since it suggests that invasion meets no resistance, whereas conservationists resist the interrogation of despoilers. Resistance means that developers (who are the perpetrators of 'rape') sometime seek and win the support of the law, but this search for legitimacy is merely an extension of the violence and does not enable developers to escape the censure of conservation groups. Nor, if it proves impossible to save the land from development, does it allow the violators to avoid conservationists' exposés of what they take to be dishonourable actions against heritage and traditional usage in the pursuit of profit.

The experience of assault and resistance is described in the book of landscape photographs by Fay Godwin entitled *Our Forbidden Land*. Altogether the work is a catalogue of what she (as a rambler) takes to be oppressive groups, particularly government agencies such as the Ministry of Agriculture, Fisheries and Food, and the Forestry Commission. She also takes issue with numerous farmers and private landowners who continuously try to close rights of way or commons to those who wish to sustain ancient patterns of use or passage, as ramblers thought might happen in the Forest of Dean (see photograph of 'Russell's Enclosure, Forest of Dean', opposite). Godwin records confrontations that involve social spatialisation: ramblers meet owners or keepers at various types of boundary, such as walls, gates, fences. More often, ramblers read the prohibitions of absent owners in signs which say 'Private', 'Danger', 'Warning', which demand they 'Keep To Footpath', or which seek to stop them with refusals such as 'No Camping' or 'No Admittance'. In this book, photographs and written text complement each other – for example, when Godwin pictures a fence or a 'No Trespassers' sign, and (as we shall see) when she reinforces these images with an account of an argument with an official or keeper.

92. Fay Godwin, 'Fence, Russell's Enclosure, Forest of Dean', 1985.

By the time Godwin visited Stonehenge in 1988 it had been fenced off by English Heritage and was heavily policed during the summer solstice to deter New Age travellers (see photographon page 279). Her approach to the Stones was determined by her own experiences of the continuing loss of public footpaths in the late 1980s. She demonstrates her fears in two ways: by using pictures to *show* how landowners ringed the land, and by *telling* what happened to her and others in her formal 'introduction' and in the commentary which runs throughout the book. She reproduces five photographs of the Stones: they depict an underpass, connecting the car-park to the area of the Stones, which has been treated to a 'theme park' approach (with signs exhorting visitors to 'step back in time more than 3,500 years'); barbed wire enclosing the Stones (see illustration opposite); a small group of Druids allowed to celebrate the solstice; women holding a 'Free the Stones' banner at a demonstration; and a perimeter fence enclosing the whole area, patrolled by the security firm 'Nightguard'. The photographs exist as evidence of permitted exclusion and resistance. Though none of the fighting is shown, Godwin writes about the threat of violence in a revealing manner. She found the atmosphere 'nasty'. This epithet, along with the brief mention of an ensuing riot begun by the 'hippies' and welcomed by the police who enjoyed enforcing order, amplify the pictures. She uses her language to counter that of the police and English Heritage.

Godwin reveals much more about the extent of violence done to her, and about her methods to confound it. She first attempted to reach the Stones in the guise of an 'insider' artist-photographer. She wrote 'a very polite letter' to English Heritage, 'complete with curriculum vitae'. At this initial stage, she tried to bypass current restrictions by appealing to the authorities at the level of art photography. She writes in *Our Forbidden Land* that she wanted to spend more time at the Stones to 'get to know' them, as had 'Bill Brandt and Paul Caponigro, and others' (Godwin 1990: 23). Here she invokes the *names* of famous, male, landscape photographers to validate an approach to the Stones. Unfortunately for her, the bureaucrats were not swayed by her art allegiances and her request to take photographs 'over a period of time, outside normal visiting hours' (23). She was told that she would have to compete with film crews making advertisments (which she was prepared for) and she would have to pay a fee of £200 per visit. She could not afford this fee, nor did she expect to have to pay it since she was engaged in 'creative work' (23).

Undeterred by this correspondence, she wrote to the Director of English Heritage, who waived the fee, but asked her to visit only once because of unspecified 'administrative problems'. Godwin did not accept this offer, since 'much time is needed to find one's personal view of a much-photographed monument'. Godwin clearly positioned herself as a serious traveller engaged in significant art photography, rather than as a tourist or a jobbing photographer working for the tourist market. Since she could not get permission to spend time there, 'From now on', writes Godwin, 'the only photographs we are likely to see of the inner circles of Stonehenge will be those *approved* by English Heritage, generally by their anonymous public

93. Fay Godwin, 'Stonehenge summer solstice, 1988'.

relations photographers' (Godwin 1990: 23). What is interesting here is how Godwin tried to influence powerful men by negotiating a place for herself as an insider. She sought to place herself among the 'masters' of photography, disguising herself among them and so divesting herself of her gender. In the end, this route was constructively blocked by the authority's granting a permission so limited that it was useless.

Godwin's second route to the Stones was in the guise of an outsider. Taking the part of 'hippies', as we have seen, she attended the solstice celebration without the protection of men's names and armed only with an amateur snapshot camera. This time she found her route blocked by the threat of violence. When she took 'a snap with a small amateur camera', a policeman threatened to 'smash' it if she tried to take any more pictures (Godwin 1990: 23). In each case, in short, she was refused. In response, she chose to depict some of the barriers to progress, and to expose the polite bureaucratic men and intimidating police in her written text. She attempted to use the word of male authority against itself, only to be defeated by the low-level embodiment of the same authority.

The accounts of two methods of approach, both of them ending in kinds of defeat, are extremely revealing. Godwin shows through her texts, her photographs and her actions how men write themselves over the landscape and how they succeed in repelling boarders at the boundaries. She draws attention to the masculine narrative by operating along the borders, which becomes a crucial space for her. She uses the strategy of adopting the guise of insider, and when her path is blocked, she aligns herself with the outsiders. In both guises, she makes herself visible and renders the duality of inner/outer problematic.

Godwin recounts an even starker example of this combination of official approval and *de facto* rejection in her visit to a Ministry of Defence (MOD) submarine base in Scotland. She wanted to photograph the perimeter fence of the base from the public road. She wrote for permission, which was granted, and reported at the main gate on arrival, apparently doing everything required to protect herself. Again, she found the men intimidating and the atmosphere 'horrible', and so decided to leave after half an hour. She was then stopped by an MOD policeman who questioned her. She produced the letter of permission but instead of it safeguarding her against him, the letter diminished her since it actually means 'on sufferance'. Clearly, she had some authority to be there, but not enough to prevent the policeman questioning her further. He insisted that she reveal the name of her employer, and 'had difficulty in understanding' that she was working for herself (Godwin 1990: 20). Accordingly, the policeman decided to 'note' every line of the letter of permission granted to Godwin by his superiors, so verifying their authority as dispensers of the Word, his status as replicator of the Word, and her position as recipient of the Word. This was a clear act of bureaucratic intimidation and, less obviously, it was an act reproducing himself as fully present against her. Already placed in the position of supplicant by the letter of permission, she was further diminished by his taking back the Word by which she sought to gain recognition, however temporarily, as an insider.

Permission and the possibility of its denial, giving it and threatening to take it away, are signs from the same axis of power designed to deny authority, security or protection to the supplicant. Permission and denial maintain the order of those men who dispense and retract. It is a practice established among the writers and copiers of the Word, and it is given to both that they may perform these actions either smoothly or magnanimously, or with condescension, intimidation and threat.

Except in her actions in operating along the borders, Godwin never made much of the *male* contribution to her exclusion. In fact, the proscribing figures of the law (the authors of the Word) were themselves absent, but embodied their authority in signs, fences, police or private security guards with dogs. Her photographs showed the signs of their authority and her defeat – the wire, the fence, the simplistic 'theme' approach to the history of the Stones. When she came up against policemen, they either threatened her directly or warned her off, rendering her the object of their authority, effectively refusing her their protection even as an artist-photographer. Thus driven to seek access through solidarity with other 'outsiders', Godwin eventually marked herself as the proper object of legal restraint and threat.

At the same time that she placed herself in the supplicant position of one who seeks to gain entry, by working on the boundaries she became what she always was in this context – her liminality is a sign of her marginalised presence and resistance. Indeed, Godwin's whole stance is one of resistance to the authorities who (in their terms) succeed in defeating her. She tells of the letters, the interrogation, the copying. She tells of manoeuvres to use 'creativity' as an open sesame to inaccessible and forbidden grounds. She prints the photographs of the fence, and other points of resistance such as the peace camp, or protesters with messages of defiance. She turns words back upon the men. She succeeds as an outsider by documenting her obstacles.

Irony and inversion provide other forms of resistance which deny domination and parody power. Terry Dennett and Jo Spence take this route in their 'photo-theatre' piece called 'Remodelling Photo History' (see Spence 1986: 118–33). There they deal with 'adversity and oppression' not through 'comradely struggles or learned exposition, but lived out through individual or group rituals like sarcasm or irony' (Spence 1986: 119). As we see in this photograph from the series, Spence places herself at the boundary of unspecified private property, in front of the gate and near a sign which addresses her as an 'unauthorised person…not allowed beyond this point' (see illustration on page 283). She registers her comedic 'dismay' and defiance in the choice to sprawl face down and naked with her head under the front wheel of a car. She mimics and (literally) turns upside down the artistic category of the (nude) female figure in a landscape. At the same time she makes a photograph in the style of a police record of a peculiar, intractable kind of death under the shadows of a barred gate and a sign of the law-made-word. The scene is sarcastic, as she and Dennett intended, and it remains opaque too, even though the caption describes the scene as 'victimisation' (see Spence 1986: 126–7). The simplest reading, perhaps, recognises Spence as 'victim' and the landowner as 'victimising'; in another reading she is 'victimising', because though she is debarred she succeeds in mocking the Word.

Arrival at the boundary is the critical moment, and if there is to be a catastrophe in that place it must be instigated by gender itself. As we have seen, there are only two characters in the mythic text, the (male) hero and the (female) obstacle or boundary. The hero is mobile, and 'moves through the plot space establishing differences and norms. The second character is but a function of that space, a marker of boundary, and therefore inanimate even when anthropomorphized' (de Lauretis 1987: 43; 1989: 250). In this scenario, only the external heroic character can cross the boundary, which is the second character, into the interior. Another way of representing the same relationship apparently reverses the roles of the two characters: in this case, the (female) character is active and meets a seemingly passive (male) character. Despite appearances, the positions have not been reversed at all, and the character in a fixed position succeeds in defeating the other's advance, thus proving himself to be the male hero. Success at repelling boarders is proof of masculinity, whereas failure to cross a boundary is proof that the character is part of the female matrix. Here we see that the estate will not admit trespass, and that it stands in for the heroic (male) defender of the ground, repelling weak opposition at its border. Jo Spence failed to cross the barrier, allowing the absent landowner (through his gate and sign) to become hero, male, the creator of difference. Spence acquiesced in this, though as we have seen, not in silence – indeed her mockery diminishes the victory won by the landowner.

As I argued above, what is socially peripheral is symbolically central (pages 109–10). The apparently disregarded spaces of wasteland, or perimeter fences, or the scrub land which runs along their edges, are never empty of meaning. Indeed, apart from a 'beauty spot', nothing is likely to excite as much attention as its seeming opposite – the abandoned or derelict site. Some reasons for the interest lie in

94. Jo Spence/Terry Dennett, 'Victimisation', from the series Remodelling Photo History, 1982.

conventional ways of seeing the picturesque, or in contemporary concerns for the environment. Most crucially, interest in desolate spaces derives from the ceaseless action of the colonising and objectifying gaze. The gaze abhors the invisible and perpetually strives to bring it to light. The gaze cast over land recognises no distinction between landscape as beautiful and wasteland as its opposite. The aim is always to bring land within range and conquer it, actually or mentally. Because the hierarchies of sight are continuous with other inequalities in culture, the gaze remains the most powerful (though resisted) of the various ways of looking, and is crucially tied to masculinity, with its object the feminine 'other'. The authority of this gaze is challenged only by inserting a third term between the observer and 'his' object. Wasteland as a peripheral space will remain at the centre in establishing the meaning of landscape, and will continue to engender anxiety as a point of resistance, with implications far beyond its function as a sign of the picturesque.

References

Adler, Judith (1989) 'Origins of sightseeing', *Annals of Tourism Research*, 16: 7–29.

Alfieri, Bernard (1888) 'On the Broads', 'Holiday Resorts and Photographic Haunts', *Amateur Photographer*, 5 October, 216–17.

Alloula, Malek (1986) *The Colonial Harem*, Manchester, Manchester University Press.

Amateur Photographer (1909) 'The exhibition of pictorial photographs by Colonial workers at the "A. P." Little Gallery', 13 July, 36.

Amateur Photographer (1910a) 'Empire Number', 8 March, 219.

Amateur Photographer (1910b) 'The second exhibition of colonial photographs at the "A.P." Little Gallery', 12 July, 41.

Amateur Photographer (1911) 'The Empire of the Camera', 20 March, 267.

Amateur Photographer (1912) 'Topics of the week and editorial comment', 12 February, 147.

Amateur Photographer (1916) 'After two years of war, the present position of photography', 24 July, 63.

Amateur Photographer (1921) 'Editorial', 16 March, 201.

Amateur Photographer (1922a) '£3,000 all-British photographic competition', 18 January, 48.

Amateur Photographer (1922b) 'The £3,000 all-British photographic competition', 27 December, 548.

Amateur Photographer (1924) 'Spirit of the times', 7 May, 425.

Amateur Photographer (1927a) ' "See Britain First", a big photographic competition', 13 April, 372.

Amateur Photographer (1927b) ' The "See Britain First" competition', 9 November, 461.

Amateur Photographer (1928) 'Metro-Land competition', 9 May, 387.

Amateur Photographer (1929) 'The golden age for amateur photographers', 10 July, 26.

Amateur Photographer (1931a) 'A £20,000 photographic competition', 1 April, 289.

Amateur Photographer (1931b) 'Topics of the week', 6 May, 386.

Amateur Photographer (1931c) 'The snapshot that won £1,000', 21 October, 394.

Amateur Photographer (1931d) 'The world's best snapshot for 1931', 25 November, 498.

Amateur Photographer (1932) 'Current newspaper competitions for amateur photographers', 13 July, 41.

Amateur Photographer (1933) 'Our annual overseas competition', 29 March, 298.

Amateur Photographer (1935a) 'Our annual overseas competition', 10 April, 316.

Amateur Photographer (1935b) 'Newspaper photographic competitions', 7 August, 144.

Amateur Photographer (1938) 'Cash prize competitions open to all amateur photographers', 6 July, 27.

Amateur Photographer advertisements (1927) 15 June, 2.

Amateur Photographer advertisements (1931) 'Another world championship for Britain!', 16 December, 2.

Anderson, A. J. (1910) *The ABC of Artistic Photography*, London, Stanley Paul & Co.

Anderson, Benedict (1989) *Imagined Communities: Reflections on the Origin and Spread of Nationalism*, London, Verso.

Andrews, Malcolm (1989) *The Search for the Picturesque*, London, Scolar Press.

Annual Report (1931) 'Kodak international $100, 000 competition', Rochester, Eastman Kodak Company, 15.

Anon. (1886a) 'Photographic industries: the dry plate factory of Mr. William Cobb', *British Journal of Photography*, 2 July, 414–5.

Anon. (1886b) 'Photographic industries: the dry plate factory of R. W. Thomas & Co.', *British Journal of Photography*, 10 December, 779–80.

Anon. (1888) 'Proceedings of the Societies', 'Birkenhead Photographic Association', *Photographic News*, 18 May, 319.

Anon. (1891) 'Photographers' jaunts, a day with the Warwickshire Survey', *Birmingham Daily Gazette*, 10 June, n.p.

Anon. (1892a) 'A photographic record and survey', *British Journal of Photography*, 13 May, 306–7.

Anon. (1892b) 'Warwickshire Photographic Survey', *Birmingham Daily Gazette*, 14 May.

Anon. (1893) 'Birmingham Photographic Society', *Photographic News*, 12 March, 246.

Anon. (1894) *Supplement to the Photographic Review of Reviews*, July, 1–4.

Anon. (1896) 'Photographic assistants and their grievances', *British Journal of Photography*, 15 May, 306–7.

Anon. (1897a) 'Class distinctions', *The Spectator*, 4 December, 819–20.

Anon. (1897b) 'The National Photographic Record Association', *Photography*, 7 October, 637.

Anon. (1897c) 'The National Photographic Record Association', *Photography*, 28 October, 683.

Anon. (1908a) 'A gigantic enterprise: a visit to Houghtons Ltd., and the new Ensign works', *Photographic Dealer*, March, 92–6.

Anon. (1908b) 'A modern camera factory', *Photographic Monthly*, 15, 118–21.

Anon. (1909) 'The moral paradox', *A Beautiful World*, X: 66.

Anon. (1910) 'The National Photographic Record

Association', *British Journal of Photography*, 3 June, 418.

Anon. (1926) *Dear Old Cornwall, The Homeland Illustrated*, London, Homeland Association.

Anon. (1928a) *Just Oxford, The Homeland Illustrated*, London, Homeland Association.

Anon. (1928b) *The Beauty of West Sussex*, London, Homeland Association.

Anon. (1929) *Leafy Warwick, Camera Pictures of Shakespeare and George Eliot Country*, The Homeland Illustrated, London, Homeland Association.

Anon. (1937) *Times Literary Supplement* , 27 March, 238.

Anon. (1940a) 'Restrictions on roadside advertising', *Hotel*, July, 200–3.

Anon. (1940b) 'The land we are fighting for', *Picture Post*, 6 July, 28–9.

Anon. (1941–42) *The Legacy of England*, London, Batsford, The Pilgrim's Library. First published 1935.

Anon. (1942) 'Bath: what the German's mean by a "Baedeker raid" ', *Picture Post*, 4 July, 20–1.

Anon. (*c.*1945) *Ourselves in Wartime*, London, Odhams Press Ltd.

Anon. (1992) 'Photography banned after National Trust treasures are snapped up', *Guardian*, 18 March.

Arbuthnot, Revd G. (1889) *Two Hours in Stratford-on-Avon*, Morgan's Penny Guide, Stratford-on-Avon, J. Morgan.

Armstrong, Isobel (ed.) (1992) *New Feminist Discourses*, London, Routledge.

Ashwin, C. (1978) 'Graphic imagery 1837–1901: a Victorian revolution', *Art History*, 1: 360–70.

Bailey, Peter (1977) ' "A mingled mass of perfectly legitimate pleasures": the Victorian middle class and the problem of leisure', *Victorian Studies*, 21: 7–28.

Ballard, Phillada (1985) *A City at War, Birmingham 1939–1945*, Birmingham, City Museum and Art Gallery.

Ballerini, Julia (1993) 'The in visibility of Hadji-Ishmael: Maxime Du Camp's 1850 photographs of Egypt', in Kathleen Adler and Marcia Pointon (eds) *The Body Imaged*, Cambridge, Cambridge University Press.

Baran, Paul A. and Paul M. Sweezy (1968) *Monopoly Capitalism: an Essay on the American Economic and Social Order*, Harmondsworth, Penguin.

Barnes, Trevor J. and James S. Duncan (1992) *Writing Worlds: discourse, text & metaphor in the representation of landscape*, London, Routledge.

Barnett, Anthony (1982) 'War over the Falklands', *New Left Review*, 134: 5–96.

Barnett, Correlli (1986) *The Audit of War: the illusion & reality of Britain as a great nation*, London, Macmillan.

Barni, Z. D. (1938) 'Sunrise', *Amateur Photographer*, 6 April, n.p.

Barthes, Roland (1982) *Camera Lucida: Reflections on Photography*, London, Jonathan Cape.

Bate, David (1992) 'The occidental tourist: photography and colonizing vision', *Afterimage*, Summer: 11–13.

Benjamin, Walter (1973) 'The work of art in the age of mechanical reproduction', *Illuminations*, London, Fontana.

Bennett, Tony (1988) 'Museums and "the people" ', in Robert Lumley (ed.), *The Museum Time-Machine*, London, Routledge.

Berger, John X. and Olivier Richon (1990) 'Sheep in wolf's clothing: myth and history, "The Art of Photography 1839–1989" ', *Art History*, 13: 232.

Blatchford, Robert (1894) *Merrie England*, London, Clarion.

'Blue Peter' (1890) *A Week in a Wherry on the Norfolk Broads*, London, Simpkin, Marshall, Hamilton, Kent & Co. Ltd.

Bolitho, Hector (1943) *A Batsford Century: The Record of a Hundred Years of Publishing and Bookselling 1843–1943*, London, Batsford.

Bommes, Michael and Patrick Wright (1984) ' "Charms of residence": the public and the past', in Richard Johnson (ed.), *Making Histories*, London, Hutchinson, 253–301.

Bond, Brian (1982) 'Dunkirk; myths and lessons', *Royal United Services Institute for Defence Studies Journal*: 3–8.

Bond, Brian and Ian Roy (eds), (1975) *War and Society*, London, Croom Helm.

Boni, Albert (1972) *Photographic Literature: an international bibliographic guide*, New York, Morgan and Morgan.

Boorstin, Daniel (1962) *The Image*, London, Weidenfeld and Nicolson.

Booth, William (1890) *In Darkest England and the Way Out*, London, International Headquarters of the Salvation Army.

Bostock, C. W. (1923) 'Pioneer and Mailman', *Amateur Photographer*, 2 May, n.p.

Brandt, Bill (1936) *The English at Home*, Introduction by Raymond Mortimer, London, Batsford.

Brandt, Bill (1938) *A Night in London*, London, Country Life.

Brandt, Bill (1948) *Camera in London*, Introductory essay by Bill Brandt, London, Focal Press.

Brassington, W. Salt (1898) 'Notes on the old houses in Stratford-upon-Avon', *Birmingham and Midland Institute, Birmingham*

Archaeological Society, Transactions, Excursions and Reports for the year 1898, Walsall, W. Henry Robinson, 33–43.

Briggs, Asa (1990) Victorian Things, Harmondsworth, Penguin. First published 1988, London, Batsford.

British Journal Photographic Almanac advertisements (1936) 'Kodak photographs the world!', 16–17.

Brittain, Harry (1891) Rambles in East Anglia, or Holiday Excursions among the Rivers and Broads, London, Jarrold & Sons.

Bronfen, Elisabeth (1992) Over Her Dead Body – death, femininity and the aesthetic, Manchester, Manchester University Press.

Brown, Charles (1886) 'Photographic haunts – Dorking', Amateur Photographer, 8 January, 19.

Brown, G. (1895) 'Another hard case', British Journal of Photography, 10 May, 303.

Brown, Ivor and George Fearon (1939) Amazing Monument: a Short History of the Shakespeare Industry, London, William Heinemann.

Browne, W. R. (1886) 'The English gentleman', The National Review, April, 261–71.

Bryson, Norman (1983) Vision and Painting, the logic of the gaze, London, Macmillan.

Buckland, Gail (1981) Cecil Beaton, War Photographs 1939–45, London, Imperial War Museum/Jane's.

Bunnell, Peter (1989) 'Pictorial Effect', The Art of Photography 1839-1989, London, Royal Academy, 156–60.

Burman, H. (1933) 'Come for a drive', Amateur Photographer, 5 April, n.p.

Burton, Cosmo I. (1889a) 'The whole duty of the photographer – I', British Journal of Photography, 11 October, 667–8.

Burton, Cosmo I. (1889b) 'The whole duty of the photographer – II', British Journal of Photography, 18 October, 682.

Butler, Susan (1989) 'Shifting Focus – observations, speculations, imaginings', in Susan Butler, Shifting Focus – An International Exhibition of Contemporary Women's Photography, Bristol/London, Arnolfini/Serpentine Collaboration.

Calder, Angus (1982) The People's War, Britain 1939–1945, London, Granada.

Calder, Angus (1991) The Myth of the Blitz, London, Jonathan Cape.

Calder, Angus and Dorothy Sheridan (eds) (1984) Speak for Yourself: a Mass-Observation Anthology, 1937–1949, Oxford, Oxford University Press.

Calder-Marshall, Arthur (1937) Time and Tide, 20 March, 382, in Jeffrey Meyers (ed.) (1975) George Orwell: The Critical Heritage, London,

Routledge and Kegan Paul, 101–3.

The Camera (1925) ' "Kodak" competition', December, 301.

The Camera (1926) 'Buy British', August.

Cannadine, D. (1983) 'The context, performance and meaning of ritual: the British monarchy and the "invention of tradition", c.1820–1977', in E. Hobsbawm and T. Ranger (eds) The Invention of Tradition, Cambridge, Cambridge University Press.

Caputi, Jane (1988) The Age of Sex Crime, London, The Women's Press.

Carey, John (1992) The Intellectuals and the Masses, London, Faber and Faber.

Carlyle, Thomas (1900) On Heroes and Hero-Worship, London, Ward, Lock & Co. Ltd.

Carrick, Edward and Gerry Bradley (c.1943) Meet '...the common people...', London, Studio Publications.

Chak, Lau Cho (1938) 'Homeward Bound', Amateur Photographer, 1 June, 623.

Chaney, David and Michael Pickering (1986) 'Authorship in documentary: sociology as an art form in Mass-Observation', in John Corner (ed.) Documentary and the Mass Media, London, Arnold.

Child Bayley, R. (1906) The Complete Photographer, London, Methuen & Co.

Clapp, George Wood (1925) The Life and Work of James Leon Williams, New York, The Dental Digest.

Clark, Lyonel (1891) 'Camera Club library catalogue', Journal of the Camera Club, March, 33–8, April, 50–64.

Clunn, Harold (1936) The Face of the Home Counties, London, Simpkin Marshall.

Coan, T. (1889) 'Bloater land', British Journal Photographic Almanac, 403–6.

Coan, T. (1892) 'A quiet nook on the Norfolk coast', British Journal of Photography, 1 January, 7–8.

Cockett, C. Bernard (1928) John Bunyan's England – a tour with a camera in the footsteps of the immortal dreamer, London, Homeland Association.

Coe, Brian (1976) The Birth of Photography: the story of the formative years 1800–1900, London, Ash and Grant Ltd.

Coe, Brian and Paul Gates (1977) The Snapshot Photograph: The Rise of Popular Photography 1888–1939, London, Ash and Grant Ltd.

Coles, Joanna (1993) 'The slick and the dead', Guardian, 6 July.

Collins, Douglas (1990) The Story of Kodak, New York, Abrams.

Collins, Norman (1936) Letter in Gollancz's records dated 22 December.

Colls, Robert and Philip Dodd (1985) 'Representing

the nation – British documentary film, 1930–45', *Screen*, 26, 1: 21–33.

Corner, John and Sylvia Harvey (eds) (1991) *Enterprise and Heritage: Crosscurrents of National Culture*, London, Routledge.

Cosgrove, Denis E. (1979) 'John Ruskin and the geographical imagination', *Geographical Review*, 69: 43–62.

Crary, Jonathan (1990) *Techniques of the Observer, On Vision and Modernity in the Nineteenth Century*, Cambridge, Massachusetts, MIT Press.

Crick, Bernard (1980) *George Orwell – A Life*, Harmondsworth, Penguin.

Culler, Jonathan (1988) 'The semiotics of tourism', in *Framing the Sign: criticism and its institutions*, Oxford, Basil Blackwell.

Daniels, Stephen (1993) *Fields of Vision: Landscape Imagery and National Identity in England and the United States*, Cambridge, Polity Press.

Danziger, James (1980) *Beaton*, London, Secker & Warburg.

Davies, G. Christopher (1876) *The 'Swan' and Her Crew, or the adventures of three young naturalists and sportsmen on the Broads and Rivers of Norfolk*, London, Frederick Warne and Co.

Davies, G. Christopher (1884) *Norfolk Broads and Rivers*, London, William Blackwood and Sons.

Davies, G. Christopher (1897) *The Tourists' Guide to the Rivers and Broads of Norfolk and Suffolk*, London, Jarrold & Sons.

Davies, Gill (1988) 'The end of the pier show', *New Formations*, 5: 133–40.

Davies, John (1987) *A Green & Pleasant Land*, Manchester, Cornerhouse.

Dawson, Graham (1984) 'History-writing on World War II', in Geoff Hurd (ed.) *National Fictions: World War Two in British Films and Television*, London, British Film Institute.

de Lauretis, Teresa (1987) *Technologies of Gender: Essays on Theory, Film, and Fiction*, Bloomington, Indiana University Press.

de Lauretis, Teresa (1989) 'The violence of rhetoric: considerations on representation and gender', in Armstrong, Nancy and Leonard Tennenhouse (eds), *The Violence of Representation: literature and the history of violence*, London, Routledge.

Deakin, P. T. D. (1896) 'South Warwickshire Survey', unpublished manuscript, Birmingham City Reference Library.

Deakin, P. T. D. (1900) Untitled diary account of survey during Easter weekend, unpublished manuscript, Birmingham City Reference Library.

Deakin, P. T. D. (n.d.) 'A South Warwickshire Survey on cycles with the camera, (the home of beauty and contentment, picturesque and pretty as a poet's dream)', unpublished manuscript, Birmingham City Reference Library.

Dixon-Scott, J. (1937) *English Counties*, London, Thomas Nelson and Sons.

Doane, Janice and Devon Hodges (1987) *Nostalgia and Sexual Difference: the Resistance to Contemporary Feminism*, London, Methuen.

Dodd, Anna Bowman (1896) *On the Broads*, London, Macmillan and Co.

Dodd, Philip (1982) 'The views of travellers: travel writing in the 1930s', in Philip Dodd (ed.) *The Art of Travel, Essays on Travel Writing*, London, Frank Cass, 127–38.

Doughty, H. M. (1889) *Summer in Broadland: Gipsying in East Anglian Waters*, London, Jarrold and Sons.

Duncan, James and David Ley (eds) (1993) *Place/Culture/Representation*, London, Routledge.

Editorial (1978) 'Mass-Observation', *Camerawork*, 11: 1.

Edwards, Elizabeth (ed.) *Anthropology and Photography 1860–1920*, New Haven and London, Yale University Press in association with The Royal Anthropological Institute, London.

Edwards, H. (1896) 'A plea for a survey of life and character', *British Journal Photographic Almanac*, 699–703.

Emerson, Peter Henry (1886a) 'Photography a pictorial art', *Amateur Photographer*, 19 March, 139.

Emerson, Peter Henry (1886b) 'The Log of the "Lucy"', *Amateur Photographer*, Supplement to the Winter Number, 10 December, 1–4.

Emerson, Peter Henry (1887) *Pictures from Life in Field and Fen*, London, G. Bell & Sons.

Emerson, Peter Henry (1888a) *Idyls of the Norfolk Broads*, London, Autotype Co.

Emerson, Peter Henry (1888b) *Pictures of East Anglian Life*, London, Sampson Low & Co.

Emerson, Peter Henry (1889) *Naturalistic Photography for students of the art*, London, Sampson Low & Co.

Emerson, Peter Henry (1890) *Wild Life on a Tidal Water*, London, Sampson Low & Co.

Emerson, Peter Henry (1893) *On English Lagoons*, London, David Nutt.

Emerson, Peter Henry (1895) *Marsh Leaves*, London, David Nutt.

Emerson, Peter Henry and Goodall, T. F. (1887) *Life and Landscape on the Norfolk Broads*, London, Sampson Low & Co.

Everitt, Allen E. (1882) 'Hampton-in-Arden', *Birmingham and Midland Institute Archaeological Section, Transactions, Excursions and Reports 1878–79*, Birmingham,

Cund Bros: 1–2.

Featherstone, Mike (1991) *Consumer Culture & Postmodernism*, London, Sage.

Field, Arthur G. (1890) 'A trade union in photography', *British Journal Photographic Almanac*, 560–4.

Field, Arthur G. (1894) 'Unity among photographic workers', *British Journal Photographic Almanac*, 668–9.

Field, Arthur G. (1897) 'A trade for photographic workers', *British Journal Photographic Almanac*, 756–63.

Field, Arthur G. (1898) 'Combinations among photographic assistants', *British Journal Photographic Almanac*, 749–54.

Field, Eleanor F. (1894) 'Photographic co-operation', *British Journal Photographic Almanac*, 671–4.

Field, Eleanor F. (1895) 'Photographic co-operation', *British Journal Photographic Almanac*, 686–7.

Fleming, Peter (1957) *Invasion 1940*, London, Hart-Davies.

Foote, Kenneth E. (1987) 'Relics of old London: photographs of a changing Victorian city', *History of Photography*, 2: 133–53.

Ford, Charles Bradley (1935) *The Legacy of England: An Illustrated Survey of the Works of Man in the English Country*, The Pilgrims' Library, London, Batsford.

Fowler, Peter J. (1992) *The Past in Contemporary Society: Then, Now*, London, Routledge.

Fox's Penny Guide to Stratford-on-Avon (1890), Stratford-on-Avon, Edward Fox.

Frow, John (1991) 'Tourism and the semiotics of nostalgia', *October*, 57: 123–51.

Fussell, Paul (1975) *The Great War and Modern Memory*, Oxford, Oxford University Press.

Fussell, Paul (1980) *Abroad: British Literary Traveling between the Wars*, Oxford, Oxford University Press.

Fussell, Paul (1989) *Wartime: Understanding and Behaviour in the Second World War*, Oxford, Oxford University Press.

Gaze, John (1988) *Figures in a Landscape: a History of the National Trust*, London, Barrie & Jenkins.

Gerald, J. Edward (1956) *The British Press Under Government Economic Controls*, Minneapolis, University of Minnesota Press.

Giddens, Anthony (1990) *The Consequences of Modernity*, Cambridge, Polity Press.

Gloversmith, Frank (1980) *Class, Culture and Social Change: A New View of the 1930s*, Brighton, Harvester Press.

Godwin, Fay (1990) *Our Forbidden Land*, London, Jonathan Cape.

Goldring, Douglas (1937) *Fortnightly*, April, 505, in Jeffrey Meyers (ed.) (1975) *George Orwell: The Critical Heritage*, London, Routledge and Kegan Paul, 108–9.

Gower, H. D., L. Stanley Jast and W. W. Topley (1916) *The Camera as Historian*, London, Sampson Low, Marston and Co. Ltd.

Grafton, P. (1981) *You, You and You! The People out of Step with World War II*, London, Pluto Press.

Green, Nicholas (1990) *The Spectacle of Nature, Landscape and Bourgeois Culture in Nineteenth-Century France*, Manchester, Manchester University Press.

Greenhalgh, Paul (1988) *Ephemeral Vistas: The Expositions Universelles, Great Exhibitions and World's Fairs, 1851-1939*, Manchester, Manchester University Press.

Guest, Anthony (1907) *Art and the Camera*, London, George Bell and Sons.

Guest, Antony (1915) 'The Colonial Exhibition at the "A. P." Little Gallery', *Amateur Photographer*, 26 July, 72.

Hall, Stuart (1972) 'The social eye of *Picture Post*', *Working Papers in Cultural Studies*, 2: 71–120.

Handy, Ellen (1989) 'Art and science in P. H. Emerson's naturalistic vision', in Mike Weaver, (ed.) *British Photography in the Nineteenth Century: The Fine Art Tradition*, Cambridge, Cambridge University Press, 181–95.

Hannington, Wal (1937) *The Problem of the Distressed Areas*, London, Victor Gollancz.

Harker, Margaret (1979) *The Linked Ring: The Secession Movement in Photography in Britain, 1892–1910*, London, Heinemann.

Harris, Neil (1979) 'Iconography and intellectual history: the half-tone effect', in John Higham and Paul K. Conkin (eds), *New Directions in American Intellectual History*, Baltimore, Johns Hopkins University Press, 196–211.

Harrison, W. Jerome (1886a) 'Bibliography of photography', *Photographic News*, 1 January, 9–10; 29 January, 65–6; 19 February, 113–15; 16 April, 242–3; 30 April, 274–5; 4 June, 361–2; 9 July, 436–7; 19 November, 749; 26 November, 764.

Harrison, W. Jerome (1886b) 'Light as a recording instrument of the past', *Photographic News*, 8 January, 23.

Harrison, W. Jerome (1887) 'Bibliography of photography', *Photographic News*, 8 April, 214–5.

Harrison, W. Jerome (1889) 'Some notes on a proposed photographic survey of Warwickshire', *Photographic Societies' Reporter*, 31 December, 505–15.

Harrison, W. Jerome (1892) 'Proposal for a National Photographic Record and Survey', *Photographic Journal*, 28 May, 226–42.

Harrison, W. Jerome (1906) 'The desirability of promoting county photographic surveys', *British Association for the Advancement of Science: Annual Report*, 58–67.

Harrison, W. Jerome (1907) *Shakespeare-Land*, in Irving, Sir Henry and Frank A. Marshall (eds), *The Works of William Shakespeare*, XIV, London, The Gresham Publishing Company.

Harrisson, Tom (1940) 'What is public opinion?', *Political Quarterly*, 11: 368–83.

Harrisson, Tom (1942) 'Notes on class consciousness and class unconsciousness', *Sociological Review*, 34, 3–4: 147–64.

Hartley, John (1992) *The Politics of Pictures: the Creation of the Public in the Age of Popular Media*, London, Routledge.

Harvey, David (1989) *The Condition of Postmodernity*, Oxford, Basil Blackwell.

Haworth-Booth, Mark (1984) *Bill Brandt: London in the Thirties*, London, Gordon Fraser.

Haworth-Booth, Mark and David Mellor (1985) *Bill Brandt Behind the Camera*, Oxford, Phaidon.

Hawthorne, Nathaniel (1890) *Our Old Home*, London, Chatto & Windus.

Hawthorne, Nathaniel (1941) *The English Notebooks*, London, Oxford University Press.

Hekman, Susan J. (1990) *Gender and Knowledge: Elements of a Postmodern Feminism*, Cambridge, Polity Press.

Hetherington, Kevin (1992) 'Stonehenge and its festival: spaces of consumption', in Rob Shields (ed.) *Lifestyle shopping, the subject of consumption*, London, Routledge.

Hewison, Robert (1987) *The Heritage Industry: Britain in a Climate of Decline*, London, Methuen.

Hiley, Michael (1979) *Victorian Working Women*, London, Gordon Fraser Gallery Ltd.

Hill, Miranda (1888) 'Life on thirty shillings a week', *The Nineteenth Century*, March, 458–63.

Hirsch, Julie (1981) *Family Photographs: Content, Meaning and Effect*, Oxford, Oxford University Press.

Hissey, J. J. (1886) *On the Box Seat from London to Landsend*, London, Bentley.

Hissey, J. J. (1887) 'Artistic photography in relation to landscape', *Amateur Photographer*, 15 April, 179–80, continuing in twelve chapters to 14 October, 173–4.

Hissey, J. J. (1889) *A Tour in a Phaeton through the Eastern Counties*, London, Bentley.

Hissey, J. J. (1891) *Across England in a Dogcart from London to St Davids and Back*, London, Bentley.

Hissey, J. J. (1908) *An English Holiday with Car and Camera*, London, Macmillan.

Hobsbawm, Eric and Terence Ranger (eds) (1983) *The Invention of Tradition*, Cambridge, Cambridge University Press.

Hodgson, Basil (1928) *The Beauty of East Sussex*, London, Homeland Association.

Holderness, Graham (1992) 'Shakespeare and heritage', *Textual Practice*, 6, 2: 247–63.

Holland, Revd B. (1899) 'Out-of-the-way villages', *British Journal Photographic Almanac*, 795.

Holme, Charles (1905) *Art in Photography*, London, The Studio.

Hoppé, E. O. (1926) *England*, Berlin, Verlag Ernst Wasmuth AG; published (1929) as *Great Britain*, London, 'The Studio' Ltd.

Horne, Donald (1984) *The Great Museum: The Representation of History*, London, Pluto Press.

Howarth, E. (1889) 'Suggestions for a photographic survey of the district of Sheffield', *Photographic Societies' Reporter*, 30 April, 185–9.

Howkins, Alun (1991) *Reshaping Rural England: a social history 1850–1925*, London, HarperCollins.

Hudson, Derek (1972) *Munby, Man of Two Worlds: The Life and Diaries of Arthur J. Munby, 1828–1910*, London, John Murray.

Hull, Isabel V. (1982) 'The bourgeoisie and its discontents: reflections on "Nationalism and Respectability"', *Journal of Contemporary History*, 17: 247–68.

Hurd, Geoff (ed.), (1984) *National Fictions: World War Two in British Films and Television*, London, BFI Books.

Ingham, John (1885) 'Submarine photography', *British Journal Photographic Almanac*, 102.

Irving, Washington (1890) *Select Works of Washington Irving, including The Sketch Book and Bracebridge Hall*, London, Thomas Nelson and Sons.

Jacobus, Mary, Evelyn Fox Keller, Sally Shuttleworth (eds) (1990) *Body/Politics: Women and the Discourses of Science*, London, Routledge.

James, Henry (1905) 'In Warwickshire (1877)', in *English Hours*, [1981] Oxford, Oxford University Press.

James, Peter (1989) *William Jerome Harrison, Sir Benjamin Stone and the Photographic Record and Survey Movement*, unpublished M.A. dissertation, Birmingham Polytechnic.

Jameson, Fredric (1984) 'Postmodernism, or the cultural logic of late capitalism', *New Left Review*, 146: 53–92.

Jeans, D. N. (1990) 'Planning and the myth of the

English countryside in the interwar period', *Rural History*, 2: 249–64.

Jeffery, Tom (1978) *Mass-Observation – A Short History*, Stencilled Occasional Paper Number 55, Birmingham, Centre for Contemporary Cultural Studies, University of Birmingham.

Jeffrey, Ian (1981) *Photography – A Concise History*, New York and Toronto, Oxford University Press.

Jeffrey, Ian (1983) 'The culture of connotation, and after: some notes on landscape photography in Britain since 1900', *Undercut*, 7/8: 62–8.

Jeffrey, Ian (1993) *Bill Brandt, Photographs 1928–1983*, London, Thames and Hudson in association with the Barbican Art Gallery.

Jenkins, Reese V. (1975) 'Technology and the market: George Eastman and the origins of mass amateur photography', *Technology and Culture*, 16:1–19.

Jerome, Jerome K. (1982) *Three Men in a Boat*, annotated and introduced by Christopher Matthew and Benny Green, London, Pavilion Books.

Jerome, Jerome K. (1984) *Three Men in a Boat*, Harmondsworth, Penguin.

Jerome, Jerome K. (1989) *Three Men in a Boat*, illustrated by Paul Cox, London, Pavilion Books.

Johnson, William S. (ed.) (1990) *Nineteenth-Century Photography: An Annotated Bibliography, 1839–1879*, London, Mansell Publishing Ltd.

Kappeler, Susan (1986) *The Pornography of Representation*, Cambridge, Polity Press.

Kaufman, Linda (ed.) (1989) *Gender & Theory: Dialogues on Feminist Criticism*, Oxford, Basil Blackwell.

Keating, Peter (1976) *Into Unknown England*, London, Fontana.

Keene, Richard (1884) 'Stray thoughts about home work', *British Journal Photographic Almanac*, 168–9.

Keene, Richard (1892) 'The Warwickshire Survey', *British Journal of Photography*, 27 May, 346.

Keith, Michael and Steve Pile (1993) *Place and the Politics of Identity*, London, Routledge.

Kemp, Wolfgang (1990) 'Images of decay: photography in the picturesque tradition', *October*, 54: 102–33.

Kharegat, Sorab J. (1932) 'Snake Charmer', *Amateur Photographer*, 4 May, n.p.

Kingsley, Rose G. (1885) 'Shakespeare's county', *English Illustrated Magazine*, January, 278–91.

Knights, Sarah (1986) 'Change and decay: Emerson's social order', in Neil McWilliam and Veronica Sekules (eds) *Life and Landscape:* *P. H. Emerson: Art and Photography in East Anglia 1885–1900*, Norwich, Sainsbury Centre for Visual Arts, University of East Anglia, 12–20.

Knop, W. G. (1939) *Beware of the English! German Propaganda Exposes England*, London, Hamish Hamilton.

Knorr, Karen (1991) *Marks of Distinction*, London, Thames and Hudson.

Kodak (1897) *Kodak Works*, publicity leaflet in the archive of the National Museum of Photography, Film and Television, Bradford.

Kodak (*c.*1906) *The Kodak Properties*, publicity leaflet in the archive of the National Museum of Photography, Film and Television, Bradford.

Kodak (1931) *Kodak International Competition, British Isles Awards*, a pamphlet held in the National Museum of Photography, Film and Television, Bradford.

Kodak Magazine (1931) 'The film that frees photography from bogies – what "verichrome" does and how', June, 102–3.

Kodak Trade Circular (1922) 'Covering the country', May, 9.

Kodak Trade Circular (1923) 'National advertising', May, 8–9.

Kodak Trade Circular (1925) 'Why we believe in advertising', April, 56–9.

Kodak Trade Circular (1928) 'Round the Empire', February, 22–4.

Laski, Harold (1937) *Left News*, March, 276, in Jeffrey Meyers (ed.) *George Orwell: The Critical Heritage*, Routledge and Kegan Paul, 1975, 104–7.

Layard, George Somes, (1888) 'How to live on £700 a year', *The Nineteenth Century*, February, 239–44.

Lears, T. Jackson (1981) *No Place of Grace*, New York, Pantheon.

Lee, Martyn J. (1993) *Consumer Culture Reborn*, London, Routledge.

Leed, Eric (1979) *No Man's Land: Combat and Identity in World War I*, Cambridge, Cambridge University Press.

Light, Alison (1991) *Forever England: Femininity, Literature and Conservatism between the Wars*, London, Routledge.

Lowenthal, David (1985) *The Past is a Foreign Country*, Cambridge, Cambridge University Press.

Lowenthal, David (1989) 'Nostalgia tells it like it wasn't', in Christopher Shaw and Malcolm Chase (eds) *The Imagined Past: History and Nostalgia*, Manchester, Manchester University Press.

Lowenthal, David (1991) 'British national identity and the English landscape', *Rural History*, 2, 2:

205–30.

Lowerson, John (1980) 'Battles for the countryside', in Frank Gloversmith (ed.) *Class, Culture and Social Change: A New View of the 1930s*, Brighton, Harvester Press.

Lumley, Robert (ed.) (1988) *The Museum Time-Machine*, London, Routledge.

Lyotard, Jean-François (1984) *The Postmodern Condition: A Report on Knowledge*, translated from the French by Geoff Bennington and Brian Massumi, Manchester, Manchester University Press.

MacCannell, Dean (1976) *The Tourist: A New Theory of the Leisure Class*, New York, Schocken Books.

MacCormack, C. (1980) 'Nature, culture and gender: a critique', in C. MacCormack and M. Strathern (eds) *Nature, Culture and Gender*, Cambridge, Cambridge University Press.

MacKenzie, John M. (1984) *Propaganda and Empire: the Manipulation of British Public Opinion, 1880–1960*, Manchester, Manchester University Press.

MacKenzie, John M. (ed.) (1986) *Imperialism and Popular Culture*, Manchester, Manchester University Press.

McLaine, Ian (1979) *Ministry of Morale: Home Front Morale and the Ministry of Information in World War II*, London, Allen & Unwin.

McWilliam, Neil and Veronica Sekules (eds), *Life and Landscape: P. H. Emerson: Art and Photography in East Anglia 1885–1900*, Norwich, Sainsbury Centre for Visual Arts, University of East Anglia.

Madge, Charles and Tom Harrisson (1938) *First Year's Work*, London, Lindsay Drummond.

Mallock, W. H. (1887) 'Wealth and the working classes', *Fortnightly Review*, March, 355–75; May, 657–75; August, 177–97; October, 514–34.

Mangan, J. A. (ed.) (1990) *Making Imperial Mentalities: Socialisation and British Imperialism*, Manchester, Manchester University Press.

Mannin, Ethel (1937) *The New Leader*, 12 March, 5.

Marsh, Jan (1982) *Back to the Land: the Pastoral Impulse in England, from 1880 to 1914*, London, Quartet Books.

Marx, Leo (1964) *The Machine in the Garden: technology and the pastoral ideal in America*, New York, Oxford Univerity Press.

Massingham, H. J. (1942) *Remembrance, an Autobiography*, London, Batsford.

Masterman, C. F. G. (1960) *The Condition of England*, London, Methuen.

McConkey, Kenneth (1986) 'Dr Emerson and the sentiment of nature', in Neil McWilliam and Veronica Sekules (eds) *Life and Landscape: P. H. Emerson: Art and Photography in East Anglia 1885–1900*, Norwich, Sainsbury Centre for Visual Arts, University of East Anglia, 48–56.

McGrath, Roberta (1984) 'Medical Police', *Ten.8*, 14: 13–18.

Mellor, Adrian (1991) 'Enterprise and heritage in the dock', in John Corner and Sylvia Harvey, *Enterprise and Heritage: Crosscurrents of National Culture*, London, Routledge.

Mellor, David (1978) 'Mass-Observation: the intellectual climate', *Camerawork*, 11: 4–5.

Mellor, David (1981) *Bill Brandt: A Retrospective Exhibition*, Bath, The Royal Photographic Society.

Mellor, David (1988) 'Romances of decay, elegies for the future', in *British Photography: Towards a Bigger Picture*, New York, Aperture, 113: 52–67.

Merchant, Carolyn (1980) *The Death of Nature: Women, Ecology and the Scientific Revolution*, New York, Harper and Row.

Meyers, Jeffrey (ed.) (1975) *George Orwell: The Critical Heritage*, London, Routledge and Kegan Paul.

Miles, Hamish (1937) *New Statesman and Nation*, 1 May, 724, 726, in Jeffrey Meyers (ed.) (1975) *George Orwell: The Critical Heritage*, London, Routledge and Kegan Paul, 110–13.

Mingay, G. E. (ed.) (1976) *Rural Life in Victorian England*, Stroud, Alan Sutton.

Mingay, G. E. (ed.) (1981) *The Victorian Countryside*, volumes 1 and 2, London, Routledge.

Mingay, G. E. (ed.) (1989) *The Rural Idyll*, London, Routledge.

MOI [Ministry of Information] (1941) *The Battle of Britain, August–October 1940*, London, HMSO.

MOI [Ministry of Information] (1942) *Front Line 1940–41: The Official Story of the Civil Defence of Britain*, London, HMSO.

MOI [Ministry of Information] (c. 1942) *The Battle of Britain, August–October 1940*, London, HMSO.

MOI [Ministry of Information] (1943) *Roof Over Britain: The Official Story of Britain's Anti-Aircraft Defences 1939–1942*, London, HMSO.

Mort, Frank (1987) *Dangerous Sexualities: Medico–Moral Politics in England since 1830*, London, Routledge.

Mortimer, Francis J. (1941) 'Photography's part in the war', *Photographic Journal*, April, 124–45.

Mortimer, Francis J. (1942) 'More about photography's part in the war', *Photographic Journal*, April, 88–105.

291

Morton, H. V. (1927) *In Search of England*, London, Methuen & Co.

Moss, L., and Box, K. L., (1948) *Ministry of Information Publications: a Study of Public Attitudes towards Six Ministry of Information Books*, London, Central Office of Information.

Mulvey, Laura (1975) 'Visual pleasure and narrative cinema', *Screen*, 16, 3: 6–18.

Naef, Weston (1978) *The Collection of Alfred Stieglitz: Fifty Pioneers of Modern Photography*, New York, The Metropolitan Museum of Art/Viking.

Nairn, Tom (1977) *The Break-Up of Britain*, London, New Left Books.

Neil, Samuel (1892) *The Home of Shakespeare*, Warwick, Henry T. Cooke & Son.

Newby, Howard (1979) *Green and Pleasant Land: Social change in rural England*, London, Hutchinson & Co., and updated version (1985) Hounslow, Wildwood House.

Newhall, Nancy (1975) *P. H. Emerson: The Fight for Photography as a Fine Art*, New York, Aperture.

Nunokawa, Jeff (1992) 'Tess, tourism, and the spectacle of the woman', in Linda M. Shires (ed.) *Rewriting the Victorians, theory, history and the politics of gender*, London, Routledge.

'Operator' (1895) 'A hard case', *British Journal of Photography*, 26 April, 272.

Opie, Robert (1985) *Rule Britannia: Trading on the British Image*, Harmondsworth, Penguin.

Orwell, George (1937) *The Road to Wigan Pier*, London, Victor Gollancz.

Orwell, George (1982) *The Lion and the Unicorn: Socialism and the English Genius*, Harmondsworth, Penguin. First published London, Secker & Warburg, 1941.

'Our Views' (1889) *Amateur Photographer*, 3 May, 282.

Ousby, Ian (1990) *The Englishman's England: taste, travel, and the rise of tourism*, Cambridge, Cambridge University Press.

Parr, Martin (1989) *The Cost of Living*, Manchester, Cornerhouse.

Paulson, Ronald (1975) *Emblem and Expression: meaning in English art of the eighteenth century*, London, Thames and Hudson.

Pearsall, Ronald (1971) *The Worm in the Bud: the World of Victorian Sexuality*, Harmondsworth, Penguin.

Pennell, Joseph and Elizabeth Robins (1891) *The Stream of Pleasure: a Month on the Thames*, London, T. Fisher Unwin.

Persons, Stow (1973) *The Decline of American Gentility*, New York, Columbia University Press.

Photographer (1907) 19 February, cover.

Picton, Tom (1978) 'A very public espionage', *Camerawork*, 11: 2.

Pimlott, J. A. R. (1947) *The Englishman's Holiday*, London, Faber and Faber.

Plumwood, Val (1993) *Feminism and the Mastery of Nature*, London, Routledge.

Poignant, Roslyn (1992) 'Surveying the field of view: the making of the R[oyal] A[nthropological] I[nstitute] Photographic Collection', in Elizabeth Edwards (ed.) *Anthropology and Photography 1860–1920*, New Haven and London, Yale University Press in association with The Royal Anthropological Institute, London.

Pointon, Marcia (1979) 'Geology and landscape painting in nineteenth-century England', *British Society for the History of Science*, 1: 84–108.

Pope-Hennessy, James (1941) *History Under Fire*, London, Batsford.

Porter, Roy (ed.) (1992) *Myths of the English*, Cambridge, Polity Press.

Potts, Alex (1989) ' "Constable country" between the wars', in Raphael Samuel (ed.) *Patriotism: the making and unmaking of British national identity*, London, Routledge, 161–86.

Powyss-Lybbe, Ursula (1983) *The Eye of Intelligence*, London, William Kimber.

Pratt, Mary Louise (1992) *Imperial Eyes: Travel Writing and Transculturation*, London, Routledge.

Prentice, Richard (1993) *Tourism and Heritage Attractions*, London, Routlege.

Prescott Row, B. and A. H. Anderson (eds) (1911–14) *Where Shall We Live?*, London, Homeland Association.

Priestley, J. B. (1941) *Out of the People*, London, Collins.

Priestley, J. B. (*c.*1941) *Britain Under Fire*, London, Country Life Ltd.

Priestley, J. B. (1943) *British Women go to War*, London, Collins.

Pringle, A. in W. Arthur Boord (ed.) (1890) *Sun Artists: Mr H. P. Robinson*, London, Kegan Paul, Trench, Trübner & Co. Ltd., Number 2, January.

Pugh, Simon (1988) *Garden – nature – language*, Manchester, Manchester University Press.

Pugh, Simon (ed.) (1990) *Reading Landscape: country – city – capital*, Manchester, Manchester University Press.

Pumphrey, A. (1880) *Twelve Permanent Photographs of Stratford-on-Avon*, Birmingham, Midland Educational Co. Ltd.

Randall, John A. (1896a) 'Assistants and their grievances', *British Journal of Photography*,

24 April, 271.

Randall, John A. (1896b) 'Co-operative photography', *British Journal of Photography*, 5 June, 360–1.

Randall, John A. (1900a) 'The economy of photographic labour', *British Journal of Photography*, 28 September, 618–19.

Randall, John A. (1900b) 'The organization of photographic labour', *British Journal of Photography*, 21 December, 809.

Reas, Paul (1993) *Flogging a Dead Horse*, Manchester, Cornerhouse Publications.

Roberts, W. (1888) 'Life on a guinea a week', *The Nineteenth Century*, March, 464–7.

Robinson, H. P. (1869) *Pictorial Effect in Photography, being hints on composition and chiaroscuro for photographers*, London, Piper & Carter. Reprinted (1971) Pawlet, Helios.

Robinson, H. P. (1888) *Letters on Landscape Photography*, New York, Scovill Manufacturing Company.

Robinson, H. P. (1897) *Picture-Making by Photography*, London, Hazell, Watson, & Viney, fifth edition. First published (1884) London, Piper & Carter. Reprinted (1973) New York, Arno Press.

Rodee, Howard D. (1977) 'The "dreary landscape" as a background for scenes of rural poverty in Victorian paintings', *Art Journal*, 36, 4: 307–13.

Rose, Gillian (1993) *Feminism and Geography: The Limits of Geographical Knowledge*, London, Routledge.

Rothnie, Niall (1992) *The Baedeker Blitz: Hitler's Attack on Britain's Historic Cities*, Shepperton, Ian Allan.

Ryan, Chris (1991) *Recreational Tourism: a social science perspective*, London, Routledge.

Rye, Walter (1885) *History of Norfolk*, London, Elliot Stock.

Samuel, Raphael (1989) 'Introduction: The figures of national myth', in Raphael Samuel (ed.) *Patriotism: The Making and Unmaking of British National Identity*, volume 3, 'National Fictions', London, Routledge, xi–xxxvi.

Sansom, Leslie (1939) 'War-time pressman', *British Journal of Photography*, 27 October, 648–9.

Scharf, Aaron (1986) 'P. H. Emerson: naturalist and iconoclast', in Neil McWilliam and Veronica Sekules (eds), *Life and Landscape: P. H. Emerson: Art and Photography in East Anglia 1885–1900*, Norwich, Sainsbury Centre for Visual Arts, University of East Anglia, 21–32.

Scherman, David E. and Richard Wilcox (1944) *Literary England: Photographs of Places made memorable in English Literature*, New York, Random House.

Schwarz, Bill (1987) 'Englishness and the paradox of modernity', *New Formations*, 1: 147–53.

Seiberling, Grace with Carolyn Bloore (1986) *Amateurs, Photography and the Mid-Victorian Imagination*, Chicago, University of Chicago Press.

Sekula, Allan (1984) 'The Traffic in Photographs' in *Photography Against the Grain: Essays and Photo-Works 1973–1983*, Halifax, Nova Scotia.

Sellar, Walter C., and Robert J. Yeatman (1989) *1066 and all That*, London, Methuen. First published in 1930.

Shakespeare's Country: views and descriptions of the places of interest on the route of the East and West Junction Railway (1886), London, MacFarlane and Co.

Shaw, Christopher and Malcolm Chase (eds) *The Imagined Past: history and nostalgia*, Manchester, Manchester University Press.

Sheail, John (1981) *Rural Conservation in Inter-War Britain*, Oxford, Clarendon Press.

Sheridan, Dorothy (1991) *The Tom Harrisson Mass-Observation Archive: A Guide for Researchers*, Brighton, University of Sussex.

Shields, Rob (1991) *Places on the Margin: Alternative geographies of modernity*, London, Routledge.

Shields, Rob (ed.) (1992) *Lifestyle shopping: the subject of consumption*, London, Routledge.

Shiva, Vandana (1989) *Staying Alive: Women, Ecology and Development*, London, Zed Books Ltd.

Shoard, Marion (1987) *This Land is Our Land: the Struggle for Britain's Countryside*, London, Paladin.

Showalter, Elaine (1987) *The Female Malady: Women, Madness and English Culture, 1830–1980*, London, Virago Press.

Showalter, Elaine (1991) *Sexual Anarchy: Gender and Culture at the Fin de Siecle*, London, Bloomsbury.

Smith, A. C. H., Elizabeth Immirzi, Trevor Blackwell and Stuart Hall (1975) *Paper Voices: The Popular Press and Social Change*, London, Chatto & Windus.

Smith, Derek and Tom Picton (1978) 'Humphrey Spender: M.O. Photographer', *Camerawork*, 11: 6–7.

Smith, Jonathan (1993) 'The lie that blinds: destabilizing the text of landscape', in James Duncan and David Ley (eds) *Place/Culture/Represention*, London, Routledge.

Smith, Lindsay (1992) 'The politics of focus: feminism and photographic theory', in Isobel Armstrong (ed.) *New Feminist Discourses*, London, Routledge.

Solomon-Godeau, Abigail (1986) 'The legs of the countess', *October*, 39: 65–108.

Solomon-Godeau, Abigail (1991) *Photography at the Dock: Essays on Photographic History, Institutions, and Practices*, Minneapolis, University of Minneapolis Press.

Sontag, Susan (1977) *On Photography*, New York, Farrar, Straus and Giroux.

Southam, Jem (1989) *The Red River*, Manchester, Cornerhouse.

Spence, Jo (1986) *Putting Myself in the Picture*, London, Camden Press.

Spence, Jo and Patricia Holland (eds) (1991) *Family Snaps: The Meanings of Domestic Photography*, London, Virago Press.

Spender, Humphrey (1982) *Worktown People: Photographs from Northern England 1937–38*, Bristol, Falling Wall Press.

Spender, Humphrey (1987) *'Lensman' Photographs 1932–52*, London, Chatto & Windus.

Spenser Allberry, A. (ed.) (1932–34) *This Homeland of Ours*, London, Homeland Association.

Squire, Shelagh J. (1993) 'Valuing countryside: reflections on Beatrix Potter tourism', *Area*, 25, 1: 5–10.

Stafford, Barbara Maria (1984) *Voyage into Substance: art, science and the illustrated travel account, 1760–1840*, Cambridge, Massachusetts, MIT Press.

Stallybrass, Peter and Allon White (1986) *The Politics and Poetics of Transgression*, London, Methuen.

Stanley, Liz (1990) 'The archaeology of a 1930s Mass-Observation project', Sociology Occasional Paper Number 27, Manchester, Manchester University Press.

Stening, J. S. (1914) 'The Pioneer', *Amateur Photographer*, 6 April, cover.

Stephenson, Tom (1989) *Forbidden Land: the struggle for access to mountain and moorland*, Manchester, Manchester University Press.

Stewart, Susan (1993) *On Longing: Narratives of the Miniature, the Gigantic, the Souvenir, the Collection*, Durham, NC, Duke University Press. Originally published Baltimore, Johns Hopkins University Press, c.1984.

Street, Paul (1989) 'Painting deepest England: the late landscapes of John Linnell and the uses of nostalgia', in Shaw, Christopher and Malcolm Chase (eds) *The Imagined Past: history and nostalgia*, Manchester, Manchester University Press.

Summerfield, Penny (1985) 'Mass-Observation: social research or social movement?', *Journal of Contemporary History*, 20, 3: 439–52.

Summerfield, Penny (1986) 'The "levelling of class"', in Harold L. Smith (ed.), *War and Social Change: British Society in the Second World War*, Manchester, Manchester University Press.

Sussex, Elizabeth (1976) *The Rise and Fall of British Documentary: The Story of the Film Movement Founded by John Grierson*, Berkeley, University of California Press.

Swingewood, Alan (1977) *The Myth of Mass Culture*, London, Macmillan.

Tagg, John (1988) *The Burden of Representation: Essays on Photographies and Histories*, London, Macmillan.

Tawadros, Gilane (1988) 'Other Britains, Other Britons', in *British Photography: Towards a Bigger Picture*, New York, Aperture, 113: 41–6.

Taylor, James (1870) *The Family History of England*, London, William Mackenzie, 1 (six volumes 1870–75).

Taylor, John (1978) *Pictorial Photography in Britain 1900-1920*, London, Arts Council of Great Britain.

Taylor, John (1979) 'Henry Peach Robinson and Victorian theory', *History of Photography*, 3: 295–303.

Taylor, John (1983) 'Picturing the past: documentary realism in the 30s', *Ten.8*, 11: 15–31.

Taylor, John (1990) 'The alphabetic universe: photography and the picturesque landscape', in Simon Pugh (ed.) *Reading Landscape: country – city – capital*, Manchester, Manchester University Press, 177–96.

Taylor, John (1991) *War Photography – Realism in the British Press*, London, Routledge.

Taylor, Roger (1981) *George Washington Wilson, Artist and Photographer (1823–93)*, Aberdeen, University of Aberdeen Press.

Thatcher, Margaret (1982) 'The Prime Minister's speech to a Conservative Party rally at Cheltenham racecourse', 3 July, London, Conservative Central Office.

Thompson, E. P. (1967) 'Time, work-discipline, and industrial capitalism', *Past & Present*, 38: 56–97.

Thomson, John (1876–77) *Street Life in London*, London, Sampson Low Marston, Searle and Rivington.

Thornton-Pickard Manufacturing Company (1896) Publicity leaflet in the archive of the National Museum of Photography, Film and Television, Bradford.

Titmuss, Richard M. (1950) *Problems of Social Policy*, London, HMSO.

Tomsich, John (1971) *A Genteel Endeavor: American culture and Politics in the Gilded Age*, Stanford, Stanford University Press.

Turner, Bryan S. (1987) 'A note on nostalgia', *Theory, Culture & Society*, 4: 147–56.

Turner, Peter (1975) *Bill Brandt: Early*

Photographs 1930–42, London, Arts Council of Great Britain.

Tweedie, George R. (1927) *The Beauty of Hampshire* (The Homeland Illustrated), London, Homeland Association.

Urry, John (1984) 'Englishmen, Celts, and Iberians. The Ethnographic Survey of the United Kingdom 1892–1899' in G. W. Stocking (ed.) *Functionalism Historicized, Essays on British Anthropology*, Wisconsin, Wisconsin University Press, 2: 83–105.

Urry, John (1990) *The Tourist Gaze: Leisure and Travel in Contemporary Societies*, London, Sage Publications.

Vergo, Peter (1989) *The New Museology*, London, Reaktion Books.

Verney, George (1885) 'A difficult landscape', *British Journal Photographic Almanac*, 102–3.

Vernon, P. E. (1941) 'Psychological effects of air raids', *Journal of Abnormal and Social Psychology*, 36: 457–76.

Vertrees, Alan (1982) 'The picture making of Henry Peach Robinson', in Dave Oliphant and Thomas Zigal (eds), *Perspectives on Photography*, Austin, Texas, Humanities Research Center, University of Texas, 79–101.

'Victim' (1896) 'A warning to assistants', *British Journal of Photography*, 21 February, 126.

Vine, P. A. L. (1983) *Pleasure Boating in the Victorian Era*, Chichester, Phillimore & Co. Ltd.

Virilio, Paul (1989) *War and Cinema: the Logistics of Perception*, tr. Patrick Camiller, London, Verso.

Walsh, Kevin (1992) *The Representation of the Past: museums and heritage in the post-modern world*, London, Routledge.

Walter, James (1874) *Shakespeare's Home and Rural Life*, London, Longmans, Green, Reader, and Dyer.

Ward, H. Snowden and Catharine Weed Ward (1896) *Shakespeare's Town and Times*, London, Dawbarn & Ward Ltd.

Warren, C. H. (1941) *England is a Village*, London, Eyre & Spottiswoode.

Waterhouse, K. (1989) *The Theory and Practice of Travel*, London, Hodder & Stoughton.

Weaver, Mike (ed.) (1989a) *British Photography in the Nineteenth Century: The Fine Art Tradition*, Cambridge, Cambridge University Press.

Weaver, Mike (ed.) (1989b) *The Art of Photography 1839–1989*, London, Royal Academy of Arts.

Whistler, J. A. M. (1967) 'The "Ten O'Clock" lecture' in *The Gentle Art of Making Enemies*, New York, Dover. First published (1888) London, Chatto and Windus.

Wiener, Martin J. (1981) *English Culture and the Decline of the Industrial Spirit*, Cambridge, Cambridge University Press.

Williams, Douglas and Quentin Reynolds (1941) *Britain Can Take It: The Book of the Film*, London, John Murray.

Williams, James Leon (1892) *The Home and Haunts of Shakespeare*, London, Sampson Low, Marston & Company Ltd.

Williams, Raymond (1975) *The Country and the City*, London, Paladin.

Williams Ellis, Clough (1928) *England and the Octopus*, London, Geoffrey Bles.

Williams Ellis, Clough (1938) *Britain and the Beast*, London, J. M. Dent and Sons.

Willis, Anne-Marie (1988) *Picturing Australia: A History of Photography*, North Ryde, Angus & Robertson Publishers.

Wojtas, Olga (1993) 'Car travellers reclaim the countryside', *Times Higher Education Supplement*, 17 September.

Wombell, Paul (1992) 'Postcards from post-industrial Britain', *Creative Camera*, CC316, June/July, 14–23.

Wombell, Paul and Gerald Deslanders (1990) *Heritage, Image + History*, Manchester/York, Cornerhouse/Impressions.

Wright, Patrick (1985) *On Living in an Old Country: The National Past in Contemporary Britain*, London, Verso.

Wright, Patrick (1986) 'Misguided tours', *New Socialist*, July/August: 32–4.

Yaeger, Patricia (1989) 'Towards a female sublime', in Linda Kaufman (ed.) *Gender & Theory: Dialogues on Feminist Criticism*, Oxford, Basil Blackwell.

Yale, Pat, (1991) *From Tourist Attractions to Heritage Tourism*, Kings Ripton, Elm Publications.

Yass, Marion (1983) *This is Your War: Home Front Propaganda in the Second World War*, London, HMSO.

Index